The Curbstone Brokers

THE
CURBSTONE BROKERS

The Origins of
The American Stock Exchange

ROBERT SOBEL

The Macmillan Company, New York, New York
Collier-Macmillan Ltd., London

THE MACMILLAN COMPANY
866 Third Avenue, New York, N.Y. 10022
Collier-Macmillan Canada Ltd., Toronto, Ontario

Library of Congress Catalog Card Number: 75-103686

THIRD PRINTING 1972
Printed in the United States of America

for Barbara

Contents

Preface

FOR A HALF CENTURY and more Wall Street has been a major symbol of finance capitalism. From turn-of-the-century populists and progressives to New Dealers of the 1930s, post-World War II reformers, and today's New Left, critics have attacked it with varying degrees of invective. In the same period it has had its defenders, to whom Wall Street has been an integral part of America's great material civilization, and a showplace for its vitality.

Visitors from all parts of the world can be found there almost every business day. They walk up the narrow street, and many are puzzled by the plentitude of umbrella-covered hot dog stands. (Although Wall Street has only a few restaurants on the east end, there are hundreds of large and small eating establishments in the area, but since the offices tend to empty between 11:30 and 1:30, they are always packed with individuals wanting a quick lunch. Thus, hot dog stands do a good business, catering to clerks and, at times, partners of important organizations.) Most stare at the impressive bank buildings, nod knowingly at the jagged scars on the House of Morgan's facade (a reminder of the bomb explosion that rocked the district in 1920), and stop to listen to evangelists preaching to passers-by. (They too, consider Wall Street a symbol, and the employees servants of mammon who badly need salvation. Thus, the preachers may be found in the vicinity of Wall and Broad, which is also believed a fine spot for politicians to address the lunchtime crowd in election years. In a different way, they too appreciate the symbol. Financial district employees who have been in the area for a while tend to ignore both, or look upon them with a bemused detachment. Tourists, therefore, make much the best audience for both preachers and politicians.)

Many visitors stand on the steps of the Subtreasury, looking up at the statue of George Washington, and down at the mass of brokers, bankers, clerks, and other district employees, who mingle with tourists and those on their way to offices in the area. Some may drive through Wall Street late at night and be amazed by the quiet of the place, interrupted only by the noise of garbage collectors and an occasional car on its way to another part of the city. They may walk the length of Wall Street in a few minutes, from the Franklin D. Roosevelt Drive and the East River on one end to Trinity Church on the other. On every fourth or fifth building they can see reminders of the past, in the form of metal plaques or similar memorials; they may visit the Alexander Hamilton and Albert Gallitan graves in Trinity Churchyard.

Some may go down Broad Street, past the New York Stock Exchange's impressive facade, eavesdrop on conversations of clerks and brokers, look into the windows of brokerages and other offices, or turn into the unusual lanes of New Street and Exchange Place. Having done this, they believe they have caught a glimpse of the center of American capitalism and the people who make it work.

There is much to be said for this view, for indeed Wall and Broad streets contain some of the most important offices in the nation, and are the business addresses of leading banks and brokerages, not to mention the Stock Exchange itself. But there is far more to the financial district than is contained in these two short streets. Larger banks have offices north of Wall Street, and southeast of Broad and Wall are several important commodities exchanges, insurance firms, and even a few old residences. And on the west side of Trinity Church, at 86 Trinity Place, is the nation's second largest securities market, the American Stock Exchange.

One would scarcely guess the building's function from the

outside were it not for the name, in metal letters, above the second-story windows. There are never large crowds in front of the American Stock Exchange, and even during lunch hour only a few clerks and runners will stand around smoking cigarettes and joking with each other. The "Amex" is bound on the north by a small parking lot, on the site of which once stood New York University's Graduate School of Business, which has moved to a new building across the street. Since there are usually more students than stockbrokers walking along Trinity Place, one might mistake the Exchange for part of an urban university rather than the giant financial complex that it is. To the south is a solid wall of tall buildings, with ground floors housing small shops and a handful of restaurants. Across the street is Trinity Church and the graveyard, which stands as though a combination barrier and buffer between the Amex and the rest of the financial district. All of this gives the area an air of spaciousness and calm. There is a great deal of open sky around the Amex; the building is not part of the canyonlike atmosphere one finds on Wall Street. This is fitting, for during most of its life, the American Stock Exchange and its direct antecedents traded out-of-doors.

The Exchange's exterior is different from that of the New York Stock Exchange. The Big Board is housed in a ponderous-looking edifice, replete with columns, friezes, and heavy doors. The Amex is a tall, graceful structure, done in the skyscraper style of uptown buildings. It has many more windows than the Big Board, and this too seems to recall the airiness of the outdoor market. The trading floors are different, although they may not seem to be so at first glance. At the New York Stock Exchange, traders stay at their posts or roam about, sending messages and orders to clerks and employees by pneumatic tubes. The Amex floor is also crowded with brokers and clerks, but on either side, like onlookers at a football game, are two banks of brokerage firms' clerks who receive and give instructions to floor brokers by a system of fast-moving conveyer rails. From time to time a broker hurrying to transmit an order to his clerk seated somewhere on these sidelines will catch his eye and wave his hands, gesticulating with fingers and arms in a manner strange to visitors. This was the way orders were transmitted when the Amex's predecessors were out in the open, when brokers transacted business on the street, while their clerks were perched at the windows of nearby office buildings, waiting to transmit and receive orders over the telephone, and then send them down to their employers. If the visitor looks carefully at the brokers on the Amex floor, he may see some older men, a handful of them in their late sixties and seventies, who were clerks, runners, and brokers in that outdoor market, and who were active participants in one of the most dramatic success stories in the nation's business history, the rise from a much-maligned unstructured group of men, known as curbstone brokers, to a powerful and respected securities market.

This book is an attempt to tell part of their story, to present and analyze the outdoor markets of lower Manhattan from the late eighteenth century to 1921, when the last of them went indoors. Many markets will be discussed, but the focus will always be on the curbstone brokers themselves. Emphasis will be placed on their business activities, but other subjects of interest will also be explored. For example, the Curb as a social institution in a time of great ethnic friction may offer some clues as to methods of dealing with present problems, as well as cast new perspectives on old battlefields. In the early 1900s, at a time when Irish and Jewish Americans were in conflict in almost every other aspect of urban life, they worked in harmony at the Curb. Indeed, from the outside it may appear the organization was dominated by an Irish-Jewish "inside group," whose members were not only able to work together, but apparently had great personal respect and affection for each other.

Another area of related interest was the impact of progressivism on the financial district, and upon the outside market in particular. The role played by government in the financial district has always been a touchy issue, setting off many arguments during the past seventy years. Those who believe governmental intervention was unnecessary may change their minds after referring to the appendices and texts, and learning how the New York Stock Exchange dealt with rivals and allies before government stepped in as a referee. Such people may also be interested in the impact of governmental investigations and legislation on Wall Street. The great turn-of-the-century reform movement had little success insofar as the financial district was concerned. It was led by ill-informed men, investigating complex institutions they little understood, intent on reform but not knowing how to accomplish it. They did cause changes in American finance, but some of these were contrary to what they might have desired. The reform movement did assist the Curb and helped prepare the way for the important move indoors. Its general failure may be seen in Wall Street's history during the 1920s, and in 1929 in particular.

Generally speaking, the curbstone brokers got along well with the reformers, and utilized their findings to assist in their business. These were the men who went indoors in 1921, the founders of the American Stock Exchange. The institution's present name was taken in 1953; before that time it was known as the New York Curb Exchange. But when the curbstone brokers went indoors in 1921, their new home was called the New York Curb Market. For this reason, the title of this book may seem a trifle misleading, since the term "American Stock Exchange" will not be found in its pages. In a second volume I hope to carry its history to the present, and show how this rather fragile institution of 1921 gained in power and prestige during the next half century.

As the reader will discover from the "Essay on Sources and Methodology" at the end of this book, not much has been written about the curbstone brokers. Without the cooperation of dozens of former out-of-doors traders, this project could not have been undertaken. The names of those most helpful in the project may be found in the Essay. In addition, Mr. Winsor H. Watson, Jr., senior vice president of the American Stock Exchange, and Mr. Robert A. Coplin, vice president of the Information Services Division, have been most helpful in arranging for me to use the Amex's facilities and library. Mr. Edwin J. Wheeler of Bregman & Co., a member of the board of governors, has taken a special interest in the book, and through his assistance I was able to meet and talk with some of the older men who were direct participants in the activities discussed in the later chapters. All of these brokers, and others at the American Stock Exchange, were eager to cooperate in this project, and were gratifyingly frank in their talks with me.

Additional material has been gathered at the Library of Congress, the New York Public Library, the George F. Baker Library at Harvard University, and the New York Historical Society Library. As usual in my work on the history of the securities markets, Miss Elsie Reynolds and Miss Viola Mooney of the Hofstra University Library were most cooperative in tracking down rare items, and their help saved me much time and effort. Hofstra University granted me a leave of absence to conduct the research for this book and its companion volume, and has allowed me a financial grant for materials and secretarial aid. Finally, Mr. Ray Roberts of Macmillan has edited the manuscript with his usual skill and tact.

New College of
Hofstra University, 1970

The tribe of curb-stone brokers, which in the greenback era swarmed like locusts and filled the air with their importunate chirk, in 1857 was comparatively few in number. Their offices, when they have offices, are merely desk-rooms in upper lofts or murky basements. More generally the flooring of their offices is the sidewalk and its ceiling the firmament "fretted with golden fire," perhaps we should say with golden fractions—the eights and quarters of the market price it is their business to catch. On a busy day they are all eyes and ears, scud and scamper, their fingers quivering like aspen leaves, their mouths pouring out a stream of bids and offers disencumbered of all the spare syllables, while they telegraph signals with the ten digits, and with nods and winks. The curb-stone broker is the financial bud which if not nipped by some untimely frost, often blossoms into the flower which blooms in the garden of the regular board. . . . The curb-stone broker is the scullion in the brokerage kitchen, feasting on odds and ends, and is obliged to serve his time there before he can be admitted to the banquets and privileges of the parlor.

WILLIAM WORTHINGTON FOWLER, 1880

The Curbstone Brokers

Introduction

THE EARLIEST TRADERS conducted their business out-of-doors. Mesopotamian merchants of the third millennium before Christ formed trading companies, dealt in what we would recognize as commodities futures, and took shares in local projects. There was an open-air market in Athens, where businessmen would gather to buy and sell grain and olive oil as well as shares in commercial ventures, and deal in gold and silver. The Romans had primitive joint stock companies, most of which were in banking and insurance, and shares in these, as well as other goods, were bought and sold in the streets in a specified part of the city. Regional fairs were an integral part of life in the Middle Ages, and much international and inter-regional trade was conducted at such gatherings. London and Stourbridge in England, Paris, Lyon, Reims and Champagne in France, Lille, Ypres, Douai, and Bruges in Flanders, and Cologne, Frankfort, Leipzig, and Lubeck in the Germanies owed much of their importance to the fact that they were host cities for such gatherings. A good deal of the fair's business was conducted in tents set up for the purpose and struck once the fair was over. But most of the action was in the narrow lanes and cleared fields, under the skies, where merchants met to transact their business.

It was at such an out-of-doors market in the Netherlands, in 1635, that the first recorded "exchange panic" occurred, when the market in tulip bulbs broke downward. The famed Mississippi

1

Scheme of the early eighteenth century, which caused a severe crash in the Paris securities market, also occurred outdoors. Writing of that market, the French historian François Guizot said:

The street called Quincampoix, for a long time past devoted to the operations of the bankers, had become the usual meeting place of the greatest lords as well as of discreet burgesses. It had been found necessary to close the two ends of the street with gates open from 6 a.m. to 9 p.m.; every house harbored business agents by the hundred; the smallest room was let for its weight in gold. The most modest fortunes became colossal, lacqueys of yesterday were millionaires tomorrow.

Even then, the actual trading in securities, gold and silver, and other items was carried on in the streets, with the rooms used as offices.

London had a similar outdoor market early in the eighteenth century. According to Daniel Defoe, in his pamphlet "The Anatomy of Exchange Alley," the narrow, twisting lane was one of the busiest thoroughfares in Europe. "The principal leaders in the jobbing trade are Whigs, Members of Parliament, and Friends of the Government," whose aim it was to "stock jobb the Nation, couzen the Parliament, ruffle the Bank, run up and down Stocks, and put the Dice upon the whole town." He wondered:

To see States-Men turn Dealers, and Men of Honour stoop to the Chicanry of Jobbing; to see Men at the offices in the Morning, at the P. House [Parliament] about Noon, at the Cabinet at Night, and in the *Exchange Alley* at the proper Intervals, What new *Phaenomina* are these? What fatal things may these shining Planets . . . fortel to the State, and the Publick; for when Statesmen turn Jobbers the State may be Jobbed. In a Word, I appeal to all the World, whether any Man that is entrusted with other Mens Money . . . ought to be seen in Exchange-Alley.

In 1720 Exchange Alley would be the scene of a severe panic, caused by speculations that originated in offices but were carried out in the streets.

Other cities had their equivalents of Rue de Quincampoix and Exchange Alley, where traders and customers met at street corners, in the entrances to buildings, or at cafés. It was in places such as these that the science and art of brokerage flourished and developed, and modern investment capitalism had its beginnings. There were many reasons for the existence of these markets. They all filled a specific need—that of bringing together men with ideas and investors with surplus capital. Later on, they would provide places where individuals who wished to buy and sell securities could meet and transact business. All of this took place amid the general dealings in commodities, and the shouts of bankers and brokers mingled with those of ordinary tradesmen and shippers. To outsiders and nonbusinessmen, the outdoor markets seemed somewhat strange and not quite respectable. It was as though a nonproductive element of society had gathered in one bustling, noisome place to make fortunes from the hard work of others in some mysterious way, and in the process produced nothing of value, no product that could be eaten, worn, or lived in. Somehow it didn't seem right; from the beginning, outsiders tended to distrust, dislike, and be suspicious of the motives and operations of those who dealt in paper rather than tilled the soil. Matters were ascerbated by the fact that these men conducted their business in the open, where all could see and hear what they were doing.

The brokers, bankers, and traders had begun outdoor dealings for a good reason. In the beginning at least, theirs was a part-time occupation, carried on for only a few months of the year in the case of the medieval fairs, and for an hour or so a day when securities first appeared. In this period there was no need for a permanent home, and no money for one should the need have existed. As securities became increasingly popular, and brokerage became a full-time occupation, the need for a semipermanent facility or facilities became evident, and so they were constructed. Later on, these were transformed into impressive edifices, but they all had small beginnings.

One of the earliest of these structures appeared in Amsterdam, just as that city had one of the first out-of-doors markets. Early in the sixteenth century brokers and their clients would gather in a street called Warmoesstraat, and by 1561 had transferred activities to Nieuwe Brug, while retiring to the Chapel of St.

Olaf during bad weather. Not until a half century later would the Amsterdam brokers go indoors for good.

A similar situation existed in London, where brokers had taken over parts of Cornhill and Lombard streets and Sweeting Alley as well as Exchange Alley by the late seventeenth century. Sometime in the 1720s, a few of the leading brokers took offices in Jonathan's Coffee-House in Exchange Alley, and from these places conducted their business. An advertisement of the time read: "John Taylor, at his office next Jonathan's Coffee-House in Exchange Alley, buyeth and selleth New Lottery Tickets, Blanck Tickets, Navy and Victualling Bills, East India Bonds, and other Publick Securities." Jonathan's burned to the ground in 1748, but the brokers helped construct New Jonathan's on the same site the following year. The building was named "The Stock Exchange" in 1773, and a securities auction organized soon after. It was not until 1801 that the first building for the specific purpose of securities dealings was constructed near Capel Court.

The Berlin merchants of the early seventeenth century also traded in the open, at the Grotte in Schlossgarten. Later on, as business expanded, they moved to a wider street in the Stechbahn, where brokers took offices in nearby inns and taverns, and went into the street for trading purposes. Berlin had to wait until 1805 for the opening of its first indoor market. Vienna had one in 1771, but it was small, inadequate, and like Jonathan's Coffee-House, used for various other purposes.

Securities dealers throughout Europe considered the move indoors a sign of permanence and status. Not only did a building symbolize the fact that the investment community had "arrived," but it provided the means whereby outsiders and the general public could be excluded.

Not all brokers were invited to come inside; generally speaking, the more substantial members of the community organized the indoor exchanges, while the rest remained out of doors, to continue trading under the sky. In the eighteenth century most cities that had an indoor market or markets also had groups of brokers who traded in the street. The two communities were at first differentiated by wealth, although in time status became the most important criterion. To the financial community in particular, but the general public as well, indoor trading appeared more honest and respectable than that which was done outdoors. At the same time, the indoor markets were usually more conservative and opposed to change; most of the innovations and experimentation which transformed the small auctions into the sophisticated, giant securities markets of today originated among the outside brokers. In addition, some of these men became wealthier and were more successful than their indoor counterparts. In the late nineteenth century, for example, the Coulisse, the outdoor market of Paris, did a greater volume of business than the Bourse, the indoor exchange. Finally, outdoor brokers had to be more skillful than the established men of the exchanges, for they had fewer rules, customs, and guidelines they could follow.

In London and Paris, Amsterdam and Antwerp, Berlin and Vienna, the outside brokers came to look upon the move indoors as the doorway to respectability and enhanced status. So it was in the United States, and in New York in particular. This book relates how the curbstone brokers of lower Manhattan made such a move, and in so doing established the foundations for today's American Stock Exchange.

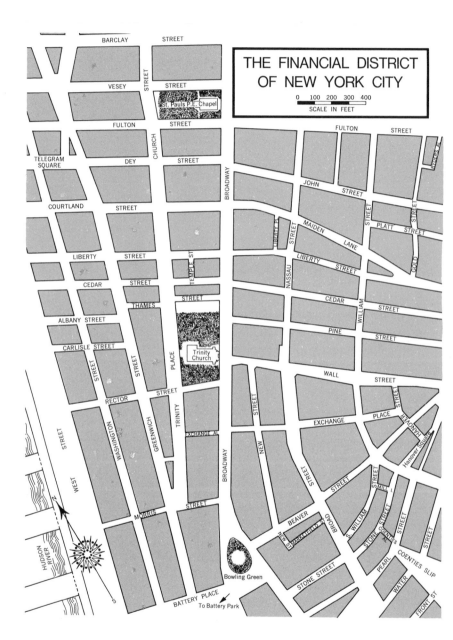

THE FINANCIAL DISTRICT
OF NEW YORK CITY

0   100 200 300 400
SCALE IN FEET

I

Some Stayed Behind

IN 1792, with a population of 34,000, New York was more a conglomeration of neighborhoods and districts than a community. There was a feeling of unity in Boston, where the old aristocracy still dominated commercial and political life. Philadelphia and Charleston were under the control of Quaker and French social and business leaders, and one could walk from one end of these cities to the other without having the feeling of entering and leaving a separate enclave every ten minutes or so. But New York was different. Even then, there was a sense of discontinuity and variety not to be found in other towns along the Atlantic seaboard. Those who held power elsewhere tended to retain it for many decades; in New York, a second-generation family of prominence would be considered a member of an old aristocracy. The early Dutch settlers were still there, to be sure, but they had more influence north of the city than on Manhattan island, where they had to share social leadership with those upper-class Tory families that remained after the Revolution and were able to adjust to the new dispensation. The city had a Jewish quarter, where the Sephardic businessmen and merchants lived and worked together, mixing only slightly with the gentiles. There was a small French community, Quakers and Baptists on Long Island, and a colony of Swedes on Staten Island. Each group was aware of the existence of the others, but were separated socially, coming together for only a brief time while the capital of the new nation was located in the city; when Washington left for Philadelphia in 1790, they drew apart once more. Social life remained segregated, although the business world was, as always, far less interested in a man's religion and nationality than with his prospects, abilities, and money.

During weekdays all elements of the population mingled in the business district, and if they did not form partnerships and combines, they would at least be willing to talk with one another, discuss common problems, and buy and sell goods and contracts in competition and cooperation. As was the case prior to the Revolution, money remained the great solvent in New York, and nowhere was this more evident than along Wall Street, the city's business district.

The life of Wall Street revolved around its docks. Within two years New York would become the leading American port in terms of total tonnage, a position it would never relinquish. Wall Street was an axle with each end a series of docks that in good weather were busy six days a week. The Rector Street and Washington Street docks on the West Side served as the terminus for the Hudson River traffic in furs and other products from as far north as the Canadian frontier. River boats would unload on the West Side, their goods to be stored in warehouses, and from there transshipped to Europe. The situation was reversed at Coffee House Slip and other docks on the East River side of Wall Street, the fast-growing importing center of the new nation. The East River warehouses were filled with English textiles, Latin American coffee, and Asian tea. In addition, American molasses, fruits, and even tobacco were sent to New York for shipment to Europe. Finally, some goods came to New York by an overland route. Cattle were driven down from New Jersey and Westchester County, to be slaughtered below Wall Street. The meat was sold locally, while hides and other by-products were processed in small tanneries and sent to domestic and foreign markets. The center for this trade, too, was located on Wall Street.

The Street itself was a wide, unpaved lane, its surface hard as stone during the dry summer, but a muddy quagmire after the long rainstorms of spring. It was lined on both sides by small buildings, none of which were more than two stories in height.

Should one leave the dock areas, he would see neat brick homes, most of which were constructed after the great fire of 1776, which had destroyed a good deal of the city. Many were business centers, with offices on the ground level and apartments on the second floor. At this time Wall Street boasted hair dressers, tailors, shoemakers, and shops where one could purchase candles, curios, and medicines. In addition to the warehouses on the Hudson end there were coffeehouses, agency offices, and boarding houses where river men would stay prior to making the trip up river. The East River side was far busier and more crowded. The city's best coffeehouses and taverns were there, as were offices of leading import firms, the Bank of New York, money lenders and a few small insurance-factoring concerns and their branches, as well as the offices of businessmen with interests in the import trade.

The East End businessmen were generalists. In 1792 none could afford to specialize in imports, private banking, land speculation, factoring, insurance, or the several other concerns of a later era. Instead, the merchant of that time would invest in land companies through the purchase of shares, insure cargoes, purchase bills of exchange, and buy and sell currencies. He might also help organize tontines, the combination insurance-gambling scheme popular at the end of the eighteenth century, and he would be drawn to lotteries, the most widespread form of speculation in America. By 1792 he might also buy and sell shares in the new banks that were being announced almost every week, such as the Tammany Bank, the Million Bank, and the Merchants' Bank, or the "blue chip" stock of the new Bank of the United States. The government's funding plan required the issuance of bonds, and these too were subject to speculation. The same man might be a director of the Tammany Bank, hold shares in the Scioto Company (which was engaged in land speculation), have an interest in a cargo of coffee due in New York the following month, be a partner in a fur business, sell marine insurance, and own a lottery. There was nothing unusual about this; such free-wheeling was the norm among merchants of stature in 1792.

Not all businessmen operated on this scale. The big businessman who insured a cargo would spread his risks by reinsuring portions with marginal tradesmen, who were sometimes allowed to take shares in land ventures if sufficient funds could not be obtained from the usual sources. Such individuals could not expect to participate in tontines organized by the city's leading businessmen; nor would they be asked to join private clubs, serve on the boards of the new banks, or be called upon to accept commissions from the new government. They made their livings in such trades as butchery, wig and candle-making, and with their surplus capital would participate as satellites in the deals of those who had offices on the East End.

Almost every small mercantile establishment offered lottery tickets, the owners receiving a commission for each one sold. They would not organize or back a large lottery, but served as subcontractors and agents on many occasions. When speculation in banks and bonds became popular, they would purchase a few shares, or a portion of a bond, but no more. These small businessmen knew their places, and they would do nothing to earn the anger of their betters, living as they did on their sufferance. Their offices—when such individuals could afford them —were not to be found on Wall or Broad streets with the city's commerical elite, but instead were farther south, in the less fashionable section around Pearl Street, near Coenties Slip, among the warehouses and naval supply stores. Thus, just as most of the New York area was divided into neighborhoods, segregated by religion and national origin, so those businessmen engaged in commerce were located in two quarters; the leaders "uptown" at Wall Street, the lesser lights "downtown," closer to the Battery.

This was the situation in early 1792, when Wall Street was in the midst of its first bull market. Speculation in treasury bonds and stock in the Bank of the United States, which was soon joined by other bank securities, sparked the increased trading. In so doing, it helped create a new kind of securities market.

As late as 1790 there had been no securities exchange on Wall Street. Should a businessman wish to sell some shares of stock, or purchase securities of any kind, he would spread the word in the coffeehouses, or at most place an advertisement in one of the many newspapers. Since there were so few public companies, and most of these closely controlled banks and insurance companies that were really partnerships in disguise, there was no need for a market or exchange. Commodities dealers met regularly to buy and sell furs, molasses, and other goods that came and went through the port, but such individuals did not consider stocks and bonds of sufficient interest, and so ignored them. This situation changed with the bull market, when on busy days more than one hundred shares in a bank might change hands on Wall Street. This increased activity led a few businessmen to keep a small supply of securities as part of their inventory, much as they would bolts of cloth or barrels of rum. McEvers & Barclay, with offices on Greenwich Street and a warehouse on Pearl, was one of the first to enter the business. John Pintard of Wall Street was another, and he was followed by Leonard Bleeker, whose office at 16 Wall Street was one of the finest in the city, and Sutton & Hardy, which was next door at 20 Wall. By the autumn of 1791 demand for securities was such that these firms and others felt the need to keep running accounts as to the securities each wanted to buy and sell. Pintard might have a request for ten shares of the Bank of North America, or five half-shares of the Bank of the United States. If he didn't have these in his office, he might send inquiries to other businessmen in order to find out where they might be obtained. This was a cumbersome procedure, and by early 1792 those interested in such paper decided to try a different operation. They would advertise for individual securities in the newspapers, but at the same time would announce auctions, to be held in their offices at specified times. This method had long been used in furs and tobacco; now it was adopted to securities.

Institutions change rapidly when they are being formed and when the need arises. John Sutton was one of the first to recognize this need. In late February or early March he formed a partnership with Benjamin Jay to engage in general business, but particularly to speculate in securities. Together with other Wall Street leaders he organized a central auction at 22 Wall Street, which held public sales in securities every day at noon. Some of the old auctions continued, but within a matter of days the new "Stock Exchange Office" had become the largest in the city.

The organization of the Stock Exchange Office was simple.

Sellers would bring their securities to the Office before noon, and deposit them with Sutton, Jay, Alexander Zuntz, or one of several auctioneers, who would receive a commission on each share or bond sold. Similarly, other businessmen would bid on shares for their own or customers' accounts, and would receive commissions from their clients. In short order, however, the system began to fail. Outsiders would attend the auctions solely to learn the going prices. Then they would offer the same securities at lower commission rates. In addition, they would trade in securities after the session was completed, in this way taking potential sales from the next day's auction. Such individuals received an increasing share of the securities business when the bull market broke in the second week of March. Moreover, members of the auction would themselves enter into outside transactions. The Stock Exchange Office, established to regularize securities dealings, was clearly unable to fulfill its function due to the interlopers and the unwillingness of the founders to give it all their business.

Wall Street's leaders met at Corre's Hotel on March 21 to correct this abuse. By then the bear market was in full swing, and many of the smaller fry as well as a handful of the city's aristocrats were close to failure. The men at Corre's Hotel represented the most powerful partnerships in New York. Now they would organize to prevent future panics, stop the wholesaling of securities, end fee-cutting, and eliminate outsiders from the securities business. In essence, they agreed to form a new auction, to be put into operation on or after April 21. The signatories would buy and sell securities among themselves at fixed fees, and would not attend other auctions. This agreement was signed on April 17 by twenty-four men or firms, including such a luminary as Warden of the Port Augustus Lawrence. All came from the Wall and Broad streets area except three merchants from the lower city, whose offices were in that section for business purposes alone. They had organized a brokers' guild, whose major function was to exclude nonmembers and maintain rates while minimizing competition.

For a while the new organization met in the street, close to the East River near what is now 68 Wall Street. Then, in late autumn, they moved indoors to the Merchant's Coffee House.

In early winter they had decided to construct their own building, close to the river on Wall Street. The brokers organized the New York Tontine Coffee House Company, chartered "for the purpose of a Merchants Exchange," and sold 203 shares for $200 each. Apparently any businessman could purchase a share, and not all the money had to be raised at once. The price was too high for most of the marginal businessmen, however, and in the end membership was virtually restricted to the wealthy members of the city's financial Establishment. Such men as Pintard, who was important in banking and insurance, helped found the New York Historical Society, and spoke several Indian languages, were leaders at the Tontine. Solomon Allen, New York's "dry goods king" was another. Nathaniel Prime, who for many years served as American agent for leading European commercial houses was one of the Tontine members, as was Samuel Ward, organizer of New York's largest brokerage.

What of the men who were not invited to Corre's Hotel that March and did not join the Tontine for financial or other reasons? They remained on the periphery of the emerging securities market, earning their livings by working with and sometimes for the Tontine Establishment. During slow periods they would go bankrupt, close their shops and work for wages, or leave the city for better prospects elsewhere. Many would return in bull markets, and new men would arrive to join them, hoping to make it big on Wall Street.

Few outsiders managed to become rich without being absorbed into what in 1817 had become the New York Stock and Exchange Board. The most powerful brokers had their offices at the Board; the most notorious speculators were among its members. Jacob Barker, the first great Wall Street plunger, operated while a Board member, as did Samuel Beebe and others who made fortunes during the great securities expansion of the 1820s. In this period only one man, Jacob Little, was able to become a Wall Street giant without having first obtained membership at the Board. Little's situation was not due to choice; he was blackballed at least three times before being admitted to the Board.

Brokerage remained a part-time pursuit during the first half of the nineteenth century. Even in boom periods volume rarely exceeded seven thousand shares a day at the auctions. The Stock and Exchange Board relocated every few years, sometimes to alleviate crowding, and on two occasions because the members thought the rent too high. The Board moved once to avoid an epidemic, and another time because its building was burned to the ground. But the organization always had a location, either a room or a building, on or in the vicinity of Wall Street. Nonmembers were seldom wealthy enough to afford even modest quarters. They would trade in restaurants and coffeehouses, or at the offices of a non-Board broker who was successful enough to have a room to rent, although not so respectable or well-connected to be granted membership at the Board.

By the late 1820s there were more nonmember brokers than ever before, as the financial boom of the Jacksonian period drew hundreds to the city. During warm weather they would trade in the open air, and former Board members who had lost their seats would mix with newly arrived hopefuls and older men who were never able to make it to the Board. Since they gathered in the streets, Wall Street thought it best to name them after their condition: they were known as curbstone brokers.

One of the more difficult problems faced by curbstone brokers was that of pricing. It was a simple matter in flour, tobacco, sugar, and other commodities. Since large quantities of these goods were sold, and most of uniform quality, potential buyers and sellers would base their bids and asks on the last quotation at the auction. Generally speaking, the heavier the trading and the greater the number of buyers and sellers, the smaller the price fluctuations from sale to sale. Such was not the case in securities in the late eighteenth century. Since there were so few public companies and only a handful of traders in this market, the last sale price had little meaning to the next customer.

Curbstone brokers were able to compete with Board members as long as this situation prevailed. They could haggle over the price of Bank of North America stock, knowing that perhaps one hundred shares would be sold at the auction that day, if indeed any transactions took place at all. The broker able to obtain one thousand shares of such a security could set prices without worrying too much about the auctions, since potential buyers would be obliged to come to him as the only source. There is some evidence that curbstone brokers were attempting to corner stocks in this manner as early as 1815.

As interest in securities grew and the financial community expanded, the Board came to resemble the commodities auctions far more than it did the gentlemanly club of the late eighteenth century. It was not unusual for four hundred shares of a popular stock to be auctioned each trading day, at a time when the firm would have fewer than sixty thousand shares outstanding. In such a situation, non-Board members were obliged to set their prices with reference to those at the auctions. The Board realized this, and took steps to prevent all nonmembers from using their rooms. Thus they hoped to exclude curbstone brokers not only from trading but also from the vital gossip that preceded the auction. It was difficult to operate on Wall Street without such information, since few brokers dared set prices or enter into negotiations before knowing what had transpired at the Board.

By the 1830s most non-Board trading took place in the afternoon, when the final sales prices reached the Street. Mornings would be spent in other businesses, or in preparation for the auction's closing. This system had its drawbacks, the most important of which were the difficulty of obtaining customers in competition with the Board and the near impossibility of making sensible decisions without adequate information. The curbstone brokers survived, apparently by paying for information, cutting prices and commissions after hours, and continuing their old practice of working for the Board members by doing errands and accepting subcontracts.

Such problems had little meaning during and after the panic of 1837, in which hundreds of businesses failed, among them the bulk of the curbstone operations and even some large Board houses. For the next few years the securities business ground to a near halt on Wall Street and elsewhere. The Board itself was in tight financial straits; it was unable to purchase a long-dreamed-of site for its own building, and had to distribute $20,000 of treasury funds among the eighty-eight members, many of whom needed the money for necessities. Once again the young exchange was obliged to seek new, less expensive quarters.

Activity increased and volume began to rise in 1845, as the worst of the depression was over; prosperity returned in 1846 with the Mexican War and hopes for territorial expansion. The Board was then situated in a large room in the Merchants' Exchange Building, which occupied the block between Wall Street and Exchange Place and Hanover and William streets. It was one of the most magnificent edifices in the city as well as the largest. The Merchants' Exchange was far too spacious for the Board alone, and brokers, insurance firms, and mercantile establishments as well as municipal agencies had offices there. But the Board was its biggest tenant, paying $1,500 yearly for its room. It could have afforded even more in the lush Mexican War period. The admission fee was $400, and through fines collected for infractions of rules the Board might expect an additional $300 or so per man. (Yearly expenditures, including rent and salaries, did not exceed $5,000 until the 1850s.) All would-be members had to apply to the admissions committee for consideration, and could not do so unless they had been in brokerage for at least one year, were solvent, of "good character," and had sponsors. Even then, three blackballs out of a membership of more than eighty would exclude an applicant from membership and the auctions.

Many curbstone brokers attempted to join the Board in this period, and most were blackballed. Reasons for such action were never given, but personal pique, bad business reputations of applicants, insolvencies, and such were probably of prime importance. Judged by membership rolls, it would seem that few if any Jews were admitted, and only a handful of members were Irish Catholic, at a time when the city directories indicate that quite a few New York brokers were of these faiths. Such exclusion was not only common, but an accepted part of New York life in that period; the city's newspapers would often identify businessmen by religion or country of origin, and anti-Catholic prejudice was at a high point in the late 1840s and early 1850s, as immigration from Ireland swelled.

For whatever the reasons, there were many solvent, aggressive, non-Board brokers in the financial district in the 1840s. These men found it difficult to conduct business without knowledge of Board transactions and resented being denied membership, which conferred not only a license to make commissions but also added considerably to one's status in the community. It was these problems and desires that led to the formation of a second securities exchange, called the New Board of Stock Brokers or, more commonly, the "Bourse."

Very little is known of the Bourse. It is referred to as early as 1834, when a group of curbstone brokers rented a small room near the Board in which to trade. Spies would be dispatched to listen in at the auction and immediately report quotations to waiting Bourse members, who would base their trades on activities at the older market. Membership was open to all who would contribute to room rental, and in early 1837 the Bourse had more members than the Board. The majority of these were small-time operators, although some were prominent businessmen blackballed at the Board, while a few were former Board members expelled for shady dealings.

Volume was higher at the Bourse than at the "Old" Board in this period. Since the latter retained the auction system, which allowed for the sale of one security at a time, there were definite limits as to how much business could be transacted at the two auctions a day then scheduled. The Bourse practiced continuous trading, with individuals moving rapidly from place to place seeking buyers and sellers of all securities. In addition, the curbstone brokers would trade before, between, and after the auctions, sometimes in their room, but more often in the Street.

Before the Board could decide on proper means of retaliation against this competition the panic of 1837 struck, and the Bourse dissolved without a trace. It next appeared in 1845, when old and new curbstone brokers rented another room, this one next door to the Board at the Merchants' Exchange. Once again the spies were sent out, and as the bull market developed, the Bourse became a large institution.

This time the Board was prepared for the competition. Regular customers were warned that the Board frowned on dealings with the Bourse members. Those curbstone brokers who joined the Bourse lost a good deal of their subcontracting business in lottery tickets, insurance, and other fields, as well as in securities. Retaliation was swift, and few small brokers could withstand it. The message was clear: join the Bourse and become the enemy of the Board. If all this failed, there was always the last recourse: the Board became a more flexible institution, and opened its rolls to some Bourse members, saying in effect that if you can't lick them, let them join you. The various stratagems worked. The Bourse was down to fewer than two dozen members in 1847, while the Board had upward of ninety. The newspapers do not refer to the Bourse after 1848; apparently the institution faded and disappeared, its members having joined the Board or returned to the outdoor market, which was now located at the corner of Wall and Hanover, a few steps away from the Merchants' Exchange.

By that time a pattern had been established that would continue for another seventy years, and to a certain degree remains intact to this day. The Stock and Exchange Board—the precursor of the New York Stock Exchange—was to be the central institution of the financial district and community. Membership conferred not only a license to dominate securities trading and underwriting, but also a status not to be found elsewhere. Those who belonged were part of a still larger community, which included the city's leading banks and insurance companies, its political and social aristocracy, and members of the best clubs. Since that period the financial district has also provided livings for other brokers and investment bankers, far more numerous than the Exchange members and in some cases wealthier and even more powerful.

The Exchange, which after the Bourse episode became more flexible than its founders might have thought wise, had three ways of dealing with outsiders. The more aggressive of those who attempted to compete with the Exchange would be opposed with whatever weapons were at hand, and others that were developed in future years. Whenever an outside group attempted to form a rival exchange or similar institution, the N.Y.S.E. could be counted upon to move quickly to check its growth, and then to administer the crushing blow.

Those exchanges and individuals that could not be eliminated were courted. After all attempts at coercion failed, the Exchange would open its doors to mavericks and enter into negotiations with rivals. On one occasion it would revamp its entire operation, and in effect become the junior partner in a merger with a more powerful but less prestigious rival. When the Exchange acted contrary to the wishes of so powerful an individual as Cornelius Vanderbilt, it was met not only with scorn but active opposition, and was forced to back down and conform to the Commodore's wishes. The Exchange was willing to do battle with opponents, but would not continue to fight should defeat appear possible.

The third method of dealing with outsiders was the most satisfactory for all concerned. Should the curbstone brokers be content to work for and not against the Establishment, they would be safe from attack. Not only would they prosper, but they could expect a niche of their own on Wall Street, with a monopoly of those securities not traded at the Exchange. Indeed, the Establishment would in time come to prefer such an arrangement, for this method kept both marginal men and securities from tainting the image of respectability it so much wanted to preserve. By the early 1850s the curbstone brokers were trading at Wall and Hanover, on the street, in the open, good weather and bad. So long as they stayed there, they were tolerated and encouraged.

It was this desire for respectability, and the belief that by leaving marginal business to the curbstone brokers they would achieve it, that almost caused the downfall of the Board. For in the next two generations the most dynamic segments of the economy would be in that very area, and the fact that the curbstone brokers were able to exploit new industries and securities while the Board preferred to concentrate on the old, enabled many newcomers to become rich. With these riches came desires to form rival organizations, which would not have been possible were it not for the Establishment's limited views on what constituted status, power, and economic growth. On several occasions these new exchanges came close to destroying the Board's power and displacing that institution. The fact that the New York Stock Exchange and its predecessors survived was due more to the nature of the business cycle and good fortune than to wise, enlightened, and farsighted leadership.

II

The Rival Exchanges

THE NEW YORK Stock and Exchange Board was more flexible in its approach to men and change in the 1850s than it had been a half century earlier. Still, it moved slowly on most issues, and tended toward a conservatism based on a desire for respectability and a reluctance to explore and innovate. During the next generation Wall Street would become a stage for some of the boldest men the nation would ever know. Cornelius Vanderbilt, Daniel Drew, Little, and Barker would remain for a while, and would be joined by Jay Gould, Jim Fisk, Addison Jerome, Henry Keep, and many more, whose speculations, corners, and dealings would determine whether or not a railroad was built, a panic occurred, or a politician nominated for the presidency. Never before or since had such a cast of colorful characters occupied the financial scene at the same time. The age of the "robber barons" on Wall Street would not come until the 1890s. This was the period of the buccaneers, and none of them was a Board member.

Such a situation was not considered unusual or undesirable. The Board had been founded by merchants who dabbled in many fields. They would buy goods from farmers, fur trappers, and others, to be sold and transshiped elsewhere. In most respects, they resembled middlemen and agents as much as independent businessmen. Furthermore, they conducted a good deal of their transactions with agents of European firms, and their social and business aspirations were derived from them rather than the back country producers; their ideas, values, and hopes came as much if not more from London than they did from the United States. The Board was an increasingly significant part of the American aristocracy, but the nation as a whole had little use for any aristocracy other than that which was natural. Such men, European in orientation and unskilled in the production of goods, were not equipped by training or desire to participate in the great economic boom of the next two decades, whose leaders they would serve but not join.

The Board members differed from their clients in still another and perhaps more important way. By the 1850s a second and in some cases a third generation of brokers was in power at the auctions. The Cutting, Brown, Clark, De Coppet, Ferris, Groesbeck, Jacquelin, Lockwood, Marvin, Rollins, Thorne, and Williams families represented the kind of father and son companies found among the Board's leaders. Such had been and was the case at the London exchange and in Paris, and so it would be in New York. In time they would be joined by the Clews and Eames families, and several others, who accepted the tradition and carried it forward. Some, like the Lockwoods, would leave Wall Street in disgrace after having been involved in a minor way in illegal transactions. Others, like the De Coppets and Jacquelins, who soon began to specialize in odd lots, continued to prosper for another century. All were alike in attempting to maintain an atmosphere more in keeping with the commercial America of the 1790s than the emerging industrial nation of mid-century.

These men and families faced a difficult task in this period. On the one hand, they hoped to participate in the growing and rapidly changing economic and financial opportunities of the next generation, while on the other they tried to erect unchanging institutions that would stand the test of time. These desires were contradictory; permanence and change can rarely exist together. To their credit, the Board Establishment did make an effort at compromise; it would admit new men, but not their ideas. Only individuals who would conform to its ethic were allowed to join the Board. But the old unwillingness to accept Irish Catholic and other religious minorities remained. Exchange rosters of this period were sprinkled with old Dutch names such as Van Vliet, Van Schaick, Stuyvesant, and Dyett, and the honored Anglo-Saxon families such as Manley, Smith, Knight, and Huntington. Of the more than five hundred members of the mid-1860s, there were only three O'Briens; no other name was clearly Irish.

The Board's unreceptiveness to new ideas and desire for respectability enabled the curbstone brokers to grow in number and wealth. Unlike the Establishment, they were willing and eager to adjust to new circumstances, enter new businesses, and explore the potential of the emerging industrial economy. As that segment of business grew, so did their fortunes and power. As early as 1857, *Hunt's Merchants' Magazine* would identify the curbstone brokers as "a very large class of speculators . . . composed of the oldest and most experienced operators in the Street. Many have been members of the Stock Exchange but from having failed to fulfill their contract during some of the numerous ups and downs of the market have been compelled to vacate their seats and lost their membership." This did not mean, however, that they were all of that stripe, for "the contracts of many of the curbstone brokers are infinitely better than many of the Regular Board. . . ."

The curbstone brokers of this period were more likely to seize the main chance than would their colleagues at the Board. Both recognized the importance of the railroad, and securities in large and small lines traded at the Curb and the auctions in the early 1840s and afterwards. Generally speaking, the larger, more solvent, and more heavily capitalized lines were to be found at the Board. The New York Central, the Harlem, the Illinois Central, the Erie, and the Reading were all considered "Board securities," and these were soon followed by others, including the Canton, the Cleveland & Toledo, the New Haven & Hartford, and even the Third Avenue Railroad of New York. By mid-decade railroad securities were more important than banks and insurance stocks at the Board. Similarly, curbstone brokers would deal in the rails. Some would attempt to make markets in Board stocks, and such men were singled out for destruction; Board members would not buy or sell or in any other way transact business with those who dared deal in securities claimed by the Establishment. On the other hand, the curbstone brokers were allowed to trade in the thinner, less heavily capitalized securities that did not interest the Board members. Such distinctions were not legal, or based on clear-cut rules and regulations; the Board did not have listing requirements before the Civil War, and any security that interested its members would be accepted for the auctions. The railroad securities experience helped set the pattern. New issues would come to Wall Street and first be traded at the Curb. Then, when they attracted the attention of the Board, they would move to the auctions. At such a time prudent curbstone brokers would cease trading in the securities; those who attempted to continue did so with clear warnings of retaliation.

Fortunately for the men of the Curb, new issues were quite common in the decade preceding the war; there was no shortage of business. Conditions improved markedly after the discovery of gold in California, an event of major importance for the nation as a whole, and one that almost shattered New York's securities market.

The Wall Street brokers competed not only with each other, but with their counterparts in Boston, Philadelphia, Baltimore, and other cities. Each market had a near-monopoly over local issues in the early days, and would retain it until the 1880s. The railroad changed the situation somewhat. It was clear that Philadelphia would dominate trading in Pennsylvania banks, while New York would control prices for local insurance companies. But what of railroads running through or between the two cities? Competition had existed as early as 1792, when the Board was first organized; now it heated up, as the contest for the rails pitted New York, Philadelphia, and Boston against each other, and all against St. Louis, Chicago, and other cities with their own, small exchanges.

The California gold rush and other mineral finds in the West further complicated matters. Almost immediately mining exchanges appeared in Colorado, California, Idaho, and elsewhere in the West. Little is known of these small, crude exchanges, in which shares of new mines traded in heavy volume and very low prices. By 1851 some mining shares appeared in St. Louis, where they were traded in low volume. Within a year, they had come to Wall Street.

The Board members did not trust the new securities. In the first place, mining securities were considered exotic in New York, since there were few mines in the area. Shares in several coal companies traded at the Board, but were inactive and generally unpopular. More important, however, was the question of distance and mystery, two elements the Wall Street Establishment of the 1850s did not appreciate. Brokers of this period did not trust intangibles; they wanted to be able to walk into a bank whose shares they purchased, or visit a canal that wanted to sell bonds. Although the railroads were speculative, the brokers could see the right of ways being cleared, the engines arriving, and the depots being constructed. Investors could not go to California very easily so as to enter the mines. Even the bullion carrying ships that left the West Coast for New York were considered unsafe and had to pay high insurance rates; as late as 1857 the steamer *Central America*, with 1.6 million in California gold in its hold, sank off Cape Hatteras, with the loss of four-hundred lives and the entire cargo. Finally, none could guarantee the honesty of mining shares, or even gauge their value. The mine might prove to have no gold, or could be worked out in a matter of a few weeks, and then be worthless. Given these risks, the Establishment refused to deal in mining shares at the auction, allowing the curbstone brokers a monopoly on such securities in New York.

The mining boom of the mid-1850s was one of the greatest the nation had seen up to that time. Far more shares were sold than rails, canals, and banks combined. Their prices were low and extremely volatile, and so attracted the gaming element of the city. Such individuals would crowd the docks whenever a California ship appeared in port. Even before it tied up, the speculators would shout questions to the crew, asking about business conditions in general and the mines in particular. Each scrap of information, every rumor, was quickly transmitted to the Curb, which by the mid-1850s had overflowed from Wall and Hanover to occupy parts of William Street as well. The "mining crowd" could be found at William and Beaver, and there were located the most powerful, the most daring of all the curbstone brokers. These men would commit tens of thousands of dollars on rumors of a gold or silver strike. Talk of a new vein at an established mine could send that stock up 200 and 300 percent in a day's trading. But the Board maintained its unofficial ban on the western mines throughout this period. Some Board members would buy and sell these shares through their curbstone allies, although apparently most continued to concentrate on the rails. One of the more conservative Board members scoffed at the new men rushing in from the "provinces" to make their fortunes in the questionable paper. "One had acquired wealth by selling dry goods, and therefore was fit to be a bank president; another had been equally successful in making shoes; another had been a ship chandler, and fortunate in the schooner coasting trade; another had been a stage driver; not a few were men of the narrowest minds, wholly lacking in mercantile education, and without the ability to conduct the simplest commercial correspondence."

The Board was affected by the fever, if only indirectly. The nation's gold production, which had been 43,000 troy ounces in 1847, reached 3,144,000 in 1853 before leveling off. This great addition to the nation's money supply stimulated every aspect of the economy, and the first to feel it were the banks. A new bank was started every month in New York in 1851, and fifteen more were added in the next two years. Their shares were traded at the Board; the Establishment avoided the mines, but was willing to deal in banks whose existence and prospects were based on California gold. In this period the financial district's prosperity was based on the Curb's, while at the same time the Curb's power and wealth grew at a faster rate than did that of the Establishment. A busy day at the Board might see six thousand shares auctioned off, while Curb volume might soar to over seventy thousand shares. During some months of the boom year of 1856, over one million shares a month were traded in the outdoor market. Still, business at the Board was good enough to necessitate another move to larger quarters. In the summer of 1856 it relocated at Lord's Court, a fine building with a main entrance at 25 William Street and others on Exchange Place and Beaver Street.

The burgeoning market for mining shares, the sudden wealth of the curbstone brokers, and the continuing desire for permanence and respectability, led to the formation of several new markets. In late 1856 Ezra Ludlow, a non-Board broker, announced that he would "hold a sale of securities at 12 o'clock tomorrow at the Merchants' Exchange." Ludlow rented a room near the Board, and apparently had some success, for there are references and advertisements similar to this one as late as January 15, 1857. Leonard Jerome, the grandfather of Winston Churchill, opened an office at 22 William Street, where he promised to "devote his undivided attention to the purchase and sale of all classes of stock securities," and he too ran a private auction. By late January, there were a half dozen such small rooms on William Street just south of Wall, across the street from the Board offices at the Merchants' Exchange. Although by now forbidden to attend such private auctions, some Board members were seen at Jerome's, Ludlow's, or other rooms.

Before the Board could act against the new auctions, their leaders met to form their own exchange. They rented an office at 29 William Street in early February, and proclaimed the existence of the Mining Exchange, which in its short lifetime had more members and traded more shares than did the Board.

Little is known of the Mining Exchange, which went out of business a half year after its founding. Most New York newspapers had financial columns in 1857, and many published quotations for Board shares. Although the Mining Exchange was larger than the Board, the newspapers did not carry its price lists, and had only an occasional paragraph on its activities. From these references and a handful of memoirs, we may piece together sufficient fragments to discover the nature and history of the Mining Exchange.

Apparently, the new market had continuous trading rather than an auction; such was the custom at the Curb, and it was carried indoors. Had the Mining Exchange used the auction method, it could not have traded as many shares as it did. Several new but wealthy brokerages dominated the Exchange and one of these, Talmadge & Mawley, was as well financed as any Board house. This firm advertised widely, had at least two and perhaps three offices, and maintained a correspondent house in

Philadelphia, a practice not yet entered into by Board members. Fulton, Cutting & Co., a major specialist in mining shares, was formed by two men who had previously been members of the Board, and who may have left of their own volition. Furthermore, all attempts on the part of the Board to prevent dealings with and on the Mining Exchange seem to have failed. The Board issued repeated warnings as to consequences should this violation continue; the very fact that many warnings were necessary indicates that they were not heeded.

One can only surmise what might have happened had not the Mining Exchange been crushed in the great panic of 1857. The Exchange had begun as a market for western gold and silver mines; by April it was also trading shares in eastern copper and lead companies, and other firms whose securities were not considered appropriate for the Board auctions. Volume at the Mining Exchange reached a peak in July, and at that time the Board was still not auctioning off mining shares. Had this continued—had the bull market been extended into 1858—it is possible that the Board would have changed its policy and admitted mining shares and so combatted the Exchange, or that the Mining Exchange would have expanded and replaced the Board as the first market of the city. By then quite a few Board members were spending much of the trading day at the Exchange as volume at the Board leveled off.

The panic began in early August, although its full impact was not felt until September, when banks closed, economic paralysis set in, and several major Board brokerages closed down. Some key houses went under in the first week in August, at a time when Board securities were not too seriously affected. It would seem that these were the concerns most heavily involved in mining shares—those houses which might have deserted the Board for the Exchange had the bull market lasted for a short while longer.

Eighteen hundred fifty-seven was one of the worst years in Wall Street history. The Mining Exchange was no more; Board auctions were poorly attended, as interest in securities seemed to evaporate. A year earlier a carriage could not pass through Wall or William street until after five o'clock due to the large trading crowds. Now the streets were deserted; the curbstone brokers were once again forced to either leave Wall Street or take employment in other businesses.

The depression was short-lived, and the panic soon relegated to ancient history. The financial district stirred with activity in 1859. Mines were still interesting, but now a new group appeared to tempt the speculators. Petroleum had been discovered in western Pennsylvania in 1858, and a year later the first of the oil stocks were traded at the Curb. Wary of such speculations, the Board refused to deal in the issues, so that by mid-year the old curbstone brokers had gained a new start, while a fresh group of speculators came in from the provinces to join them. Some were wildcatters who had sold their wells and then taken their money to Wall Street to learn the arts of speculation. A syndicate of gamblers arrived from Buffalo, hoping to make fortunes in the financial district. Late in 1859 several Baltimore commodities speculators united to bull and bear mines and oils in New York. Good economic news was added to reports of gold, silver, copper, and petroleum finds. Such Curb securities as North State Gold & Copper and Gardner Hill Gold & Copper rose from less than a dollar a share to as much as $10 in a few weeks. Some Board members participated in the speculation, but the Establishment refused to trade questionable securities at the auctions, and so once again the demand for a new exchange was heard.

In the spring of 1859 several specialists in mines and petroleum stocks joined forces to rent a room at 25 William Street and organized a new Mining Exchange. As had been the case with the old Mining Exchange, trading was continuous and open to all. Within a month the facilities were so jammed that the Exchange had to move to larger quarters across the street at 24 William Street. Board members were admonished not to trade at the new market; these warnings and threats were ignored. Before the Mining Exchange could seriously challenge the Board, however, politics intruded on the financial scene. Lincoln was elected in 1860 and South Carolina promptly announced it would leave the Union. A new panic hit Wall Street, forcing the Mining Exchange to close its doors. As had been the case so often in the past, the Curb felt the affects of the bear market more severely than did the Board. Out of the liquidations and disasters of 1860 came the most exciting period of Curb history.

The Civil War marked a new watershed for the nation and transformed the financial district. Prior to the war, most brokers still could not afford to concentrate on securities alone, and had to be active in several areas. This situation changed once the North realized the war would be a long, drawn-out struggle. Hundreds of new companies were organized to supply the Union war machine. At the same time Jay Cooke and others formed syndicates to market federal bonds. For the first time, the average American was introduced to the mysteries of securities, and this increased interest in Wall Street happenings. In addition, railroad construction was stimulated both by the war and the desire to effect a transcontinental linkage with California, and speculation in these securities was also popular. Finally, the federal government issued some $400 million in "greenbacks"— paper money unsecured by gold. Since such money might be worthless should the Confederacy win the war, an active market in currency was created. All of these changes came in rapid succession; those who understood them and had the daring to take advantage of new opportunities were able to gain power and wealth.

The Board had been unable to meet the challenge of the two mining exchanges; it was even less prepared to adjust to the swiftly evolving world of the early 1860s. The increased volume of business required a reconsideration of auction practices, and perhaps its complete abandonment and replacement by continuous trading. Those conservative brokers who still controlled the Board refused to alter their methods, perhaps because they were unwilling to admit Curb practices were better than theirs and that they could learn from inferiors. Furthermore, the Board was still reluctant to admit unseasoned securities to the auction, and since the vast majority were of this variety, it meant that the Curb by necessity was bound to increase its share of dealings. Only a half dozen mines had their shares listed at the Board in 1864, while more than one hundred were traded at Curb organizations. On a typical day fewer than fifty issues would be auctioned at the Board; although it is impossible to gain exact figures for Curb operations, as many as 130 issues might trade there on the same day. While one hundred thousand shares might change hands at the Board in 1863, there is some evidence that the Curb had its first million share days that year. Finally, the Board remained an exclusive organization. Many Curb brokers clamored for admission; had they become Board members, they might have "modernized" that organization and repulsed threats from rivals. Perhaps for this reason rather than in spite of it the Board leaders closed ranks to exclude the interlopers. In 1861 twenty-nine Curb brokers applied for acceptance to the Board. Their applications underwent a total of sixty-six ballots, at the end of which only seven escaped the blackball. As a result, fewer than one hundred brokers belonged to and attended the auctions, while at least twice that number were in the securities business elsewhere in the financial district.

The rapid and dramatic change in the securities markets and the inability of the Board to meet these new conditions enabled the curbstone brokers to enjoy their golden age. From 1861 to 1869 they would set the tone for the financial community as the Board stagnated, unable to adjust to and compromise with the forces unleashed during the war.

At least eleven exchanges of varying sizes, importance, and longevity were formed in this period. This does not include over twenty minor organizations that were little more than floating crap games, and new regional exchanges, most of which disappeared after the war. All of these were led by curbstone brokers; all but one were dominated by non-Board members. Four were larger than the Board and one of them, in effect, later forced the older institution to capitulate. Throughout this entire period the out-of-doors market continued to operate on William Street, between Beaver Street and Exchange Place.

The new exchanges may be divided into three categories: those specializing in gold, the exchanges that attempted to supplement the Board, and one that tried to supplant it. The older organization cooperated with the first for the most part, ignored the second, and tried unsuccessfully to discover a method to combat the third.

In mid-1861, as Secretary of the Treasury Salmon Chase had difficulty selling federal bonds, raising funds for the war effort, and in general proved incapable of organizing the nation's finances, the hoarding of gold began in the North. By December it was clear the war was going badly, and there were fears Britain might support the Confederacy. At this time Chase was obliged to admit he had failed in his attempts at mobilizing northern capital, and acknowledged the continuing gold drain. He recommended a series of taxes and a tariff increase, but before they could take effect the nation's private banks were forced to suspend gold payments. Two months later Congress authorized the first of the greenback issues; by April the new paper money was in use throughout the North and gold coins had dispapeared from circulation, to be sold at a premium. Silver was also "demonetized" and went into hiding or, as was more often the case, was sent to Canada, where $100 in silver could be exchanged for $97 in gold, which could be sold in New York for $120 in greenbacks.

Many curbstone brokers mastered the art of currency arbitrage, which actually had been quite popular throughout American history. Others were quick to realize that the demand for gold would grow in proportion to the Union's losses and the weakness of the economy. Whenever reports of a Union defeat reached Wall Street, people would rush to get rid of their greenbacks, using them to purchase gold, the price of which would rise. Union victories would lessen the demand, leading the gold price to decline. There were no public opinion polls in the 1860s; we have no clear-cut way of knowing whether northerners expected to win the war. The gold price, however, was perhaps a more accurate barometer of such sentiments than any poll conducted by today's social scientists. In the dark days of 1863, as Lee advanced toward Gettysburg, it took $170 in greenbacks to purchase $100 in gold. A few months later, before it became evident that Grant and Sherman had turned the tide, the price of gold in terms of greenbacks reached a high point of $285. Fortunes could be made and lost quickly by buying and selling gold at the right or wrong times.

The New York newspapers carried stories of gold transactions as early as November, 1861. It was not until the following month, however, that speculation in bullion became widespread.

Recognizing the need for a market, the Board began auctioning gold in January, before the morning and afternoon sessions. Word of the last sales would be quickly transmitted to the Curb, where outdoor dealing in the metal would be continued. Some Establishment leaders protested that such trading was unpatriotic, since the gold brokers were, in effect, betting on or against a Union victory. In early summer of 1862 they introduced a resolution to stop such business. Despite vigorous protests, the motion carried. Gold speculation did not end. Instead, some Board members joined with the gold dealers on the Curb to organize a separate market at 23 William Street. The room was hot and poorly lit, and so was called the "Coal Hole" by the Board. In April of 1863 some of these brokers relocated to Gilpin's News Room, on the southeast corner of Exchange Place and William Street. Since there was no broker by that name registered at the Board, and no landlord named Gilpin on William Street, we may assume the man was a curbstone broker.

As had been the case with previous non-Board organizations, membership at Gilpin's was open to all who would pay the $25 a year fee. At first it was merely a place where buyers and sellers could meet to haggle over prices. By summer, there was a regular auction at Gilpin's. A few months later it was revealed that some gold dealers had sent representatives to the front, to learn of and report on any activities that might affect the gold price. Such knowledge could enable a speculator to make a fortune, since frontline news was the major determinant for Gilpin's prices. This market had a better information-gathering operation than any newspaper or even the government; Wall Street learned of Meade's victory at Gettysburg before Lincoln. "What do you think of those fellows in Wall Street who are gambling in gold at a such time as this?" asked Lincoln. "For my part, I wish every one of them had his devilish head shot off."

Speculators could count on "action" at Gilpin's, where the slightest fluctuations could mean the making of a fortune. Gilpin's became the largest exchange in the district during its short life, attracting most Board members at one time or another. By autumn over $5 million in gold a day might be auctioned off, and on such occasions the Board would have small attendance and low volume. Once again, the majority of Board members, forced to select between the Establishment's dictates and high profits, chose the latter.

Both to conclude this speculation and to satisfy the Board, which had representatives in Albany and Washington, government leaders attempted to close down Gilpin's and other, similar organizations. On February 18, 1863, the state prohibited banks from lending money on gold. This effectively ended some of the trading on margin that was then being practiced. Two weeks later Congress outlawed the use of gold as collateral for cash advances, thus plugging another loophole. Finally, on June 17, 1864, Congress passed a law declaring the buying and selling of gold to be penal offenses, unless the transactions took place in a private office. In effect, the bill aimed at closing Gilpin's and minor gold exchanges. But the government, no more than the Establishment, could stop this speculation. For a while the brokers would deal in the metal at the Curb, while some used their offices to set up masked auctions which conformed to the letter while violating the spirit of the edict. Since there was an element of risk in running such exchanges, sellers were able to ask for and get a higher price than might ordinarily have been the case. Thus, the legislation backfired. Congress repealed the law on July 2, and Gilpin's resumed operations.

By late September interest in gold was so great that Gilpin's could no longer admit new members to its crowded quarters. E. O. Read and John Bloodgood, two gold brokers who were also Curb leaders, rented a room at William and Beaver and transferred Gilpin's operations there. Annual membership cost $200, and was open to all. The new room began operations on October 1, 1864, with a membership list of over one hundred which included Curb as well as Board establishments. Such prominent Board concerns as Fisk & Hatch, Clark, Dodge & Co., Livermore, Clews & Co., and P. Speyer & Co. were members, as were Levi P. Morton & Co. (whose head would become Vice President of the United States), Brown Brothers & Co., and J. P. Morgan & Co. They were joined by leading non-member firms, including Hallgarten & Herzfeld, Escoriaza & Gimbernat, M. C. Klingenfeld, and C. Unger & Co.

The informal alliance between the Curb and the Board took

on enhanced meaning on October 14, when the new market was incorporated as the New York Gold Exchange, more commonly known as the Gold Room. So as to prevent the organization of a rival curbstone exchange, membership remained open to all who could pay the $200 fee, although this was raised to $1,000, and finally to $2,500 within a year. Henry Benedict and Thomas Akers were selected as president and vice president; both men were Board members. Joseph Moses, a second vice president, was not on the Board roster, however, and neither was treasurer Theodore Gentil.

For a while speculators would deliver bullion by horsecar, but this was inefficient and tempting to the criminal element. After several robberies, the Exchange entered into a relationship with the Bank of New York, which for a fee of $1,000 per account would keep deposits of gold in its vaults and honor drafts against them. This, too, proved dangerous; Ketchum & Sons, a member firm, forged over $1.5 million in drafts before being discovered. Finally, the Exchange organized the Gold Exchange Bank, with new safeguards including daily statements to all subscribers. In late 1865 almost all members had accounts at the Bank, making transfer simpler and safer. By bending to the needs of the time in this fashion, the Board did more than merely indicate its willingness to accept some minor changes; it began to transform itself into a modern institution.

For the first time curbstone brokers were allowed to join an organization that had status on the Street. They mingled and dealt with Board members, and this helped break down business barriers. For its part, the Establishment was so secure insofar as the social world was concerned, it no longer needed to exclude powerful though parvenu brokers from polite company during working hours. Never again would the Board be as rigid in its membership rules; in the future, commercial dealings with "outside brokers" on the basis of equality would not be frowned upon. In addition, the experience with gold trading taught the Board the importance of regulation and the need for a larger community of interest than had previously been the case. Gilpin's had been an unorganized market, where only the alert could avoid scoundrels. The Gold Room, in contrast, was well policed, though its trading sessions were the wildest Wall Street would ever know. The Gold Room–Board–Gold Bank nexus, when combined with the authority of leading curbstone brokers, enabled it to provide as open and honest an exchange as could be expected at that time. Furthermore, the Establishment realized that the government's action in closing Gilpin's was based as much on its thievery and shoddy nature as the desire to stop speculation in gold. For its own sake as well as to prevent outside control, the Establishment now recognized the need for realistic regulations, framed so as to facilitate business operations and not merely to freeze in power a brokerage elite.

Other, even more important changes, would come as a result of competition from a rival exchange which, ironically, would begin as a creature of the older market.

The Board's membership was small and its leaders old when the war began. By systematically excluding new men and making the Board a closed guild, the Establishment had failed to provide the means for its own renewal. This situation was further complicated by the enlistment of several young Board members, officers in local militia organizations, who now went off to war. The Board had fewer active members in 1862 than it had two years earlier. Thus, it was less prepared to meet the challenges of increased business and opportunities than ever before.

The Board's old men rose to the occasion, and began to make adjustments. Some were symbolic: on January 29, 1863, they changed the designation of their organization to the New York Stock Exchange. The name had been used earlier, but now that rival "boards" were forming in the city, the Establishment felt the need to make it official. More important, however, was a new willingness to consider outsiders for membership, which began to expand slightly in 1863.

This openness could not prevent the formation of a supplementary market late in the year. By then the auctions were hectic, crowded, and more important, far longer than ever before. Furthermore, the Curb had grown in size and threatened to set prices for Exchange securities as well as its own. For this reason, the elderly brokers were obliged to hire younger men to act as their representatives both at the Exchange and on the Curb. Prior to this time, only partners conducted business; by late 1863, representatives were handling an increasingly significant share of the transactions, and in the process learning the trade and making contacts that would prove useful in future years. Some of these apprentices hoped to be admitted as full members at the Exchange. When their petitions were refused, they sought other means of gaining independence. At that time those brokers who remained at the Coal Hole after the gold traders left for Gilpin's had united into what was called the Public Stock Board, with offices at William and Beaver. The Public Board was poorly organized and contained a shabby crew of marginal brokers as well as some honest but minor newcomers. On December 31, 1863, the latter group joined with some Exchange representatives and several Curb houses to form the Public Stock Exchange in the City of New York, which was to begin operations once fifty members had paid an entrance fee of $500. That many individuals and firms had paid their money by March, 1864, when the new organization, renamed the Open Board of Stock Brokers, rented a room at 16–18 Broad, and started dealings in securities.

The Open Board differed from the Exchange in two important respects. In the first place, although there were two, and later on three auctions, these were less important than the continuous trading that went on throughout the business day in an adjoining area called the "Long Room." Each security was traded at a specific place in the Long Room, in a combination of old Board and Curb methods. A potential buyer would go there and, shouting, ask for prices. Sellers would then bid against each other, until the buyer accepted an offer. Similarly, sellers would call out for purchase orders. In effect, there were several dozen small auctions going on simultaneously in the Long Room. Since no broker could hope to participate in all, they began to station themselves at one location or another, and concentrate on individual securities. Brokerages might have one partner at the auctions and another in the Long Room. The latter would command several representatives, each of whom was to stay at a different place and was charged with bidding for certain securities. In this way, the present specialist system was born.

True to its name, the new organization was an open one. Any trader who was not a member but was willing to pay an entrance fee of $50 per day was entitled to use its facilities. As the Open

Board grew in popularity, many brokers applied for regular membership, and the fee was raised to $2,000 before the war ended. As might be expected, promising young men who had thought themselves doomed to serve as Exchange clerks for the rest of their lives left the older organization to go to the Open Board. The Exchange recognized this threat, and raised its admissions fee to $3,000, but provided that representatives with three years service might join for half that amount. Doubtless this helped persuade some to remain at the Exchange, although the outpouring of talent to the Open Board continued.

Within a year the new organization was doing ten times the business of the old, and had attracted the most ambitious of the men then crowding into the financial district. Some of them were Jews and Catholics. Such people could work as clerks and runners at the Exchange, and had done so in the 1850s. Unconvinced that they could hope for membership there, and unwilling to wait out the three-year trial period only to be blackballed and denied admission, they went to the Open Board. In 1865 several prominent members of the new market were of foreign birth; Irish, Spanish, and middle European accents were not unusual at 16–18 Broad Street, where Charles Hallgarten, William Henriques, Mendes Nathan, J. E. P. Lazerus, Soloman Levy, and E. L. Oppenheim were founding members and B. F. Gallagher, Morris Nathan, and William Kennedy were officials. The largest Open Board brokerage, Hallgarten & Herzfeld, which was also active at the Gold Exchange, bought and sold over $169 million of securities and metal in 1865, a far larger volume than any Exchange house.

Finally, there were new markets that attempted to supplement the Exchange rather than challenge it. For the most part, these were organized by and for marginal dealers and those adventurous speculators whose appetites for action were not slaked by the dealings at Gilpin's.

In 1861 a group of these men, led by Nathaniel Godwin (sometimes reported as Goodwin) rented a room at Lord's Court, not far from the Board. Their spokesmen made it quite clear that they had no desire to do anything that might arouse the Establishment's anger. Rather, they hoped to trade in Board securities between the calls in such a way as to service rather than undercut the older institution. The Board concurred; volume was low in 1861, and Godwin's did not seem a rival organization. Under the agreement, Godwin's was allowed to have one of its representatives stand in the vestibule during the auctions and shout prices to his fellows, who would then trade in the securities between calls. Since many Board members had clerks at Godwin's, they viewed the innovation as an extension of, rather than a challenge to, their postions.

The Board took a less favorable view of the evening exchanges, the first of which appeared in 1862 at the Fifth Avenue Hotel. Brokers and speculators would retire there after the exchanges and Board closed, to continue trading. By mid-year an evening market had been established at Fifth Avenue and 23rd Street, which did a small business for the "uptown crowd" during the day, and was jammed with regulars after working hours. During the war, the 23rd and 24th Street areas, between Broadway and Fifth Avenue, became a nighttime financial district, with brokers' offices, its own curb market, and several rival exchanges.

In March, 1864, a curbstone broker by the name of R. H. Gallagher (sometimes spelled Gallaher) leased part of Republican headquarters at 23rd Street and Broadway, which he converted into an evening exchange. The Republicans met there during the day; the brokers took over at night. The new market was a success, and Gallagher took his earnings, purchased property on 24th Street and Fifth Avenue, and erected a building that he called the New York Evening Exchange, which opened for business in April, 1865. Gallagher charged a membership fee of $250 a year, but would allow speculators to enter for a nightly fee of 50 cents. The new market, the only building in the city designed primarily for securities trading, attracted most of the Wall Street crowd to its evening dealings. During the summer of 1865, as speculation established records in the district, the Evening Exchange might accommodate over one thousand brokers at a time, among them most of the Exchange and Open Board members. By then, too, volume at Gallagher's was larger than that of the two major daytime exchanges combined.

The Open Board, which was a much more flexible organization than the Exchange, considered Gallagher's an asset to the community. The Establishment, however, thought the Evening

Exchange a den of thieves, which might try to threaten its position. Warnings to members began in mid-summer, but these were ignored. Then, after the Ketchum forgeries were discovered, and a reaction against marginal dealings began, the Exchange took its strongest action to date, promising that "Any member who shall be present at or indirectly send orders to be executed at what is commonly designated as the Evening Stock Exchange, shall cease to be a member of this Board." The Open Board and the Gold Exchange cooperated with the Establishment, and within a short time, Gallagher closed his market. For a while, however, New York had 'round-the-clock trading, the only place in the world with this innovation. And Gallagher had his imitators. In the half year after Appomattox, there were at least seven evening exchanges in the city, most of which moved from hotel room to vacant office every week or so.

Then there was the old Curb, still a leading market for non-listed securities. The curbstone brokers had cordial relations with the Open Board, since so many founders of that market had begun their careers as out-of-doors brokers. During the next four years other successful curbstone brokers would be admitted to the Open Board, while their places in the street were taken by newcomers and fallen members of indoor markets. The combination of Open Board and Curb was far more powerful than the Exchange, and this was known to all perceptive members of the financial community. The major question of this period seemed to be, "Would the Exchange prove flexible enough to meet the challenge?" For if it were not, then it would surely disappear.

III

Consolidation and the Consolidated

THERE WERE FOUR separate related communities in the New York securities business at the end of the Civil War. First and foremost was the New York Stock Exchange, which did not have the authority it wielded in the antebellum period, but still listed the most prestigious, trusted, and powerful of the Wall Street houses and individuals on its rolls. The Open Board of Stock Brokers was larger than the Exchange, with more members and a greater volume of trading. Its leaders were either first-generation Wall Streeters or individuals who before the war had been on the Curb. The Open Board counted among its members some of the wealthiest people in the city, and several had the proper credentials to seek admission to the Exchange. That they did not do so indicated that the Open Board had visions of replacing the Exchange as the city's leading market. Just as a new industrial elite was rising to take power from the partnerships of the 1850s, so the Open Board thought it could supplant the family concerns and old aristocracy that still led the Exchange Establishment. The third group was comprised of those brokers who belonged to the evening exchanges, the mining and petroleum boards, and to other tertiary markets. Like their betters at the Open Board, they actively competed with the Exchange for business. Although they had little hope of ever rising to great power or prominence, such men thought they would be able to win customers by offering slightly lower prices and shaving commissions. As a rule, they were the least reliable or honest group on the Street. The fourth was the old Curb, where brokers still traded out-of-doors, mostly in securities not carried on the Open Board or Exchange lists.

Members of the two major markets fought for customers, but joined with leading Curb houses in organizing the Gold Room and closing such marginal operations as the evening exchanges. The curbstone brokers would accept orders from both large markets, and since they did not deal in the same securities, were able to retain the good will of the district's leaders. Furthermore, the exodus of prominent curbstone brokers to the Open Board did not abate, giving these two communities an even closer connection. Finally, members of the tertiary markets also operated at the Curb, where they competed with the regulars of that group, and at the Gold Room, where they sometimes joined in the speculations. Some Open Board houses, such as Hallgarten & Herzfeld and Gentil & Phipps, had memberships at the Gold Exchange, Gallagher's, and several of the mining boards, as well as clerks at the Curb. Leonard & Manley, an Exchange firm, also belonged to the Gold Room and was represented at Gallagher's. This overlapping of interests would continue, even as each organization battled the others. But one line was clear throughout the postwar period: the Exchange and the Open Board were willing to join with the Curb to eliminate the tertiary markets. For the next generation, this fact would dictate the organization of the financial district and would set a pattern that determined the shape of that community for a century and more.

The Exchange and Open Board drew closer together soon after Appomattox, and by 1867 were cooperating in several joint ventures. The two markets remained separate and competitive, but the Exchange abandoned hope of destroying the Open Board, which on its part devoted more attention to Long Room operations than auctions, and showed a willingness to allow the tone of the market to be set at the older institution. This *rapprochement* was not due to a recognition of the benefits to be derived from cooperation, but rather was forced on both markets by circumstances beyond their control.

The postwar period saw a continuation of the wartime

economic boom, and the securities and gold markets were busier than ever before. Now that the fighting was over and the nation secure in its future, speculators were wilder and more numerous than they had been earlier. Daring operators and outright swindlers had accounts at several brokerages, and rejecting the business code of the antebellum period, would cheerfully default on obligations. The Open Board and Exchange houses entered into an arrangement in 1866 whereby they would pool information on such individuals, who would be blacklisted and forbidden from dealings. In this way the community of interest which was already in existence at the Gold Room was enlarged, while the marginal operators were forced into cooperation with the smaller exchanges, making these more suspect than before.

Technological change also forced cooperation. The Atlantic cable was completed in 1869, making possible almost instantaneous communication between the London Exchange and New York. Foreign investments in American stocks and bonds, which had risen sharply in the immediate postwar period, now skyrocketed. These securities were traded at the London and Paris markets with greater ease and confidence, since brokers in those cities were always apprised of the New York closings of the previous day before going to the trading areas. As early as 1867 American railroad bonds were becoming London favorites, and such issues as Union Pacific, Norfolk & Western, and Louisville & Nashville were familiar to British traders. Now many other securities joined them in English portfolios.

European banking houses refused to be drawn into the competition between the Open Board and the Exchange, and in fact discouraged it, since it increased the uncertainties of the American market. Thus, any attempt on the part of the Exchange to destroy the Open Board would be frowned upon by America's best securities customers. Similarly the London Establishment, which had strong ties with its counterpart in New York, would not permit Open Board incursions against the Exchange. Insofar as the burgeoning foreign securities trade was concerned, then, the two rivals cooperated and shared the business.

E. A. Calahan patented the first practical stock ticker in 1867. Calahan, an employee of the American Telegraph Company, was backed by leaders of the Gold & Stock Telegraph

Company, a firm organized to exploit the new invention. The New York brokers quickly recognized the ticker's value, since it would enable them to get rid of their small armies of runners while speeding up and facilitating trading. There is no evidence that the Open Board or the Exchange attempted to monopolize the tickers. Had either done so, the other would have suffered a damaging and perhaps destructive blow. David Groesbeck, an Exchange member, had a ticker installed in his office late in 1867; Lockwood & Co., an Open Board leader, advertised such a service in January, 1868. By that time, it would appear the two exchanges were moving closer to cooperation in such matters.

A common desire to regularize methods and exclude interlopers also united the exchanges. In 1864, the Establishment reorganized the New York Mining Exchange. Unable to compete with the Curb in the more seasoned issues, it concentrated on new mining and petroleum offerings. Since most of these were swindles, it took a daring (and usually marginal) speculator to buy stock at the Mining Exchange. In 1865 such companies as Woolah-Woolah Gulch Gold Mining and Gulliver Canyon Gold and Silver Mining were speculative favorites at the Mining Exchange. As far as can be learned from meager reports, none of these new issues found its way to the established exchanges.

Since the Mining Exchange operated under Establishment control, Open Board members were barred from its sessions. The younger organization retaliated by organizing the New York Petroleum Stock Board in 1865. S. B. Hart, then Open Board president, encouraged his members to trade there, hoping to put the Mining Exchange out of business. The Petroleum Board also dealt in new issues, and even had a longer list of stocks, since it aggressively sponsored petroleum companies as well as mines. The two markets attracted shady characters, however; after the war the original sponsors left, and both were controlled by near-criminals.

Since these new men were not concerned with pleasing the major exchanges, they united in January of 1866 and reorganized as the Petroleum and Mining Board, with hopes of becoming a permanent institution. At this point the Open Board and the Exchange joined forces to expose the shady element there, while at the same time fraudulent dealings led the few remaining respectable brokers to quit the organization. Some of them attempted to organize a second new market, called the Public Petroleum Stock Exchange of New York, but both tertiary markets declined and soon after went out of business.

The common effort to rid the district of corrupt (and possibly rival) organizations further united the Exchange and Open Board leaders, and encouraged a movement toward amalgamation that was evidenced as early as 1865. The great expansion in trading of that year forced a search for a new Exchange site. Some Establishment members formed the New York Stock Exchange Building Company, purchased land at 10–12 Broad Street, and constructed a four-story building which became the Exchange's home on December 6. Now the Exchange and the Open Board were neighbors, and this close proximity led to greater social and business contacts. It also resulted in a series of friendly overtures.

The Exchange expanded by adding a separate wing devoted to government bonds in 1867. Since Exchange leaders had important contacts at the Treasury Department they were able to win many flotations, in effect monopolizing the transactions in New York. The Exchange also indicated a willingness to share this business with the Open Board, and allowed its members to attend the bond auctions, with full privileges of dealing.

The Open Board reciprocated the following year. By that time several marginal brokers had joined the Long Room crowd, and that market was now viewed as a den of thieves. President J. L. Brownell ordered the room closed to such individuals and ended the practice of admissions on a daily basis. An exception was made for members of the Exchange, who continued to trade at the Long Room. The Long Room was closed in mid-1868 and its operations transferred to the basement of the New York Gold Exchange, which itself relocated to 12–16 New Street, with an entrance at 14 Broad as well. Thus, the block bounded by Wall Street on the north, Broad to the east, Exchange Place on the south, and New Street to the west (the site to today's New York Stock Exchange) housed the city's three leading indoor markets, with the Exchange and the Open Board on either side of the Gold Exchange, where they shared in currency trading on the first floor and coordinating continuous trading in the basement. Furthermore, they united to exclude nonmembers from dealings in both rooms.

The next step came in October, when the Exchange voted to allow the transfer of membership by sale. New members had to be accepted by a committee on admissions, rather than the old method of vote by the entire membership, where blackballs were still the practice. Since the Establishment controlled the committee, and was leading the movement for union with the Open Board, brokers at that market were assured membership if they desired to purchase a seat. As it happened, few chose to join the Exchange. T. S. Vanderhoef did become a member on March 26, but his brother and partner, Edgar, remained at the Open Board. In any case, by that time the question was almost academic, since merger talks had begun in early autumn.

The coming union would create an organization with great power, one that had a near-monopoly on dealings in leading securities. For the past few years, stock manipulators and leading railroad tycoons had played the two exchanges off against each other. The Exchange was rebuffed whenever it attempted to obtain financial statements from companies whose shares were traded at the auctions. It could scarcely take action against such firms, for if its shares were delisted they could still be traded at the Open Board. As a result, speculator-businessmen were able to do what they wished with their company's securities, without fear of retaliation. Stock watering and other dishonest dealings were considered the privilege of those who controlled any railroad's treasury and printing press. Unusually adept at these practices were Commodore Cornelius Vanderbilt, Jim Fisk, Jay Gould, and Daniel Drew, an unholy foursome who took turns milking the Erie Railroad dry. Drew in particular was an expert in such maneuvers. He would enter into short sales in Erie, and when asked to deliver would print new shares for the purpose. Exchange leaders objected, but Drew and his sometime partner Vanderbilt ignored them.

In December of 1868 the Exchange announced that in the future all outstanding shares in firms whose securities were traded at the auctions would have to be registered. In addition, listed companies would be obliged to submit periodic financial reports to the Exchange. Within a week the Open Board released similar statements. Although few such reports were forthcoming, all firms with securities at the two exchanges complied with the registration requirement, except the Erie. As a result, that line's common stock was removed from both the Exchange and the Open Board, and rejected for trading at the continuous market in the Gold Room basement. For the first time, Wall Street attempted to regulate the quality of its merchandise. This could not have happened were it not for the joint action taken by the two leading markets.

Drew and Vanderbilt were quick to retaliate. Their first step was to encourage curbstone brokers to specialize in Erie. Curb leaders, many of whom needed Exchange business in unlisted securities to exist and who had close personal and social relations with the Open Board, refused to deal in Erie. Others, especially marginal brokers, leaped at the chance, and with Vanderbilt's blessing and aid from the Erie directors formed a new indoor market, the National Stock Exchange, more commonly known as the Erie Board. This organization occupied a room on William Street which was open to all brokers who would pay the $500 admission fee. There were no other membership requirements, and none for listing of securities. The Erie Board attracted some men from the Petroleum and Mining Board and the Public Petroleum Stock Exchange, as well as those curbstone brokers who had little to do with the Open Board and the Exchange. It soon had over three hundred members and was trading in most of the issues listed at the two major exchanges, whose leaders warned that any broker seen near the Erie Board would be ejected from their midst. Wall Street was divided into rival camps. On one side was the Exchange, the Open Board, the Gold Room, and leading curbstone brokers, while the marginal men were on the other, together with Drew and Vanderbilt and their allies. The Gold & Stock Telegraph Company, which was allied with and controlled by the Exchange, refused to lease tickers to the Erie Board. The Erie Board was denied clearing-house facilities, its members were rejected in polite society (since few could aspire to social acceptance, this meant little), and were subject to threats. Still, they did a respectable volume of business, an indication that such an organization had a chance of succeeding in the financial district. Then, in early autumn, Vanderbilt left the Erie board of directors and lost interest in the enterprise. Without his backing, the Erie Board collapsed and went out of business. Erie registered its shares, and was readmitted to trading at the established markets.

While battling the Erie Board, officers of the Exchange and the Open Board also met to discuss common problems. Accord was reached between the two groups in late April. The Exchange rewrote parts of its constitution, and on May 1 announced that in the future all power would be vested in a new governing committee consisting of twenty-eight members. A week later leaders of the two markets released their merger agreement. Twelve Open Board brokers would be selected for the governing committee, and more would be named to other Exchange committees. All those who were members of the Open Board and the Government Bond Department would automatically obtain seats at the Exchange. The new organization would have 1,060 members, of which 527, or three less than half, came from the two newer markets.

The Open Board held its last sessions on May 10, 1869. The brokers let up a shout as the final trades were made at 3:00, and while singing "Auld Lang Syne," raised Vice President George Henriques to their shoulders and marched to Delmonico's for a round of drinks. Afterwards, they joined the more austere Exchange community to ratify the articles of agreement. Thus ended the Open Board of Stock Brokers, the most successful of all curbstone organizations, and the only one to defeat the Exchange in battle. The next day saw the beginning of the revamped New York Stock Exchange.

Consolidation soon brought an end to the Open Board auction and introduced members of the old Exchange to the continuous market (but not too detailed an initiation, since most of them had representatives and correspondent houses at the Open Board much earlier). The Long Room was reopened for this purpose, and although often undergoing renovation and expansion, would serve as the Stock Exchange's major market until 1903. The auctions would become increasingly less important, and were finally abandoned for stocks in 1882, and for bonds in 1902. In 1870 the Stock Exchange purchased the land and edifices on 10–

18 Broad Street from the Building Company for $575,000, and in 1879 additional land to the south on Broad was obtained for $377,488. In this way, the revamped Stock Exchange indicated that Wall and Broad would be the center of future securities dealings in New York.

Not all agreed to accept Stock Exchange leadership. Some Open Board members, for example, had opposed the consolidation. Feeling that they were asked to give up too much for what was received, they voted against the plan. As they saw it, the Open Board had proven its superiority to the Exchange, which had been forced to seek a union in order to survive. If this were so, then the Open Board deserved to be the senior partner in the merger, and should have more than half the members of the governing committee. In addition, these individuals had fought the Exchange for a long time; the idea of joining their adversaries was repugnant. The fact that the enlarged exchange intended to maintain strict standards indicated to some of this group that a good portion of their business might be lost to the curbstone brokers. Finally, these men viewed the consolidation as an act of desperation, a major effort at restraining competition which was doomed to failure. The early success of the Erie Board was one sign of this, and the continued prosperity of leading curbstone brokers another. New opportunities were continually opening up, and those who opposed the merger felt reasonably certain the Stock Exchange would be unable to meet these challenges, just as it had so often failed in the past.

Soon after the consolidation went into effect, these individuals joined together to form the Unlisted Securities Market. Its purpose was to make markets for those issues that had been traded at the Open Board but were not acceptable to the revamped Stock Exchange. In other words, they would concentrate on stocks in companies whose leaders had opposed the Stock Exchange's attempts at regulation. The Unlisted Securities Market seemed to have a bright future. It initiated talks with the Erie Board with an eye toward a merger, and began trading in Curb issues as well as inviting important outside brokers to join their ranks. There is little written about the Unlisted Securities Market. The newspapers mentioned it in passing the summer of 1869, but it disappeared from sight in autumn. In all probability, it disbanded about the same time as the Erie Board. During its short existence the Unlisted Securities Market provided an indication of the district's future. Among other things, it demonstrated that not all brokers accepted Stock Exchange leadership. Given the opportunity to do so, such men would organize similar markets.

To have any chance of success they would have to fulfill a need not being met by the Stock Exchange and the curbstone brokers. The former controlled trading in seasoned securities, while the Curb concentrated on smaller companies. At that time both markets tended to cater to the more sophisticated investor and speculator, while during strong bull markets they would also handle transactions for newcomers. Neither market attempted to provide services for the small investor. Finally, both the Stock Exchange and Curb tried to regularize trading and at least give the semblance of discouraging "gaming tactics." As a result, those outside brokers who hoped to compete with rather than act as satellites of the major exchange tended to exploit these areas; they would specialize in new issues, fill small orders for occasional investors and speculators, and seek clients among gamblers and other "disreputable" elements. At the same time, they would offer rebates, lower commissions, and special prices to speculators in Stock Exchange issues, in the hope of winning their business. During the last quarter of the nineteenth century, these markets were enormous, and the potential for success considerable.

Gold was discovered in the Black Hills in 1874, setting off what would prove to be the last of the major gold rushes for a quarter century. Soon after copper and lead became important in the West's development. Additional transcontinental railroads were constructed, and their spurs went to the mines to bring the minerals back east. Information regarding new mining companies came to Wall Street earlier, as did a large number of fresh mining companies for the district's speculators. Some of these companies would prove sound and well managed; Anaconda Copper dates its origin to the 1880s, when it was a small outcropping near Helena, Montana. But most were swindles, marginal speculations, or at best inflated hopes of unrealistic promoters. Such firms could not hope to have their securities traded at the Stock Exchange, and many curbstone brokers—especially those with close affiliations with the Establishment—shied from them. There were customers for the new shares, however, and brokers to underwrite the issues, make markets for them, handle orders, and benefit from these transactions. The 1873 panic had sent many brokers into hiding or bankruptcy; now such men returned to participate in the new bull market for mining shares. Once again, the district was ripe for another wave of "exchange-formations" similar to that of the mid-1860s.

Twenty-five of these men organized the New York Mining and Stock Board in an office at 60 Broadway, in September of 1875. This action was discouraged by district leaders, and those curbstone brokers who joined it lost a good deal of Stock Exchange business in unlisted securities. The risk seemed worthwhile; interest in mining shares was growing, and the new Board's organizers thought that, given time, its members would attract enough business to prosper. Meanwhile, there was insufficient volume to support the membership. Therefore, the new Board announced it would also buy and sell "odd lots" (less than one hundred shares). The Stock Exchange had previously refused to accept such orders, although bidders and sellers of large blocks were permitted to deal in irregular amounts. Thus, Wall Street offered no facilities for the small investor. Now these individuals flocked to the Board's new office at 24 Pine Street. Unfortunately for them, its members were usually fly-by-night operators whose shady dealings became evident shortly after the new Board was organized. The market was dissolved in February, 1876, amid a flurry of bankruptcies and lawsuits. Writing of the new Board that year, the *Engineering and Mining Journal* said, "It contributed, more than any other cause, to bring mining interests into disrepute in the East, for it was made the agent for floating all kinds of swindling enterprises."

The demand for new mining shares did not abate, and as might be expected, promoters set to work organizing a new exchange. The American Mining Stock Board made its appearance in September, 1876, announcing its intention to create an honest market for mining company shares, and by implication, to avoid dealing in Stock Exchange securities. By November, however, its brokers had learned that there were still insufficient customers for such securities to make a large market, and so they changed the name to the American Mining and Stock Exchange and began trading in odd lots of listed securities.

The new market did better than its predecessor. It was a fairly honest exchange for the time, had some substantial members, and was able to ride the crest of a bull market. The fact that several important businessmen, including Jay Gould, supported the organization, afforded it additional strength. Although it did not prosper in a spectacular fashion, the American Mining and Stock Exchange was able to gather sufficient business to indicate that it might become a permanent market, and in the future rival the Stock Exchange.

The Establishment used a variety of weapons against the new organization. After ignoring it for a few months, during which time the mining shares were traded out-of-doors, the Stock Exchange warned that it would consider relocation to an indoor site a declaration of war. When such a place was found, and the marginal operators had a roof over their heads, the Stock Exchange demanded a state investigation of shady dealings in the financial district. Affiliated curbstone brokers were told that any hint of connections with the Mining and Stock Exchange could mean an end to their privileged positions in regard to outside stocks. The most effective move, however, was to initiate the revival of the New York Mining Stock Exchange early in 1877, which was located at 18 Broad Street, in the New York Stock Exchange Building.

At first this market was controlled by the older organizations, whose members were encouraged to purchase seats. It was to deal only in mining securities but later on, when the Stock Exchange showed little interest in new industrial firms, these were included. The Mining Stock Exchange vowed not to allow the purchase or sale of any listed security and to immediately stop dealing in any security should it be accepted for trading at its parent market. Since the Mining Stock Exchange would not handle marginal railroads, gas companies, coal mines, and other curbstone favorites, it would not threaten the business of outside traders, either. In effect, the American Mining and Stock Exchange was left with only the odd lot market. Such business was insufficient to support the organization's brokers, and it conceded defeat; in June, 1877, remnants of the distressed market were permitted to join the Mining Stock Exchange, which now had a near-monopoly on such securities in New York. In order to accommodate the enlarged membership, the Mining Stock Exchange moved to a large hall at 60 Broadway near Exchange Place.

This victory was hollow, however, especially for those members who did not have Stock Exchange affiliations. The great mineral boom appeared over; new issues no longer had glamour on Wall Street. As business declined, the independent members petitioned for a union with the older exchange, asking to be made affiliates but not members of that market. Such a limited merger might place them in a position to become junior partners in some underwritings and large block sales, which in the late 1870s seemed necessary for survival.

The Stock Exchange refused such requests. Throughout its existence the Establishment would accept change only when forced upon it by outside pressures. Since there were no such problems at that juncture, the Stock Exchange tended to go along in the same ways as it had since the consolidation. From time to time new markets would appear, but these were short-lived, and could be readily absorbed into the Mining Stock Exchange. There are some scattered references in the newspapers to an "open board," which apparently specialized in odd lots, but this was a minor organization, and could be ignored. Some Pennsylvania brokers had formed a New York Petroleum and Stock Board in 1877, although this too was unimportant at the time.

Aware that any attempt to expand beyond the narrow limits of mining shares would bring Stock Exchange opposition, but unable to survive on that business alone, the independent members of the Mining Stock Exchange searched for expansion in other fields.

In 1879 the petroleum pipeline that originated in western Pennsylvania reached its terminus at Bayonne, New Jersey, where the crude oil was refined and stored for transshipment throughout the East. Ever since the mid-1860s there had been a petroleum exchange at Oil City, Pennsylvania, where shares in exploration and production companies were bought and sold, and new money raised for speculative ventures. In addition, the Oil City market transacted business in a new kind of security, called pipeline certificates. Despite their name, these were really commodities futures. A petroleum producer would sell contracts for crude oil, which would be delivered at a specified place at a mutually agreed upon price on a designated date. Such contracts had existed in an informal way before the Civil War, and were used then as now in farm products. After the war, when demands for capital were high and producers unwilling to tie up funds until their goods were sold, they became more popular, and were an important speculative vehicle. Grain, beer, and pork "futures" were bought and sold in several New York locations by organizations specializing in that trade, the largest of which being the New York Produce Exchange. At this time, there was no clearcut connection between securities dealers and commodities brokers, although occasionally each would transact business in the other's markets.

Pipeline certificates presented the Mining Stock Exchange with a badly needed opportunity for profit. Trading commenced in 1880, and at the same time the Petroleum and Stock Board, working in conjunction with the Oil City crowd, began dealings in the paper. To further complicate matters, some members of the New York commodity markets joined to form the Miscellaneous Securities Board, which also competed for customers. Thus, a three-way struggle erupted, which did not involve either the Stock Exchange or the mass of curbstone brokers. Large profits were to be made, both in speculation and brokerage. Certificates for more than one million barrels of crude were traded at the Mining Stock Exchange in 1883, while stock sales amounted to some 1.5 million shares. The following year, 3.2 million barrels were sold at the Mining Stock Exchange, and stock volume was two million shares. By that time, it was evident that more money was to be made in certificates than in stock. Such profits resulted in the formation of still a fourth minor market, the National Petroleum Exchange.

Competition between these four markets was fierce, so much

so that their leaders were obliged to seek accommodations with each other. At the conclusion of several meetings, the National Petroleum Exchange joined the Mining Stock Exchange on March 16, 1883, to form the rather awkwardly named New York Mining Stock and National Petroleum Exchange. This organization took over the Miscellaneous Securities Board on November 16, and then entered into merger talks with the Petroleum and Stock Board. After much discussion, including trips to Oil City to win that market's approval, the two rivals united on March 19, 1885. In view of the complex mergers and changes of the past decade, the new organization took the name of the Consolidated Stock and Petroleum Exchange. Since each merger resulted in the joining of two sets of brokers, the Consolidated started its life with a membership of 2,403, or more than twice that of the New York Stock Exchange. It was, for the time being at least, the largest securities market in the world in terms of members.

The new name indicated the nature of its business and structure; the Consolidated was, in fact, an amalgam of four smaller organizations and had a special interest in pipeline certificates. Its large membership was by no means homogeneous. Some were interested solely in pipeline certificates, others specialized in mining shares, and a handful were really odd-lot dealers. Approximately four hundred members of the Mining Stock Exchange also held seats at the Stock Exchange, and they joined the Consolidated. Now that they were together in a single organization, the founders had to decide the nature of their market and, most importantly, its relationship to the Stock Exchange.

It is at this point that accounts and reports begin to differ. Leaders of the Consolidated would claim that they tried every avenue of cooperation with the Stock Exchange, and at no time attempted to rival it. According to them, their market was designed to service customers and transact business not being satisfied by Stock Exchange instruments or brokers. Pipeline certificates, commodities, mining shares, and odd lots had no place at Wall and Broad, and were almost the entire business of the Consolidated. The older organization had consistently refused to list shares in the newly formed industrial sector, especially steels, mercantiles, and petroleum companies, and these too were traded at the Consolidated. Younger brokers, those rejected for membership at the Stock Exchange, and certain specialists, would comprise the bulk of the membership; these men were of no interest to the Establishment. Volume was rising on Wall Street, and at times the senior market was flooded with orders it could not handle. At such moments, those four hundred or so brokers who held dual memberships could transact business at the Consolidated, making it a supplementary market for the district. Finally, the Stock Exchange was still in competition with markets in Chicago, Boston, Philadelphia, and other cities, and would not deal in securities listed on their boards. The Consolidated, which had no reason to oppose out-of-town exchanges, could provide services for those New Yorkers who wanted such stocks and bonds.

The Stock Exchange took a different view. In the opinion of its officers, the Consolidated was a rival market, and not merely a supplemental one. While it conceded that the new organization had sworn not to admit those issues already listed at the Stock Exchange for round-lot dealings, its members were even then conducting a lively, surreptitious business in listed rails. Furthermore, Consolidated officials were considering the listing of small railroads, the type of company that in a few years would ordinarily apply for admission to the Stock Exchange trading sessions, and this seemed to indicate a desire for expansion and competition. Many of the Consolidated's members were suspicious characters, whose past activities had bordered on the criminal. Their presence in a supposedly reputable organization cast aspersions not only on their fellow-members, but the entire financial community. Cooperation with out-of-town exchanges, while not directly competitive with the Stock Exchange, gave aid and comfort to the enemies of the Wall Street Establishment and could not be countenanced. The odd-lot business attracted small speculators to Wall Street, and this was considered dangerous to the district's stability. Although the Consolidated claimed that it was interested in the Stock Exchange's overflow alone, the fact that listed securities were traded on quiet days seemed to prove the new organization planned to aggressively challenge the older one.

As usual, both sets of charges contain half-truths and exaggerations. What does seem clear, however, is that the Consolidated's trading volume and the number of customers it was able to attract exceeded all predictions. From the first, the organization was solvent, successful, and secure. (According to its own figures, which unfortunately are not accurate, the Consolidated dealt in 5.8 million shares in the last five months of 1885, 41.7 million in 1886, and 57.8 million in 1887, a year in which Stock Exchange volume was 84.9 million.) Obviously, the Consolidated represented a threat. Stock Exchange leaders, some of whom were former members of the Open Board, remembered the earlier experience with a strong rival, and had no desire to undergo a second period of competition. Almost immediately, they set about nipping the danger in the bud.

In late March of 1885—only weeks after the Consolidated's opening—the Stock Exchange announced the formation of a special department to handle unlisted securities. The official statement said nothing of the Consolidated. Rather, it noted that during the panic of the previous year many of these stocks declined in such a way as to wipe out hundreds of speculators. Furthermore, state legislation had made some railroad securities almost worthless, and the public had to be assured that a Wall Street agency would vouch for their financial statements. Finally, the Stock Exchange was obliged to recognize and satisfy the increased demand for industrial securities, which the committee on stock list still felt were unsuited for regular trading. Writing of this period a generation later, a Stock Exchange president said, "But the public had shown a disposition to buy the 'industrial shares,' and members of the Stock Exchange felt compelled to buy those shares for customers and assume the risk of carrying them without the safeguard of a public market. Stocks, which were not in a position to meet the requirements of the Committee on Stock List, were admitted to the 'Unlisted Department.' This department did not create the industrial stocks. The creation of that department was a result which followed the public demand for such stocks at a period when other stocks had been discredited." In actuality, however, the Unlisted Department was the first salvo in the attack on the Consolidated, and an attempt to win customers from the rival organization.

The second came a few days later. Those Stock Exchange members who were also founders of the Consolidated were forced to relinquish their business at the latter market, and all transactions with Consolidated brokers were banned, under threat of severe disciplinary action. Simultaneously, the Establishment warned satellite curbstone brokers that they would be cut off from Stock Exchange orders if they persisted in dealing with the Consolidated, tried to purchase a seat at the new market, or transacted business with it. As a result of these bans and threats, over five hundred Stock Exchange and curbstone brokers left the Consolidated; by 1887 the organization had fewer than 1,200 members, or half its original number.

Still, the Consolidated was able to expand. Many of those brokers who held seats at both markets and relinquished their offices at the Consolidated were represented there by sons, brothers, or friends. In time, an affiliation at the Consolidated came to be considered one way for such individuals to learn the securities business, after which they would apply for and often receive Stock Exchange seats. So many members of the senior market retained their ties with the Consolidated that the older organization dared not enforce its bans, but for the time being was satisfied to repeat them periodically. The odd-lot business and pipeline certificate sales continued to rise, even though volume in mining shares declined. It was possible to make a living at the Consolidated, and so long as this was the case the Stock Exchange could do little to destroy that market.

The Consolidated began a search for a new site in mid-1887. Business was expanding, and the old quarters were inadequate. There were several large halls in the financial district, but any landlord who might rent rooms to the Consolidated realized that he could hope for no business from the Stock Exchange. Finally, the Consolidated decided to erect its own building. Land was purchased on Broadway and Exchange Place, and the cornerstone laid on September 8. Noting the occasion, the *Times* editorialized:

Whether there is "room" in New York for a second Exchange is a question that can be answered only by experiment and that seems to be the way of receiving a favorable answer. The position of the Stock Exchange toward the new Exchange is understood to be that the new

Exchange is a "bucket shop," meaning that it allows dealings in lots beneath the dignity of the older body. As a matter of fact, this difference by no means indicates that the business of the new Exchange is at all more aleatory than the business of the other. There is an official pretense of referring to people who gamble in stocks as "investors" even when their investments consist in betting on a fall. Nevertheless, there are such creatures as investors, though a broker may pass a busy life without falling in with one. The Stock Exchange recognizes as investors only persons who wish to buy and sell 100 shares of stock at each operation—that is to say, still in theory and assuming all stocks to be at par, persons who have not less than $10,000 to invest upon every occasion when they invest at all. . . .

It should be noted, however, that the *Times* was a conservative newspaper, and had often written of the entire Wall Street community as a den of thieves, waiting to plunder all who entered its confines. At this time too the newspapers were carrying stories of the decline of Henry Ives, a noted plunger who had looted several railroads, and then went bankrupt in an attempt to corner the stock of the Baltimore & Ohio. Ives had close Stock Exchange connections, and this seemed an added reason to criticize that market, especially when it attempted to blacken its rival's reputation. But the key charge made by the Stock Exchange at this time was that the Consolidated was a bucket shop operation. These were fighting words in 1887, and an exploration of them will reveal a good deal about Wall Street's topography and infrastructure in the late 1880s.

IV

Bucket Shops on Broadway

THE *New York Times* regularly worked for an end to bucket shops in the financial district. James Gordon Bennett's *Herald* considered them to be the city's worst blight. The legislature in Albany would demand investigations at almost every session, and no gubernatorial candidate could consider his campaign complete without at least one speech against bucket shops. The Stock Exchange accused the Consolidated of being "nothing but a den of bucket shops," while the new organization promised to "refuse admission to any of the many bucket shops that now abound in the financial district." Both exchanges warned the curbstone brokers to refrain from "bucketing operations," and the most damaging rumor that could be started regarding a Curb regular was that he ran one. Clearly, the fact that so much attention was paid to these places indicates that they were believed to be a significant part of the financial district in the 1870s and 1880s, and their presence, absence, actions, and operations would determine the future not only of individual brokers, but of such important institutions as the Curb and the Consolidated.

Like most expressions that become epitaphs and curses, there is no clear meaning to the term, "bucket shop." Just as in the 1950s the word "communist" was hurled about so casually as to lose its original meaning and become synonymous with any individual with whom the speaker disagreed on political, economic, or social questions, and as in the 1960s "racist" came to indicate a person whose ideas on specific social questions differed from one's own, so it went with bucket shops in the two decades prior to the turn of the century. The words did originate to describe a specific place, and then their meaning expanded to include many similar locations. The first bucket shops appeared in London in the early nineteenth century, and were unrelated to either securities or brokerage. At that time it was customary for some of the city's mendicants to go from tavern to tavern carrying buckets, begging to take the last, bitter dregs from the bottoms of beer barrels. Should they cause no trouble and amuse the paying customers, permission was often granted, and fortunate "bucketeers" might also be allowed to empty mugs and wine bottles and squeeze the bar cloth, the contents of which would go into the buckets. Afterwards, such individuals would gather in a den to pool their resources and drink it down. These rooms came to be known as bucket shops, or places for disreputable drinkers.

Whenever a London broker wanted to indicate that a rival was not above engaging in shady operations, he would charge that he ran his office like a bucket shop. It was a common invective, taken as seriously as minor curses are today. Although the term was not mentioned in American newspapers at the time, antebellum brokers probably used it to describe their enemies and operators in other cities.

The words appeared with greater regularity during and after the Civil War. At first they were applied to newcomers and those Stock Exchange members forced to leave that organization due to irregularities or failure. Such men would rent shabby offices, store fronts, or hotel rooms, to be used as brokerages. Since they had no connections with the larger exchanges, and could not wrest business in unlisted securities from leading Curb houses, they were obliged to support any and all new markets that appeared in this period. The evening exchanges and some of the mining boards in particular became hangouts for bucket shop brokers. There they would transact business in competition with the Big Board, getting away with it by charging lower commissions, handling odd lots, and offering securities loans to their clients. For a while—especially during bull markets

—such brokers were able to prosper. With each crash, hundreds would be wiped out, and their clients would suffer due to foreclosed accounts and undelivered securities. This happened in the panics of 1873 and 1884, and the several minor fluctuations between. The bucket shop operators always returned afterwards, however, in many cases renting their old offices and soliciting business from the same speculators they had hoodwinked earlier. Since the latter often had no credit at the Stock Exchange houses, they had little choice but to patronize the bucket shops.

Lower Broadway was lined with these marginal brokerages in 1885. Most were on the east side of the avenue between Wall and Beaver streets, some overflowed into Exchange Place and New Street, while there were a handful of offices as far north as Pine Street. Ignored by the Stock Exchange when they concentrated on unlisted securities, snubbed when they tried to mingle with the more secure and accepted houses, and condemned should they attempt to compete for clients, bucket shop proprietors tended to stay away from Wall and Broad, and confined their operations and social lives to lower Broadway and the Bowery.

These were the kind of men who had founded the New York Mining and Stock Board in 1875. The fact that the organization was put together at 60 Broadway was no accident, for John Stanton, a leading bucket shop operator of the period, had his offices there, and became the Board's president. It is worth noting too that the Mining Stock Exchange, the marginal organization set up to rival the Mining and Stock Board, generally followed Establishment leadership and dictates until mid-1877, when it took in members from the defunct Mining and Stock Board and the American Mining Stock Board. Then its policies began to change, and one indication of this was the move to 60 Broadway in July of that year. Finally, when the Consolidated was organized in 1885, many of its members were former leaders at the Mining and Stock Board, including Stanton, Joseph Gay, and R. H. Rickard.

Charles Wilson, the Consolidated's first president, who held that office from 1885 to 1899, was forty-two years old at the time of the founding. His career was typical of the new exchange's leadership. Wilson was born in Baltimore, studied law, and came to New York in 1876. He quickly learned there was money to be made in the financial district. Wilson opened a brokerage, and although he had arrived too late to join the Mining and Stock Board, he did become a member of the American Mining Stock Board. After that organization closed down Wilson applied for and received membership at the Mining Stock Exchange. While there he became a leader of the anti-Establishment forces, and attempted to convince the membership to deal in odd lots. Failing in this, he left to join the newly formed National Petroleum Exchange, and in mid-1882 became that organization's vice president. Wilson returned to the Mining Stock Exchange the following year, when it merged with the Petroluem Exchange. By that time his kind of broker dominated that market, and in 1885, when the Consolidated was formed, he was the popular choice for the presidency. Throughout this entire period—from 1876 to 1885—Wilson's own business continued to prosper. He was considered an expert on copper stocks and the district's shrewdest dealer in pipeline certificates. Wilson used his office to further expand his operations, so that before the end of the decade his was Broadway's leading nonmember house. Wilson purchased a fine mansion in Brooklyn (a separate city until 1898, when it was incorporated into New York City), became a factor in that city's Democratic party, and even dabbled in the arts. Of course, he was not accepttable in polite society, but in his own circle Wilson was king.

Men like Wilson saw nothing wrong with their exchange or the way they conducted business. As far as they were concerned, the Consolidated filled an important need on Wall Street. If this were not so, they argued, how could they exist? Stock Exchange members continued to ignore the odd-lot customers, charged high commission rates, were reluctant to deal in the stocks of new industrial companies, and in general were at least a generation behind the times. Furthermore, the Stock Exchange had all the earmarks of a trust, and this was a time when that word too had begun to take on evil connotations.

Originally, trusts were organizations—usually industrial—to which the stockholders of several corporations had assigned their shares, receiving trust certificates in return. The word itself was derived from the term "trustee," meaning one who acted for other individuals. Those who joined new trusts would have the benefits of sharing risks and rewards, and since most of the early ones were also near-monopolies, they would avoid the wastes and troubles that came with competition. Certainly the New York Stock Exchange, which resulted from the merger of two rivals and dominated the city's securities market, appeared as much a trust to the Consolidated as Standard Oil did to its smaller rivals.

The first companies resembling trusts were formed in 1879; the Standard Oil giant was organized three years later. By that time an impressive antitrust movement had also begun among small businessmen and reformers. To these individuals, trusts were not merely communities of interest or attempts to pool resources, but rather "combinations in restraint of trade." Congress passed the Interstate Commerce Act in 1887; this legislation was aimed specifically at railroads, but some reformers hoped to broaden its scope to include the industrial corporations. In 1890 a similar small businessman-reformer coalition was able to gain sufficient support through persuasion and vote-swapping to help pass the Sherman Anti-Trust Act. Under Section 2 of the Act, "Every person who shall monopolize or attempt to monopolize, or combine to conspire with any other person or persons to monopolize any part of the trade or commerce among the several States, or with foreign nations, shall be deemed guilty of a misdemeanor."

The Sherman Act was a sweeping piece of legislation, so much so that it was difficult to apply, even had the President the desire to enforce its provisions. Still, it served as a warning to the nation's industrialists of growing antitrust sentiments. The New York Stock Exchange made no official statement regarding the Sherman Act, and individual members said nothing about it that was reported in the press. Some Consolidated brokers thought the legislation would make their tasks easier. On the surface at least it would appear a valid assumption, for the words of Section 2 seemed to have been written with the New York Stock Exchange in mind.

The terms "trust" and "bucket shop," thrown across Broad Street and Broadway, set the stage for the great struggle between the two markets. Without a doubt the Stock Exchange was a trust in spirit if not in form. Exchange leaders would take pains to observe that their organization was unincorporated —more a club than a company, they said—and so did not fall under the purview of the legislation. Through court actions, threats, and warnings issued behind closed doors, it attempted to destroy its rival, and at the same time tried to prevent the Curb from altering its subordinate role. Fearful of the law, however, Stock Exchange leaders would deny vigorously all wrongdoing, and in some cases go so far as to disclaim any knowledge of Curb or Consolidated activities, even when contrary evidence was presented. Similarly, the Consolidated took pride in the fact that some of its leading houses had long records of solvency, and that the district's most sensational scandals usually involved Stock Exchange houses, and not Consolidated brokers.

Just as the Big Board denied being a trust, so the Consolidated rejected the notion that it harbored bucket shops. Every year or so, the Consolidated would mount a campaign to rid its ranks of these organizations, and the membership came to expect that each time Wilson accepted a new presidential term, he would vow warfare on such operators. Thus, toward the end of the nineteenth century, pressures were mounting for an end to corruption and the curbing of big business. New York had two major securities markets at the time. One was a reasonably honest near-monopoly, and the other a fairly corrupt small business; one group of reformers attacked the Stock Exchange, while a second castigated the Consolidated. The appearance of a revived public interest, manifested in the form of government agencies, regulations, laws, and investigations, meant that both exchanges would have to act in a more circumspect fashion toward each other and their customers.

Insofar as the speculating public was concerned, the reformers were both a blessing and a curse. Large and small speculators applauded efforts geared at obtaining full disclosure, honest reporting, and open dealings. The campaign against bucket shops was something else. Some considered them an abomination, while others preferred bucket shops to regular brokerages, asking only that they clarify their methods of operation and be solvent.

There were two methods of purchasing securities at the Wall Street of the 1880s. A person might pay cash for them, and in a short period of time receive his certificates from the company, duly registered and notarized. Or he could buy stocks on margin, meaning that he would open a "margin account" at a brokerage, purchase securities by paying a fraction of the price in cash, while borrowing the rest from the broker, who charged interest for the loan and kept the securities as collateral. Almost all the brokerages were able to handle both kinds of transactions, although at that time most securities purchasers, investors and speculators alike, operated on margin. This meant that brokerages had to have sources of funds in order to carry their customers. Some were affiliates of commercial banks, which considered margin loans as an important part of their business. Others had accounts at large banks and trust companies, drawing upon them for funds when needed. A third, very small group, was comprised of wealthy individuals who loaned money from their own resources. At this time none of the major banks would admit to "carrying" Consolidated brokers, although it appeared that some did advance funds to the more secure houses. No bank had an affiliate with a seat at the Consolidated, for to do so would earn the wrath of the district's leaders. This meant that the vast majority of Consolidated brokers had to support their own margin loan accounts if they were to attract business. Few could afford to handle more than a small amount of such business, and so those customers hoping to purchase stocks on margin naturally tended to patronize the Stock Exchange houses. Had the Consolidated been limited to these brokers and this kind of business alone, it would have either disappeared or shrunk to a fraction of its size.

There were, however, two other ways by which a speculator could participate in the market. He could purchase put and call options, which gave him the right to sell or buy a particular security at a specified price within a limited number of days, weeks, or months. The option business was a large and growing one, but was controlled by such Stock Exchange leaders as Russell Sage and a handful of others. The speculator could also place a wager on a stock, in much the same way as he might bet on a prize fight or a horse race. He would enter any one of the many small brokerage offices in the lower Broadway area and find knots of men gathered around the several tickers. At the entrance would be a cashier in a cage, with stacks of markers and a cash box. The client would approach the cashier, and perhaps ask the price of one or several stocks. These quotations would either be listed on a blackboard, attended by two or three clerks with chalk and erasers, or on long sheets of foolscap tacked to the side of the booth. Then, should the customer wish to "purchase" a stock at the ask price, he would pay for it by giving his check for 10 percent of the price, in theory borrowing the rest. He knew, however, that the broker would not buy that stock, but merely put him on the book for a specific number of shares and give him a receipt. Should the price rise and the client desire to sell, he would present his ticket at the cage and receive the price at the last Stock Exchange transaction, minus the amount of his loan and the commission. Once again, the broker did not sell the security when he received such an order, but obtained the quotation from the ticker. Similarly, should the ticker price fall by 10 percent or more, the client would be asked to "get up more margin." Should he fail to do so, his position would be "wiped out"; in effect, he would have lost his bet.

Clearly, such an organization could not exist without the ticker or the Stock Exchange, for these were the focuses of attention. Many customers, fully aware of the methods used by such establishments, preferred them to regular brokerages. Although both enabled speculators to operate on 10 percent margin, the regular brokerage would take orders and execute them at the Stock Exchange. This took time, and in the interim the price could easily have changed. In addition, the very act of purchasing shares would change their price. This point meant little to the buyer or seller of a hundred shares, or a "round lot." But speculators who dealt in thousand-share lots, and did not want their dealings to distort prices, preferred to "wager" on stocks rather than purchase them. Thus, these gambling parlors were able to draw a good deal of business from the regular brokerages.

There were many establishments in the financial district that were not what they seemed to be. They claimed to be legitimate brokerages, although in fact their operations were closer to those of the gaming rooms. When turn-of-the-century writers and critics talked of bucket shops, they usually referred to these. Clients there might purchase stocks on margin, and be assured the transaction had taken place. If pressed, the broker would show his client the tape, and point out the place where the trade was registered. Since the securities were needed to collateralize the loan, the client might deal with such an establishment for years without realizing that these were phantom transactions; that no shares were purchased or sold by the broker; that the tape had shown someone else's shares going over, and not his; and that the apparently conventional, honest, brokerage was actually a gaming room. It was entirely possible for a broker to get away with such an operation for years without being discovered.

The brokers changed their methods of operation when speculators caught on to this fraud. Should a client with a margin account (and these made up the bulk of the customers in the late nineteenth century) place an order for one hundred shares of XYZ, the broker would purchase the stock, which the buyer would see going over the tape. If the price were $50 a share, the transaction would come to $5,000 plus commission, and the client would give the broker $500, since the usual margin was 10 percent or so. The broker would be empowered to hold the stock certificate against the $4,500 loan. The customer did not realize, however, that the broker would almost immediately sell the security, in many cases at the same price as it had been purchased.

At this point, the client and his broker would have a wager going on that security. Should the stock fall below $45 a share, the client would be asked to deposit additional margin. Should he not do this, the transaction would be closed, with the broker pocketing the original $500. If the client placed a sell order at any price above $45, the broker would pay him off, in much the same fashion as was done at a racetrack. In either case, however, the client would have to pay interest on the $4,500 phantom loan, and rates of 25 percent in busy times were not unusual. These brokers were, in fact, combination bookmakers-loan sharks. They were wagering against the client, and lending him money (in theory, at least) for the bet. Since the money rates were so high, they seemed assured of a good profit at the end of most weeks.

Should the client repay his margin loan and demand delivery of his certificate, the broker would be obliged to purchase the securities at the market. If they were unavailable, or too richly priced for his purse, the broker might declare bankruptcy or leave town, forcing the customer to assume the loss. When clients purchased large amounts of securities, and then after a rise sold out and demanded payment, the broker could find himself short of cash, and close his establishment. Thus, bucket shops were capable of closing down in bad times and good; no one could tell when such a failure might occur. These brokerages were the bane of the financial district, condemned by both exchanges and the Curb, by regular brokers and operators of gaming rooms.

There were many of these marginal operations at the Curb, where regulations were nonexistent. The Consolidated's by-laws provided for regular reports as to the status of each broker's accounts. Applicants for membership were asked, "In case you are elected a member of this Exchange, do you promise not to engaged in any 'bucket shop' business?" Unless the membership committee received positive answers, and was convinced the candidate could be trusted, he would be denied admission. Few men were rejected, and fewer still expelled for running bucket shops. Throughout its history, many important bucket shops in this category found their homes at the Consolidated.

The Stock Exchange attempted to rid the district of gaming rooms and bucket shops as early as 1880. In that year it asked Western Union to remove its tickers from all brokerages that had reputations for such dealings; in effect, the Stock Exchange wanted to determine which brokers had access to information regarding its transactions. The company refused, and in retaliation the Stock Exchange established its own ticker and reporting services, and tried to have the Western Union wires removed from its floor. This ploy failed, however, and the gaming rooms and bucket shops continued to thrive. By 1887 several had branch offices throughout the city, and correspondent houses in other parts of the country. During the great bull market of the late 1890s every important resort had at least one gaming establishment for the speculators, who gambled while on vacation. By then too, several major bucket shops could claim to be larger than the average Stock Exchange firm, and a few held seats at the Consolidated, thus giving the Big Board additional reason to oppose their activities. Some specialized in outright wagering, not only in securities, but athletic and political events as well, but most tried to give the appearance of being a regular brokerage, and dealt in securities listed at the Stock Exchange. Often when they had to purchase or sell stocks they would do so through Big Board firms, especially when the Consolidated couldn't handle a large block. The Establishment railed against this practice, and promised to retaliate against member firms with bucket shop or Consolidated connections. These warnings were generally ignored at the time, and the bucket shops were able to thrive.

Such were the methods and fortunes of the Consolidated's gaming rooms and bucket shops. The popularity of the former establishments and the aggressive salesmanship of the latter enabled them to win clients from Stock Exchange firms. More important, however, was the fact that Consolidated commission fees were somewhat lower than those at the Big Board, and even these were flexible, for regular customers could count on reduced rates, and could haggle over these at times. Since membership at the Consolidated was inexpensive—rarely rising to more than $200 before the turn of the century—many heavy speculators would go so far as to purchase a seat for trading purposes alone, and this too provided a different atmosphere there from that of the Stock Exchange. The older organization was led by specialists, who concentrated their time and money on a few stocks apiece, and did a wholesale business on the Exchange floor. They were followed by general brokers, who bought and sold for their clients, and who usually transacted their business with specialists. Then there were the two-dollar brokers, men who handled business for other members, charging a commission for their services which initially had been $2 per round lot (one hundred shares of a given security). Finally, the Stock Exchange had a small group of men who used their seats to speculate for their own accounts.

The Consolidated's membership differed in its composition. There were no specialists there; since the Consolidated took its cue from the Big Board, none of its members could hope to set prices for a listed security. Similarly, there was little business for two-dollar brokers; volume was so low that the individual members did not require their assistance. But there were many bucket shop brokers, who handled any kind of transaction that came their way. In addition there were the arbitragers, who made money by purchasing and selling securities when their Consolidated quotes were lower or higher than those of the Big Board. Finally, there was a large group of men speculating for their own accounts. As a Consolidated spokesman of that period wrote:

Large traders having accounts with established brokerage houses can make substantial savings in commissions by purchasing a Consolidated membership and then trading through a fellow-member in the commission business for 1/32nd commission. This applies particularly to active traders who trade in active stocks. A number of traders having adopted this method have discovered that the saving in commission amounts to a handsome income in itself. . . . More than one manipulator in the primary market has discovered that the Consolidated market affords facilities for the acquisition and marketing of lines of stocks. This has been true of Reading, Brooklyn Rapid Transit, Union Pacific, Copper, and Sugar in their periods of speculative activity. As the Consolidated opportunities become better known it is probable that there will be a disposition on the part of the leading operators to avail themselves on a larger basis of this market.

Several important Wall Streeters took advantage of this opportunity to save on commissions and purchased Consolidated memberships. Among their number were Henry H. Rogers and John D. Archbold of Standard Oil, William Nelson Cromwell and William J. Curtis, senior partners at Sullivan & Cromwell, one of the city's leading law firms and general counsel for the Consolidated (their young clerk, John Foster Dulles, was not a member, however). Traction magnate Anthony Brady, several state supreme court judges and four state senators also had seats. Some of these men were members of the Stock Exchange too, contrary to Big Board rules. In the late nineteenth century, however, this breech was overlooked.

The situation appeared somewhat different to outsiders, and especially to those reformers intent on clearing the district of all bucket shops, ending bucketing operations, and in general enforcing a code of good conduct. Had they realized the true state of things, they might have understood that the district would be a lonely place if all who engaged in such operations were barred.

The reformers' major difficulty lay in their insistence on lumping together those establishments where the clients knew they were betting on a rise or fall with those where the customer was being deceived. This may be perceived in the final report of the Hughes Commission, more formally known as the New York State Committee on Speculation in Securities and Commodities. After a careful examination of district policies, and the issuance of a series of promises to protect the "lambs" from the bulls and bears, the Commission recommended a series of changes in district operations. But in the body of the report the members showed a lack of sophistication—a simplistic view toward wrongdoing, and how it might be corrected. Writing in 1910, the Commission said, "Bucket shops are ostensibly brokerage offices, where, however, commodities and securities are neither bought or sold in pursuance of customers' orders, the transactions being closed by the payment of gains or losses, as determined by price quotations. In other words, they are merely places for the registration of bets or wagers; their machinery is generally controlled by the keepers, who can delay or manipulate the quotations at will." The Commission members might have been shocked to learn that the operations described in the first sentence were not considered immoral or unethical by speculators and brokers. The practices described in the second, however, were condemned by all speculators, and most vigorously by the brokers who ran gaming parlors, which were sometimes confused with the bucket shops.

It would be trite to observe that toward the end of the nineteenth century the nation was in the midst of rapid change, for there never has been a period in American history when such a statement would not be true. The only difference between one era and another is the areas in which important changes were taking place, and their directions. At the end of the nineteenth century the nation was undergoing rapid industrialization, one sign of which was the growth of corporations and the emergence of what has often been called finance capitalism. The builders were still there, to be sure, but the organizers, rationalizers, and financiers had become increasingly important to the proper functioning of the industrial economy. Concomitantly, the role played by government was being enlarged; even under the administrations of such conservative politicians as Cleveland, Harrison, and McKinley the federal government was beginning to assume a regulatory function, mirroring the even greater vigor shown in the states and on the municipal level. Finally, the United States was coming to realize that it had to play a role in international affairs. Sometimes reluctantly, often eagerly, American Presidents and Congresses asserted their views of the national interest in Latin America and the Pacific. These changes were interconnected. American business, now more aggressive than before, was expanding rapidly into world markets, and its activities were aided by a business-minded federal government, and watched warily by those rural Americans who were losing power and moderate reformers fearful of basic changes in the nation's economic and social life.

If the rise of finance capitalism was the most obvious aspect of the new economy, the rapid growth of the cities must be considered its most important institutional change. At the time of Lincoln's inauguration 6.2 million Americans lived in what the census bureau called "urban territories," while 25.2 million could be found in rural areas. Twenty years later there were eight million more urban residents and eleven million more people in rural America, and at the time it still appeared the nation's future would remain on the farms. Then the tide changed. In 1890, one-third of a population of 63 million lived in urban territories. New York's share was near the 1.5 million mark, while the adjoining city of Brooklyn had 800,000 residents. Philadelphia and Chicago were also past the million mark, while St. Louis, Boston, and Baltimore each had half that amount.

Although urban growth was a nationwide phenomenon, the greatest increases took place in the eastern seaboard states, where some 80 percent of all city dwellers lived. The rapid expansion of the eastern cities was due to several causes. In the first place, farmers leaving for urban areas tended to go to those cities where jobs were available. Thus, midwestern rural dwellers relocated to Chicago and Cincinnati, while easterners tended to gravitate to New York, Philadelphia, and Boston. Since the eastern farms were smaller and marginal, they were more susceptible to foreclosures than their western and midwestern counterparts. Although a larger number of western farmers were obliged to become city dwellers, a greater proportion of eastern farmers had to leave the soil.

In the years after the Civil War—and especially in the last two decades of the century—many southerners came to the northeastern cities to seek employment. By then such men were either resigned to the fact that their section had become stagnant, or were hopeful that greater opportunities could be found in the North. Antebellum dreams took a long time to die, although by the 1880s some realized the old ways were gone, and that the South had to accommodate itself to a new role, that of economic colony for northern interests. Rather than accept this humiliating situation, the sons of Confederate veterans went North—many to New York—to seek wealth and power.

More important than this internal migration, however, was the wave of immigrants from overseas. Over three-quarters of a million foreigners came to the United States in 1882, a figure that would not be surpassed until 1903. Of those who arrived in 1882, one in three came from Germany, and an additional third from Great Britain or Scandinavia. Irish immigration, which had been a steady stream since the 1830s, was below its peak of more than 221,000 reached in 1851, but 76,000 Irish did arrive in America in 1882. More important numerically and socially, however, was the great increase in immigrants from southern and eastern Europe. Driven by famine and persecution, 32,000 Italians and 16,000 Russians arrived in 1882, an impressive jump from the figures of 15,000 and 5,000 respectively of the previous year. Over 82,000 Russians came in 1892; in 1907 the figure crossed the quarter million mark. Some 100,000 Italians arrived in 1900, and 286,000 in 1907, which was also the peak year for this national group.

The influx of south and east Europeans was of great demographic significance, as important as the Negro migration of the seventeenth and eighteenth centuries. Prior to the mid-1880s, the white population of the nation was basically Anglo-Saxon and Germanic. The major non-Protestant group, the Irish, tended to congregate in eastern cities, although a number became farmers in the upper Midwest. Now they were joined by millions of south European Catholics and east European Jews. In the 1870s, New York was essentially a Protestant, native-born city, with a large number of Irish-Americans, and smaller enclaves controlled by handfuls of other groups. In 1890, some 40 percent of all New Yorkers were of foreign birth, and much of lower Manhattan was in their hands. Those retail merchants who remained after the great immigration were obliged to learn several languages in order to deal with their customers, and stock new foods and different types of clothing. One could cross the city, from river to river or from the Battery to 34th Street, without hearing a word of English.

Naturally, ghettos appeared, as each nationality and religion made claims to one area or another. The Italians gathered along the East River side of Manhattan, and to this day one can find vestiges of "Little Italy" in that part of town. The Irish, already established along the Hudson River below 34th Street, now tightened their grip on that section. The east European Jews, the last to arrive, formed their community out of the tenement areas between the Irish and Italians. By coincidence, east European Jews fell heir to the neighborhood north of the financial district, and could easily reach Wall Street by taking the Broadway horsecars.

These waves of immigrants, some from the South, others from rural areas, and the bulk from overseas, changed the tone of the financial district just as they transformed New York into the most cosmopolitan city west of Constantinople. In 1882 the Establishment was still dominated by old Anglo-Saxon and Dutch families, although others were permitted to enter and in some cases even assume leadership since the 1869 merger with the Open Board. In particular, German-Jewish families like the Seligmans and the Lehmans, and investment bankers like Kuhn, Loeb, had joined the Morgans and Vanderbilts in prestige and power. To a limited extent at least, they were prepared to accept some newcomers to Stock Exchange membership. The change began in the late 1870s, when men with names like Herzog and Freed were admitted. They were followed by Cantoni, Speyer, Wasserman, Levy, Kelley, Stern, Gross, O'Dell, Kennedy, Cohen, Cochran, and Blumenthal among others. By the early 1890s, the Stock Exchange could point to a scattering of east European Jews, newly arrived Italians, and several Irish brokers who had been accepted to membership.

The Stock Exchange roster is only one indication of the impact of the new immigration on the district. It is not as significant as the Consolidated membership roll, however, since that market was easier to join. There one could find more Irish names, but fewer Jewish and Italian brokers. The Consolidated list shows members who gave as their home addresses such cities as New Orleans, Nashville, and Charleston. There is no record of the Consolidated's having issued a membership roster prior to 1900, but the one for that year indicates that slightly more than 20 percent had southern origins. The presence of many Grand Army of the Republic members at the Stock Exchange and Confederate veterans at the Consolidated doubtless added to the antagonisms between the two organizations.

The best way to measure the impact of foreign-born Americans on the financial district is, unfortunately, impossible to obtain. No records were kept of clerks, runners, board men, and others who had the apprentice or semimenial jobs which grew rapidly in the expansion period of the late 1890s. The few men still alive who remember that era speak of leaving school at an early age, hearing of opportunities for employment in the financial district, and going there to seek jobs. Photographs of runners and stock clerks also appear to indicate that many of them were of foreign birth. At the time, those young men who had the proper connections could obtain trainee jobs indoors, where there was much to be learned. But an immigrant who knew no one in the district could expect little better than an outside job, carrying messages and papers from one office to another. With a combination of hard work, good fortune, and a keen mind, those runners who worked for Stock Exchange houses could hope to rise as high as chief clerk if they stayed with the firm for twenty years or so. Such a position was respectable enough, but for young men of talent, surrounded by individuals who made more money in one turn of a stock than they earned in a year, it hardly seemed satisfactory. The temptation to enter the market directly, either as a speculator or a broker, was a driving force for aggressive foreign-born clerks and runners. Having no outlet at the Stock Exchange, many of these boys tended to gravitate to the Consolidated and the bucket shops. The majority, however, drifted toward the Curb market on lower Broad Street.

No Curb directory appeared prior to 1904, but survivors of that period indicate that life then was little different from what it had been a decade earlier. There were approximately 150 curbstone brokers in 1896. A few gave addresses on Wall Street and some were on Nassau; these were the cream of the Curb community, the men most admired and looked to for leadership. Most had offices on lower Broadway or Broad Street, the former the heart of bucket shop territory, the latter the location of the outdoor market. Then, as earlier, the Curb was comprised of solid brokerages, Stock Exchange satellites, and gamblers.

The Curb was an even more complex community than the Consolidated or the Stock Exchange. These indoor markets had organizations; there were no rules at the Curb other than those which grew naturally out of the trading arena, and no group or individual empowered to punish or reward a firm or individual. To be sure, those brokers who attempted to shave points, did not pay debts promptly, and stole clients were known to the others. The curbstone community had a good idea which of their number were bucket shop operators, who had the outside business of this or that large Stock Exchange house, who had a sense of honor, and which set of brokers could not be trusted.

To the outsider, the Curb appeared a jungle, with no rules and few scruples. Members of the community knew this to be untrue. The Curb had a "natural aristocracy," comprised of men with reputations for honest dealings and good connections with Stock Exchange houses. Since anyone could enter this community, it also appeared to be a hodgepodge of various nationalities, religions, and backgrounds. Sons of Stock Exchange members went to the Curb to learn the business and would work side by side with sons of recently arrived immigrants, still struggling to master English, hoping to make their fortunes in finance. As might be expected, the Curb became a magnet for the new Americans, especially the Irish and the east European Jews, whose numbers there were disproportionate to their representation in the financial community at large; at the turn of the century the leading Curb houses were Ackermann & Coles, Megargle & Co., Reilly & Co., Siegel, Heilner & Co., and Goldfinger & Co., while Oscar Bamberger, J. H. MacMannus, Carl Pforzheimer, Julius Rosenbaum, S. F. Sullivan, and L. A. Norton were well-known brokers. Stock Exchange houses usually sent young relatives of partners to represent their interests at the Curb, or lacking sons and cousins, hired Irish and Jewish brokers to deal for them there. F. R. Lockwood handled F. M. Lockwood & Co. business, and H. L. D. Lewis spoke for Lewis & Vredenburgh; James O'Brian was the Bache representative, G. L. Meehan worked for Chapin & Co., and Samuel "Kitty" Frank dealt out of Sutro Brothers.

The Curb underwent a major transformation in the late 1880s and the 1890s. In the past, its position in the brokerage picture had been fixed, secure, and accepted. Curbstone brokers were men who dealt in all issues not handled by the Stock Exchange, and who in return for their willingness to keep their places would be given commissions by the Establishment. Regularly, however, one or more groups of outside brokers had united to form their own market, often but not always in competition with the Stock Exchange. Such was the case with the Bourse, the Open Board, the various mining exchanges, and even the Consolidated. These markets had varying fates; some would disappear in panic times, a few would be incorporated within the Establishment, while the rest were crushed by Stock Exchange pressures. In the last decades of the century, the Establishment felt that all other exchanges in the city were its natural enemies, and had to be destroyed. The symbol of rebellion would be a move indoors. In the past this had always marked the beginning of a rival organization, and the Stock Exchange had no intention of allowing another indoor market to exist in the city. Thus, it opposed its greatest antagonist, the Consolidated.

The situation had changed; the lessons of the past had little meaning in the late nineteenth century, although few realized it. In the first place, the Stock Exchange had never been as powerful as it was then. It was able to oblige listed companies to release information, conform to its rules, and accept its dictates. At an earlier time some leading businessmen thought of the Stock Exchange as a place of plunder, and its leaders as willing dupes or—should they insist on maintaining standards—men to be ignored or destroyed. Such had been the case during the age of Vanderbilt and Gould. But this was no longer true in the J. P. Morgan era. Morgan did not have to disobey the law or attempt to evade it; so great was his power and that of his allies that they could help frame legislation, elect congressmen and even presidents, and speak as equals with their European counterparts.

Morgan and his circle had a stake in honesty and high standards, and so they supported as well as dominated the Stock Exchange hierarchy. The chance of a new Open Board appearing to challenge the Stock Exchange on its own grounds was so remote that it could be ignored. The Consolidated survived by concentrating on the leavings, such as odd lots, commodities, and bucketing. Throughout its entire history, the Consolidated never made a primary market in any of the hundreds of Stock Exchange securities; had the Establishment been willing to lower its standards and compete with the Consolidated, the latter would have vanished in a matter of weeks. Wall Street was unwilling to get into the gutter with lower Broadway, and so the Consolidated survived and even prospered. Just as Andrew Carnegie did not try to put some of his smaller rivals out of business, the Consolidated's initial successes were more the result of Stock Exchange indifference and disgust than an inability to dominate the district. To the Establishment, the Consolidated was a pain in the neck, but not a dagger at its bosom. It had almost no chance of attaining the power once held by the Open Board, and any curbstone brokers who might consider going indoors to form a third market would have even less chance of success. Still, the Stock Exchange did not want the slightest sign of a new organization, or a whisper of a third indoor market. And since it had the power of life and death over the Curb, it could easily prevent such talk and actions.

The historical perspective of most curbstone brokers was

changing during the late nineteenth century. Earlier there had been a curbstone tradition that was passed down from father to son, from one generation of provincial newcomers to another. Now much of this was gone. The Curb, once the domain of lower- and middle-class Protestants who could trace their ancestry back to the nation's farms, was now the home of many Irish and east European Jewish sons of immigrants, whose roots were in Europe, not America. It meant little to these men that the Bourse and the Open Board had existed. Just as the reading of colonial history indicated something different to them than it would to a native-born citizen, so the traditions of the old Curb had less relevance than did the pressing problems of the day. Better than the Establishment, they realized that open competition with the Stock Exchange was absurd, and they also knew they hadn't much of a chance of acceptance on Wall Street, where a Protestant-German Jewish nexus of investment bankers did not want them to be. For the time being at least they had as little hope of leaving their business ghetto as they did in relocating from their tenement homes to Park Avenue, although a handful were able to do both. But just as they tried to make their neighborhoods more livable, so the new curbstone brokers had aspirations for their businesses. They would try to make an orderly market at the Curb, isolate and possibly expel shady characters, and some even spoke of moving indoors to escape the elements in winter. All such talk made Establishment leaders wary; they confused a desire for order with one for competition. For the next two generations, these two perspectives of the nature and future of the Curb would cause frictions, misunderstandings, and difficulties for the brokers who traded out-of-doors on Broad Street.

V

The Broad Street Jungle

THE CURB was no place for philosophers in the late nineteenth century. The struggle to achieve and then maintain a
position was even more difficult in the out-of-doors market
than at the Stock Exchange, and required more energy and
perspicacity. The curbstone broker had to juggle his relations
with clients, Stock Exchange correspondent houses, the local
police who charged him with blocking traffic and other minor
offenses, the banks with which he dealt, rival brokers out for his
business, and cope with additional problems that scarcely
bothered or interested his Stock Exchange counterparts. These
men had no time for diaries, what letters they may have written
no longer exist, they did not will their papers to libraries (or
even consider the possibility), and were of little interest as human
beings to newspapers and magazines. Their children were married
without notice being taken in the society pages; they died
without obituaries. One may trace their actions as a group, but
not as individuals. Even their names are all but forgotten, remembered today only by octogenarians and septaugenarians,
most of whom are now retired from active brokerage at the
American and New York Stock Exchanges, who have dim
memories of old men dealing on the Curb at the time they came
there as clerks, or who repeat anecdotes told them by their
fathers.

Visitors to the financial district in the late 1870s considered the Curb the most picturesque, exciting, and incomprehensible segment of American business. Brokers would congregate at William and Beaver, mixing with clerks, runners, and secretaries. Most had at least one runner stationed at the Stock Exchange house whose orders they filled, and another by their side, prepared to take buy and sell messages to that house. Should the curbstone broker receive an order for shares, he would shout it out to his fellows, and hopefully receive a screamed reply. Each man would then rush to the other's side and negotiate prices and terms. On concluding the transaction, the broker would scribble it down on a slip of paper and hand it to his runner, who would then carry it to the Stock Exchange house. The broker would record the transaction on a second piece of paper or in his "book." Wealthier curbstone brokers had their secretaries keep this book, although there were few of them at the time.

The advent of the telephone in the early 1880s changed all this. Those runners who brought orders back and forth disappeared, or joined others whose job it was to deliver or pick up securities. Brokers rented offices along William Street, where they stationed subordinates who manned the phones. Stock Exchange houses would telephone their orders, which were screamed at the broker who waited in the street below. After the order was filled the broker shouted it back to his clerk, who then transmitted the information to the correspondent house.

Technology and the Curb market's growth led to rapid changes in the early 1890s. William Street was too narrow to accommodate all the brokers comfortably, and there were ·insufficient offices in the area for all who wanted them. Thus, the Curb moved to Broad Street near Exchange Place, and many brokers took offices in the Mills Building, located on the northeast corner of Board and Exchange Place, across the street from the Big Board. At this time too, the practice of hand signaling became standard. Some brokers found it impossible to understand the bellowed orders from the telephone clerks, and developed an informal series of signs, one for each security, others for the number of shares to be purchased or sold. The Curb adopted the hand signals, which soon became a second language for brokers and clerks, one they had to learn quickly if they were to function in the area. In addition, each broker tried to wear some distinctive article of clothing, so that his clerks could pick him out in the crowd. In summertime many wore cream-colored jackets with unusual hats; in winter brokers took to furs, bright mufflers, and the like.

The visitor would be baffled by all of this. He would see several hundred men shouting at each other, waving their hands, and constantly looking up at the proper window in the Mills or adjoining buildings. Should he enter the lobby and go into one of the busier offices of an important broker, he might see four or five clerks and a battery of telephones, several as open lines to different Stock Exchange houses and two or three others used to contact and receive orders from independent customers. The place would be strewn with paper, a blackboard on the side would contain scribbled messages, and there would be leavings of coffee and sandwiches. The windows were always open, no matter what the weather; in snowstorms the clerks would be swathed in coats, waving their hands, with their eyes narrowed against the elements. In summertime the clerks would stand on the outer window ledges in precarious fashion, searching out their brokers.

Of course, not all offices were so large or busy. Some were the size of a broom closet, in which a single clerk would operate with one or two telephones. The casual onlooker might reasonably assume this to be the office of a minor broker or a lone speculator, and in some cases he would be correct. But not always; a cubbyhole in the Mills Building could indicate its tenant to be either very marginal or quite successful. It could be the office of a broker who had his main offices elsewhere, usually on Wall Street or Broadway, and transmitted orders from the Curb to there. Or it could be the telephone drop of a specialist, some of whom were the backbone or the Curb, and its natural leaders.

Visitors to the out-of-doors market might initially think that all brokers were engaged in the same pursuits, wandering from place to place, giving and taking orders, and relaying them to clerks and secretaries. After a while they might discern order in the seeming chaos. Most brokers moved about but tended to circle a particular spot, where their fellows and customers knew they could be found. Such a place was theirs by unwritten rule. A few brokers would travel from one end of the Curb to the other, seemingly always on the go, while a handful would be immovable, as though rooted to their particular place.

The first and largest group were the commission brokers. Such people might be the junior partners of a large Stock Exchange house, although few sent their own men to the Curb; in the 1890s there was an informal understanding between the two markets that the Curb would not deal in Stock Exchange securities, and in return the Establishment would place all orders for unlisted securities through curbstone brokers. Most of these were individuals who in one way or another had managed to win the confidence and favor of a partner or chief clerk at a Stock Exchange firm, and received orders from him for unlisted securities. Such contacts or the lack of them could spell prosperity or annihilation for this category of broker, since almost all transactions at the Curb still originated at Stock Exchange houses. The relationships were initiated and maintained in a variety of ways. A curbstone broker could have received his first job at a member firm, where he managed to acquire a reputation for honesty, intelligence, and ambition. Should he be able to maintain this standing with the firm after going to the Curb, he might receive some of its business on a commission basis. Very often he would pay "kickbacks" to his contact there, or do him favors of one sort or another. It was common practice for a commission broker to keep a second book, which contained the amounts of money he owed each house with which he dealt, or have several envelopes, into which he would place a percentage of his commissions, to be delivered at a fixed time at the end of the week to the men who gave him orders. This was not considered unethical, but rather was the norm of that period. Both curbstone broker and Stock Exchange contact would receive benefits, and the relationship might continue for as long as each man trusted the other. Some of these affiliations would last for more than a half century, although the practice of kickbacks ended in the New Deal era.

The second kind of broker—the individual always on the move—was one who was dealing for his own account, or trying to pick up whatever business might come along. They were marginal brokers, often men getting their start on the Curb, or those engaged in shady dealings. The out-of-doors market had many such people, and since there were no regulations, listing requirements, or committees on standing or admission, their numbers were always being replenished. A dishonest broker in this group rarely rose any higher; once his fellows realized the nature of his business, they would shun him whenever possible. The worst were simply ostracized, and soon left the arena. The others were dealt with only when regular brokers had no other choice. For example, a broker might have an order for a thousand shares of a stock. He would call it out, and several answers would be heard. The voices and faces would be identified, and although the custom was to split the orders between those with the same low bid, the caller might ignore the marginal broker for the more reputable ones in order to assure his safety and peace of mind. Given this kind of situation, newcomers were obviously encouraged to maintain their reputations or, if they engaged in questionable practices, to make whatever money they could and get out.

The specialists remained immovable and inobstrusive, talking to few men, joking among themselves, and handling a relatively small number of orders. These were among the wealthiest and most successful of the curbstone community. In one way or another, they controlled the trades in several issues. Buyers looking for purchasers would head in their direction; sellers knew that should their issue be a popular one, a specialist for it would be at hand; dealers in large lots realized that each active security had its own specialist, and he could handle their business.

There were several ways by which a broker could come to specialize in a security, but the most common was to bring it to the market and stake a claim. Should a broker learn of a new mine being opened in the West, he might assist in its underwriting, keep a block of stock for his own account, and let it be known that he was prepared to "make a market" in that security. In essence, this meant that he promised to buy and sell the security, and offer quotes to all who asked. Thus, a fellow broker might shout, "How's XYZ?" and receive an answer of "18⅝ bid, 19⅛ ask, 18⅞ last," indicating that the specialist would buy shares at the first price, sell at the second, and his last transaction in the stock was at the third price. These quotations had to be chosen with great care; if bids were too high, a rival might try to undercut his price. On the other hand, if he were too generous with his quotes, he might receive a large buy or sell order which he could not handle, and this would be a serious blow to his reputation. Or should he enter into a transaction and then not be able to deliver, he could expect to be shunned by his fellows. These men had to be fairly well-to-do, for they held large blocks of stock for their own accounts when the need arose.

Several specialists were well connected, trusted, and respected; generally speaking, the higher the price for a Curb security, the greater the prestige of the specialists who "made the market" in that stock. Some were wealthy enough and had such good reputations that had they so desired, they might have gone over to the Big Board, and in fact some did. But a variety of social pressures, added to the fact that they were doing so well in the out-of-doors market that to forego safety there for an uncertain future indoors seemed unwise, caused most to remain at the Curb.

Not all specialists were rich and powerful. Those who made markets in low-priced mining shares, some of them quoted in pennies, could be quite shabby. A marginal broker might decide that the specialists in a minor security were sluggards, and he would attempt to take the market from them by aggressive dealings and rapid deliveries; this was not only accepted at the Curb, but expected. Or a new man might know of a stock that no broker specialized in; he could rent a sandwich sign, put it around his neck, and flash the message that he was prepared to buy and sell that security. It was a tough business, but a talented newcomer could rise to the top more rapidly through specialization than any other aspect of Curb life. A generation later Louis Cartier, then a young man in his twenties, thought the specialist in Chevrolet was mishandling that high-priced security. Cartier moved in, and by offering to buy at a slightly higher price, and sell at a lower one than his rival, was able to take the stock away from him, and go on to become one of the most respected men at the Curb for so doing.

The general, or retail brokers, individuals whose major concern was transacting business for and with the general public, and who were an important part of the Stock Exchange membership, were relatively unimportant at the Curb, where the bulk of business was based on orders from Stock Exchange member firms. One might say that the Big Board was comprised of those who were in the wholesale end of the business (specialists) and the retailers (regular brokers), while the pre-1900 Curb was largely a wholesale market.

The fact that there were several categories of brokers at the Curb does not mean that the community was rigidly stratified by occupation. Commission brokers would handle all business they could get from other sources, and might also dabble in specialization by taking on a mining stock or two. Marginal operators would at times perform the functions of commission brokers, but whenever they tried to act as specialists, one could be sure theirs was not an important issue, and might even be tainted. Specialists, in particular the less important ones, might be involved in other dealings as well. Withal, there was a pecking order of sorts at the Curb; the community was led by the specialists, followed by commission brokers, and trailed by the marginal operators and bucketeers. The first group was semi-independent; theoretically, they might function without direct support from Stock Exchange firms, but for the most part they tried to be on good terms with Big Board leaders. The majority of brokers, who handled orders for member firms and lived off commissions, existed or disappeared at the Stock Exchange's will, while the bucket shop operators were condemned and avoided by the Big Board and at best tolerated by Curb leaders. And it was evident, even then, that if the Curb were to challenge the Establishment at any time, over any significant issue, its leadership would have to come from the major specialists, men who were not as reliant upon Stock Exchange approval as the others of the Curb, and who were of sufficient wealth to risk such a fight. Conversely, the commission brokers would be the most timid in such a confrontation, since they had the most to lose should the Big Board attempt to crush the Curb.

All of this may be gleaned from newspapers and reminiscences; curbstone brokers of the late nineteenth century remain faceless for the most part. Not until after the turn of the century can we talk of them as individuals. There were, however, a handful of curbstone brokers who made minor reputations outside their own circles, whose names might be recognized by the Establishment, and who were accepted as spokesmen by their peers. These were the leaders of the group that came to the Curb after the Civil War, who were well established and often substantial figures when the immigrant waves came to the financial district, and the last of whom had retired or was dead by the early years of the new century, when the Curb was on the verge of its most important period. The only one of them who remains more than an indistinct shadow, however, was Emanuel S. Mendels, Jr.

Mendels was born in New Orleans in 1850. His father was a small businessman who had been active in Whig politics and had taken stands against secession. As party lines hardened toward the end of the 1850s, the elder Mendels' position became more unpopular in the Deep South, and he decided to leave. In 1861, a few weeks prior to the outbreak of the Civil War, he moved his family to Newark, New Jersey, and found a position as a business secretary in New York. Perhaps through an interest born of his father's work, young E. S. Mendels, Jr. came to the city after graduating high school in 1868. The postwar boom was in full swing on Wall Street at this time, and Mendels had no trouble in finding a job at a brokerage house. After four years, when he had learned how the district operated, Mendels left his position to seek a place at the Curb. There is no way of knowing why he took this route; perhaps he felt that a young southern-born Jew had little hope of going far at the Stock Exchange, or he may have been impatient to be his own man.

Whatever the reason, Mendels was successful as a curbstone broker. He was friendly, honest, and intelligent, as well as being young enough to take advantage of new opportunities and sufficiently mature to win the confidence of other southerners and sons of Jewish and Irish immigrants who came to the district later on. Although little is known of his business activities, he apparently became a specialist in several mining stocks, and did well enough to open an office at 6 Wall Street, a prime location and one few curbstone brokers could have afforded. Later on two of Mendels' sons joined the firm, and according to those who remember them, they were considered substantial brokers. Two other sons became lawyers and practiced in New Jersey, while his daughter married a local businessman. Mendels himself remained in Newark, purchasing a house at 50 Broad Street in 1876 and living there for the rest of his life.

Considering his wealth, good reputation, and the easing of restrictions on Wall Street, a man like Mendels might easily have expected to be admitted to the Stock Exchange. There is no evidence that he applied, although ambitious brokers like him were then taking the trip. The reason appeared to have been more emotional than financial; Mendels was a sentimental businessman of the type often found during the late Victorian age. He quite simply liked the Curb, its people, and the way it transacted business. Rather than elevate himself, his ambition was to purify the Curb and make it a safer place in which to function.

Mendels became a curbstone broker in 1872; soon after hundreds of young men in his position would be wiped out in the panic of 1873. The fact that he was not destroyed indicates that he was either too marginal a broker to have heavy losses, or was sufficiently conservative in his methods to ride out a panic. Mendels' rapid rise at the Curb would appear to prove the latter was the case. At a time when some brokers could not purchase securities unless they paid for them with cash on order (and not delivery), Mendels' accounts would be carried for many days without fear of loss. He seems to have been prim and stiff-necked on questions of honesty and corruption, while also possessing leadership qualities. Such individuals were needed in the 1880s, when bucket shops, bankruptcies, dishonest brokers, and worse were common at the Curb. Problems like these were compounded by the great rush of new mining issues that came to the district at that time. Reputable brokers were confused by the torrent of paper, and most of them had difficulties distinguishing honest from misrepresented issues. These men might try to obtain information on the companies, analyze their reports and balances, and find out all they could about their managements and underwriters. This was tedious, costly, and difficult work, and even had the brokers the time for such research, most lacked the abilities to carry it out. There was, however, a far simpler way of finding out which were the sound securities. Those brokers who tried to be straightforward would watch Mendels and the few like him—men who were intelligent and knowledgeable as well as honest. If Mendels dealt in an issue, they reasoned, it was probably all right. This method was not blessed by official approval; there were no officials at the Curb to give it. In a way, Mendels and others like him acted as an informal committee on listing for a segment of the out-of-doors community.

A similar situation developed regarding appraisals of newly arrived brokers. The Curb had no way of judging such individuals, and generally tried to avoid doing business with a man until he had a reputation for honesty. Because of this, many decent men were unable to last more than a few weeks at the Curb, since without orders and commissions they could not survive. Equally troublesome was the fact that some dishonest brokers managed to mask their operations, in this way trapping unsuspecting colleagues by failing to live up to their orders. Here too Mendels and the Curb leaders performed a valuable function. Once these highly regarded brokers accepted a new man, indicating this by dealing with him, the rest of the community would recognize their judgment. Thus, the Curb also developed an informal committee on membership. The procedures worked both ways; should Mendels let it be known that he would no longer deal in a security or with a man, the more scrupulous curbstone brokers would follow suit.

By the mid-1890s, the Mendels group acted as an *ad hoc* committee on membership, ethics, and listing. This is not to say that they could ban a stock or a man from the Curb; rather, it meant that the most prominent out-of-doors brokers would be wary of anything Mendels and his group refused.

The "Mendels Circle," if we may call it that, had several concentric rings. At the center was Mendels himself and a group of curbstone brokers, most of whom had Wall Street offices. Oscar Bamberger, a leading specialist in unlisted tobacco stocks who had an office at 15 Wall, was of this group, as was Carl Pforzheimer of 25 Broad, who had excellent connections in several important Stock Exchange houses and specialized in copper stocks like Butte and Braden; later on Pforzheimer would dominate Standard Oil securities, the blue chips of the Curb. Spencer Koch of 30 Broad was one of the ambitious new specialists accepted to the inner circle. John L. McCormack, who began his career as a representative of the Stock Exchange firm of Moore & Schley, was another. The brokers in this group were either specialists in the more important unlisted securities or representatives for those Stock Exchange firms which had the largest business at the Curb. At this time—in the years just prior to 1900—no Consolidated broker or marginal, independent trader exercized much power on Broad Street.

Associated with the Mendels group although not of the leadership were James O'Brian of Bache & Co. and "Colonel Washington" Content, the brother of leading Stock Exchange broker Harry Content. William Marko of Wasserman Brothers, one of the half dozen most successful curbstone brokers, was friendly with Mendels, as was young Tom Marsalis, who later on would have a spectacular career as a Standard Oil specialist. Further removed were a group of approximately one hundred specialists and commission brokers who indicated a willingness to accept Mendels' view of honesty in Curb dealings. There is no way of knowing how many brokers operated at the Curb at this time; certainly there were more than three hundred, not including those who functioned at two or more exchanges, but counting those who appeared only occasionally. Of that number fewer than half could be counted as adhering to the Mendels' positions, and although these included the most prominent of the curbstone brokers, their disciplinary powers remained informal, and their organization nonexistent.

There were three general categories of wrongdoing at the Curb. The least important of these were those practices all condemned publicly, but engaged in as a matter of practical necessity. For example, a commission broker might receive an order from a Stock Exchange house, which he would then take to the part of the Curb where specialists in that security were to be found. He would ask for quotations, let one or two specialists know of his order, and then make it clear that he meant to make a certain amount of money on the transaction, above and beyond his regular commission. He might learn that

94 · *The Curbstone Brokers*

ordinarily the price would be $15 a share for the lot. But the commission broker and the specialist would agree to enter it at $16, and split the extra point between them. Each man had made extra money, which came from the pocket of the Stock Exchange firm's client. Since there was no exact way of finding out bids and asks at the Curb, such a deal would be extremely difficult to uncover.

At other times brokers might shave commissions to obtain an order. Kickbacks by commission brokers to Stock Exchange firms were of this category. The illegal switching of tax stamps from one security to a second, so as to avoid paying the government, was another. Clerks and runners were almost expected to engage in petty thievery, such as charging for horse-car rides not actually taken. Representatives of a Stock Exchange house might enter into transactions for other firms, some of which might harm their own concerns. In all, these practices never hurt another curbstone broker directly or in an important way. The men of the Curb saw little wrong with making extra money from the Stock Exchange or the government. Since most were engaged in what amounted to a wholesale business, rarely coming into contact with actual clients buying and selling securities for their private accounts, the ultimate sufferer was always a faceless, unidentified person or a huge, impersonal organization. This business was petty when compared to the far greater wrongdoing and thievery then taking place elsewhere in the district, especially the more obvious malpractices at the Consolidated, but it did go against what the curbstone brokers publicly preached. Even then the Curb thought of itself as a community, just like similar groupings of businessmen. It had a dual standard, one for Curb dealings, the other for transactions with outsiders, and a double code of honor, the public and the private.

In the second category were those practices all curbstone brokers considered unethical, and were prepared to act against whenever uncovered. Just as Mendels, Pforzheimer, and Marko, the shakiest marginal brokers would not countenance welshing, and the man who refused to or could not deliver on orders and pledges made to other Curb brokers would be sent to Coventry; to allow him to continue his business would be to tear down the entire fabric of trust upon which every securities market in the world was constructed. Those brokers who attempted to deal with the Consolidated or transacted business in Stock Exchange securities would be avoided; the Establishment would wreck them should their activities be discovered, and those who were associated with them might also suffer, as could the Curb in general. Any dealings that endangered the community as a whole could not be permitted.

The stealing of hand signals was likewise considered a major crime, and one that deserves some explanation. The Curb could not survive without the complex arm, hand, and finger waving between broker and clerk. All of this was done in the open, in sight of everyone, but it was a matter of honor and practical necessity for each broker to avoid observing and acting upon the signals of others, for to do so would cause a breakdown of the system. For example, a broker might receive a signal from his clerk to purchase 5,000 shares of ABC Mining "at the market." Should another broker see the signal, he might rush to the "ABC crowd," getting there before the first man could arrive, and buy a block of shares at the going price. Then, when the first broker asked for prices of his 5,000 share block, the second could sell him his newly acquired shares, usually for a small but quick profit. In itself such a situation might not present a serious threat to the Curb, though had it become widespread the entire mechanism by which the out-of-doors market operated could have ground to a halt, as brokers would have run from place to place, effecting small corners with each sizable order from a window clerk. Of course, it would be difficult to prove infrequent sign-stealing, and a broker might get away with it on occasion. But should he try to make a practice of stealing signs and acting upon them, he could expect retribution, which might take the form of being frozen out of business, the ill wishes of his fellows, or a swift knee to the groin.

Finally, there were those abuses that fell into a shady area; some thought them legitimate, while others, especially Mendels and his circle, believed them inimical to Curb interests. A broker or chief clerk might leave one firm and join another, using information gathered at his previous place of employment at the new job in such a way as to harm the first employer. This was a common occurrence at the Stock Exchange as well as the Curb. Mendels didn't like it, although he saw no way of preventing the practice.

Curbstone brokers usually began business at 10:00 A.M. and closed down operations at 3:00 in the afternoon, as did the Stock Exchange, but some began earlier and stayed after 3:00. Saturday trading was from 10:00 to noon, and since many Jewish brokers were not there for religious reasons, business that day was irregular and fitful. Mendels would have preferred strong enforcement of trading hours, with penalties for those who transacted business before and after hours. On the other hand, many brokers saw no harm in early and late trading, since it did not hurt anyone directly.

The methods for delivery of certificates and payment for them were haphazard, and violations of agreements, most of them petty and in some cases accidental, were not uncommon. Here, too, Mendels would have preferred a system of penalties so as to further professionalize the Curb, but most disagreed with him in the matter. The registration of certificates was shabbily handled, and at times unregistered, illegal shares were sent to the purchaser. Some Curb leaders were unhappy about methods of fee splitting, the ways orders between specialists and commission brokers differed slightly from man to man, and the possibilities for fraud that existed. There was no way of preventing corrupt newcomers from dealing at the Curb, and no way to distinguish between honestly represented securities and those of bogus companies. Others thought the Curb as a body had no right to question such transactions, men, and securities so long as none of the regulars were harmed. One might say there were some practices that all agreed were right or wrong, but many that divided the Mendels circle from those outside of it. The former group wanted to regularize the Curb, while the latter insisted on complete freedom in their business. The stalemate that developed between these two forces was resolved, in part at least, from the outside, where pressures were building for regulation and self-policing.

The decade that began with McKinley's victory over Bryan and ended with the worst stock market crash to that time was one of the most productive in American history; from 1896 to 1907, the United States fought a "splendid little war" with Spain, rode the crest of a wave of economic advance that affected every nation in the Western world, and began the process of adapting political forms to the kind of economy that had emerged toward the end of the nineteenth century. The old problems remained; the cities continued to grow and finance capitalism remained unchecked. These seemed of secondary importance when compared with the great opportunities that were opening up in all parts of the nation.

As usual, these advances were mirrored on Wall Street, where finance capitalism was in its golden age. From 1895 to 1904, over three thousand firms disappeared as a result of mergers, and most of these were organized by New York investment bankers. In 1899, the peak year for such activities, 1,208 companies with a total of $2.27 billion in securities went into consolidations. Two years earlier there were but eight industrial firms capitalized at over $50 million, and only a scattering of industrial securities were traded at the Stock Exchange. By 1903 the number of these giants reached forty, and the industrial list was the most rapidly growing speculative arena at the Big Board. This six-year span saw the formation of such firms as International Silver, National Biscuit, American Car & Foundry, Borden's Condensed Milk, National Distillers, and United Fruit; Standard Oil of New Jersey was reorganized at this time; Electric Boat—the forerunner of General Dynamics—made its appearance. The steel industry flowered, with the formations of Tennessee Coal & Iron, American Steel & Wire, American Tin Plate, Carnegie Steel, and Colorado Fuel & Iron. Writing in *The Wall Street Journal* on March 3, 1900, Charles Dow said, "It is as certain as anything in the future that industrial securities will form the principal medium for speculation in this country. The field for the formation of industrial corporations is vast and varying degrees of skill in management, coupled with the succession of good times and bad times, will make constant changes in values which will be discounted by movements in the prices of stocks." Such a period would also bring problems; Dow noted that "It is impossible that any large portion of the industrial stocks created in the last six months should have been marketed."

The financial district rose to the occasion by expanding

rapidly so as to distribute these securities. In the first quarter of 1899 alone, new industrials capitalized as $1.59 billion were incorporated, and the total for the entire year was well over $3.5 billion, two-thirds of which represented common stock and the rest preferred and bonds. Nor was this the only area for expansion; in 1899, $67 million in new rail issues were floated on Wall Street; by 1901 the figure was $434 million, and it would reach $527 million in 1902. Most of these issues began their trading lives at the Curb.

As new issues were being marketed, the old ones disappeared through mergers. On balance, the actual number of shares listed at the Stock Exchange declined from 1897 to 1903, while those for new companies, which were traded at the Curb, increased dramatically. The general public, now more interested in speculation than ever before, came to both markets seeking "action." The impact of these forces on the Stock Exchange and the Curb was strikingly different.

The declining number of shares available and the increased desire to purchase securities led to a great bull market at the Stock Exchange. The Dow-Jones Industrials were at 34.74 and the Rails at 47.51 on October 12, 1896, when it seemed that William Jennings Bryan might win the presidential election. On January 19, 1906, the Industrials reached 103.00 and the Rails 138.36, as the bull market hit its peak. Trading volume rose along with prices; never before or since have the turnover rates for listed stocks reached such figures. During four of the years from 1900 to 1907, it exceeded 200 percent; even 1928, the wildest year of the 1920s, had a turnover of only 28 percent. In 1900, the Stock Exchange reported a volume of 102.4 million shares, when fewer than 60 million shares were listed, for a turnover of only 172 percent. On the most active day of the year, November 12, some 1.6 million shares changed hands, which in terms of today's trading-to-listed-shares ratio would be equivalent to a 105 million share day. The turnover was to go still higher. In 1901 it reached an all-time high of 319 percent, leading Jacob Shiff, the head of Kuhn, Loeb, to remark, "It is almost terrifying to contemplate the way in which the market has risen, by leaps and bounds." Schiff was concerned: "The reaction must come; it is only a question of time." Schiff and men like him who predicted disaster were worried about wild speculation. On January 19, 1901, the Industrials were at 64.77; Schiff wrote these words in late March, as it crossed the 70 level. On June 16, the Industrials hit a high of 78.26. In a period of five months, the Industrial Index had advanced what in terms of today's market would be more than two hundred points. Business continued to churn and boom. Writing in late May, E. C. Stedman of the Stock Exchange said:

The business of commission houses swelled beyond all precedent, and weary clerks toiled to midnight adjusting the accounts of lawyers, grocers, physicians, waiters, clergymen, and chorus singers who were learning to acquire wealth without labor. From every lip dropped stories of fortunes gained in a week by this or that lucky strike. Florists, jewellers, perfumers, restauranteurs, and modistes rejoiced in the collateral prosperity secured to them by the boom in stocks.

By that time million-share days were regular occurrences; the Stock Exchange trading floor and back offices could not accommodate the additional volume. The board of governors announced its plan to construct a larger building to house the Exchange on April 2. Later in the month the Big Board moved to temporary quarters at the New York Produce Exchange at 2 Broadway, and soon after workmen tore down the old building to make way for the new one. The transfer of activities took place on April 28, when Stock Exchange volume—racked up while movers sweated and cursed and brokers ran from building to building—topped the 1 million mark. On April 30, when the new quarters were barely livable, volume reached 3,250,000 shares. Without first having had a 2-million-share day, the Stock Exchange struggled through its first 3-million-share session.

If anything, the Curb was a more frantic place. The Stock Exchange was plagued by a huge volume of paper work, an increased demand for securities, and a smaller supply of stocks. The Curb had even greater problems, since it lacked clearance facilities. The number of securities traded at the Curb rose dramatically, from the hundred or so issues of 1899 to the 263 of 1901, and the more than five hundred of 1906. The speculative fever of the time, and the inability and unwillingness of the Stock Exchange to admit many new industrials to trading, caused volume to swell more rapidly at the Curb than it did at the Big Board. Some $10 million in bonds were sold at the Curb in 1900. The figures were approximately $26 million in 1907 and $66 million a year later. Fewer than 300,000 shares of industrial stocks were traded in 1900; these securities traded almost 3 million shares in 1907, and reached 4.8 million in 1908. Mining stocks, the bulwark of the Curb, recorded a 21-million-share year in 1900, and was over 32 million in 1907, and 42 million in 1908. And stock prices reflected the boom; United Copper, a small mine in the West, sold at less than seventy cents a share in 1904, but reached $77 just before the panic of 1907, after which it declined to $2.

One must view all of the above figures with great suspicion, however; the lack of trustworthy information regarding activities was a major problem at the Curb. In an attempt to bring some order to the market, Mendels and his friends approached the Bennett Press, a small job printer with offices at 48 New Street, with a proposition: if Bennett would undertake to gather information regarding quotations and volume, and print them so as to arrive at the Curb prior to the next day's trading, Mendels would guarantee the purchase of the information. Sometime in 1903, Bennett began printing his daily "flimsies," which were taken not only by curbstone brokers, but by Stock Exchange members with Curb affiliations as well. Unfortunately, even the figures printed by Bennett were inaccurate. A reporter would approach a specialist to ask about his volume and quotations, and receive replies that often bore little resemblance to the truth. Should the specialist want the public to think one of his securities was active when it was not, he might inflate a day's trading of forty shares to four hundred, and would minimize the figures should he want to mask his operations. Similarly, the broker might attempt to manipulate quotations, raising or lowering them to suit his own purposes. The Bennett Press experience was an unhappy one, but the reports continued, perhaps on the theory that even this news was better than none at all. Indeed, so successful was the venture in terms of sales that a rival service, the Curb Quotation Company, with offices at 51 Broad Street not far from the actual market, was formed in 1905, and issued its own prices and volume figures, which differed somewhat from Bennett's and served to further complicate the issue and confirm the general suspicion that neither was accurate insofar as specific securities were concerned. The experience nevertheless demonstrated that such information was not only useful, but would fetch a price, and this indicated to Mendels that the Curb desired an information-gathering agency of one kind or another. Late in 1903 he proposed the issuance of a directory, which would list all Curb brokers whom he and his friends believed reliable. The directory would sell for a modest price, be updated regularly, and could be considered a listing of reputable brokers. The plan was adopted, and in January, 1904, the first issue of the "Official Curb Directory of New York Curb Market" appeared. The publisher was an associate of Bennett's, L. T. Davis of 48 New Street, and the price was 50 cents. Mendels and other prominent brokers took advertisements in the Directory so as to defray expenses. The body of the publication contained the names, addresses, and telephone numbers of 209 brokers, some of whose names were misspelled and their offices misnumbered. Still, the 1904 Directory, together with the Bennett lists, marked the first move toward regulation and organization—feeble though it was—at the Curb.

VI

The Curb Community

THE SPECTACULAR turn-of-the-century bull market sparked a series of dramatic changes at the Curb, the most obvious of which was the move to a new location. This need was recognized as early as March of 1901, when the sidewalks in front of the Mills Building were so crowded that pedestrians could not pass; knots of brokers blocked the streets, preventing automobiles from getting through and frightening horses with their loud shouts and strange garb. The police issued another in a series of warnings: either move or be moved. The brokers were not too concerned with this; the police had been paid off in the past with Christmas gifts and the like, and would not act against the Curb unless forced to do so by higher authorities.

There were other, more pressing reasons for a move. The new interest in securities had resulted in an enlarged Curb market, and there simply were not enough offices with windows to accommodate the augmented army of clerks. Then, when the curbstone brokers learned of the new Exchange building to be erected at Wall and Broad, they were struck by mingled feelings of envy and concern. The Stock Exchange was moving ahead while they seemed to be standing still; since construction workers would soon flood the area, and remain for the next two years, creating noise and fears of swinging girders, the Mills Building would be an impossible place from which to work.

Then came the panic of 1901, shattering the euphoria of the

past four years. James Hill and E. H. Harriman, the railroad tycoons, struggled for control of the Northern Pacific, and their investment bankers, J. P. Morgan & Co. and Kuhn, Loeb, bid the price of the line's common stock to record heights. Volume increased rapidly during the week of May 6, as each side believed it had cornered the stock, while the speculators dumped all they owned so as to be able to cover their short positions in Northern Pacific. The Stock Exchange, still not settled in its temporary quarters at 2 Broadway, struggled to keep pace with the trading, but fell behind and failed to carry out thousands of orders in the confusion of that week. Lower Broadway was clogged with brokers and clients seeking to sell out before it was too late. The situation eased somewhat by mid-month, though for a few days it appeared the great bull market had come to an abrupt halt.

What if the panic had taken place a month earlier? It would have occurred at Wall and Broad instead of lower Broadway, and the horde of people would have crushed the curbstone community, which would have been forced to close down. This near disaster spurred those who wanted to move. The new Stock Exchange building would be ready for occupancy in two years. Should a panic like the one just ended occur after 1903, it might damage the Curb seriously.

The need for greater office space, the police harassment, the construction activities at Wall and Broad—all contributed toward pushing the Curb a block southward that autumn. There were three low-rise buildings at the southwest corner of Broad and Exchange Place with large windows and fine ledges, just right as perching spots for telephone clerks. The location was close enough to the Stock Exchange to enable the curbstone brokers to retain their contacts, and yet far enough away to placate the police and enable the brokers to avoid the crush when construction began. The move proved satisfactory, and by 1902 almost all the curbstone brokers were at the new location. Some had taken offices across the street, at the Broad Exchange Building, which by 1906 had more Curb brokers' offices than any other structure in the city. By then, fully one-third of all out-of-door traders had offices in from 25 to 40 Broad Street.

The bull market of 1906 also served to augment the curbstone community, so that by 1907 there were well over four hundred specialists and commission brokers at Broad and Exchange Place. Some would leave in quiet periods, while others would join the crowd during hectic sessions. This was another important difference between the Curb and the Stock Exchange. The Big Board had 1,100 members when the bull market began, and did not expand its membership. Thus, each broker had to work harder, but was rewarded with far higher commissions. On the other hand, the member firms were obliged to hire more clerks, runners, and back office help to prevent the paperwork explosion from burying them. The Curb's methods were different. The market's core remained intact; Mendels, Pforzheimer, Marko, and a few others continued to lead while at the same time expanding their own shares of the business. Whenever the need appeared, so would newcomers, who could rise rapidly to positions of prominence and wealth. To be sure, there were many new clerks and runners at the Curb in this period, but the most dramatic change was the addition of more specialists and commission brokers.

As had been the case earlier, bright young men were quick to read the message contained in this expansion. Stock Exchange firms desired their services. Newcomers could do fairly well should they remain there, but could hardly expect to join a community where the membership was fixed. On the other hand, the same person could aspire to become a specialist at the Curb whenever he felt ready. Then, too, the Stock Exchange preferred high school graduates, young men with references, or individuals with some proof of character and ability for a clerk's position. East European Jews and Irish would be hired, but such men knew their ancestry would hold them back at the Big Board. It was different at the Curb, where Irish and east European Jews were often given preferential treatment by brokers with those backgrounds. Boys drawn to the Curb didn't need an education or references to apply for and get a runner's job. A person might be a driver of an ice wagon, with a route in the district, and be attracted by the excitement and glamour of the Curb. After asking around, he would discover that he could make more money as a runner than as an iceman, and would change his job. Printer's devils from New Street, learning that clerks made a good living with hopes of advancement, would get rid of their aprons and take employment at the Curb. Telephone installers would listen to the messages, and apply for posts as telephone clerks. A man with average skill might expect to earn $40 a week in 1906; this was a fine salary at a time when a good lunch at the Exchange Buffet, a favorite restaurant at 39 Broad Street, could be had for twenty cents, and fifteen dollars bought a business suit with two pairs of pants and a vest. Should the clerk or runner begin to specialize and have even modest success, he could earn over $200 in a fair week. Or if he remained a telephone clerk he might handle orders for several brokers, collecting a regular salary from each. Never before or since—not during the Civil War, not even in the wild 1920s—have so many men with so much ambition and talent arrived at the Curb at the same time. This rush of new men was halted only temporarily by the 1907 panic; it started again the following year, and continued to 1917, when many of these newcomers went off to war.

Although the new men came from a variety of backgrounds, in some ways they constituted as homogeneous a group as did the Stock Exchange community. Most were aggressively ambitious, and found they could do well by playing the game by emulating the Mendels Circle insofar as trading ethics and relations with the Big Board were concerned. Although they would rarely overlook an opportunity to make extra money at the expense of outsiders, they held to the code in reference to transactions with fellow-brokers. In the past, the combination of intense investor interest plus a weakness at the Stock Exchange had resulted in the formation of rival organizations; at the turn of the century there seemed room for a third indoor market, which could have specialized in those industrial issues not traded at the Big Board in addition to the overflow business from that market. Mendels dictated a policy of cooperation and not competition, however, and at no time did the curbstone brokers attempt to challenge Stock Exchange domination of Wall Street.

The Curb was bifurcated at this time. At one extreme was a group of old-timers who had come through the lean years of the early 1890s and were now prosperous, while at the other was the younger crowd, men who had never known bear markets and times of despair. At other places and other times, this kind of situation could have led to a clash—the generation gap is not unique to the present. There was little evidence of this having been the case at the Curb. Mendels, Pforzheimer, and other older men were usually tolerant of the antics of the newcomers so long as they remained honest and decent, while the younger brokers looked upon these veterans as models, individuals to be emulated rather than challenged.

The Curb had a toleration for eccentricity and an easy humor not to be found elsewhere in the financial district. Hetty Green, the "Witch of Wall Street," and the richest woman in America, used to invade the area regularly, to be feared and shunned by Big Board members, who felt a trifle uneasy in speaking with this strange woman, with her old, frayed black dress, stained hat, and ragged veils. Hetty was welcomed at the Curb, where people of this description were not so unusual. "Gowanus Pete," a dog meat dealer of reknown, used to come down regularly, to sell his wares and pick up a few stock tips. "Shoestring Bill," who was known as "the poor man's Russell Sage," was a Curb regular who, after losing spells, would have himself committed to a municipal hospital, where he would recover his strength for another foray with the bulls and bears. Needless to say, such characters would have been out of place at Big Board sessions, although they were considered part of the scene at the Curb.

The young curbstone brokers of 1905 were capable of antics which would seem rather childish to a more sophisticated financial community of a half century later. They would pour buckets of water over each other during the quiet days of mid-summer, duel with water pistols, hide each other's automobiles, make passes at attractive women visitors, and wear garish clothing during nights on the town. Such pranks as handing out exploding cigars, sending novice clerks on errands to a nonexistent Mr. Bull or Mr. Bear, and dining together and conspiring to stick a fellow-broker with the bill, were considered great sport. In so doing they were little different from their counterparts at the Stock Exchange, who would pitch pennies on the trading floor, throw rubber balls to each other during lulls on quiet Saturday sessions, and toss dollar bills from the Exchange windows the last trading day before Christmas.

But there were differences between the two groups. By this

time the Stock Exchange had refined its earlier aristocratic ethic; its leaders were men of culture, education, and social pretentions. Those who lacked these qualifications soon learned that in order to be successful at the Big Board, these values and aspirations would have to be cultivated. E. C. Stedman was a poet of some reputation; Henry Clews wrote an interesting set of memoirs; President A. S. Hatch was a leader of the Methodist Church; Brayton Ives had a fine collection of old books; and S. V. White was a noted astronomer as well as a highly successful broker. J. P. Morgan, who though not a member was the Big Board's dominant figure, was also a leading art collector, and would go on annual purchasing expeditions to the Continent. He was a graduate of Göttingen, where he was considered a brilliant mathematician, and he headed an old family establishment. The Morgan yacht, *Corsair*, was one of the finest ships of its type afloat, and the pride of the New York Yacht Club, whose commodore, James D. Smith, as well as many of the members, was a Stock Exchange member.

There were no poets, authors, or book collectors at the Curb. Edward McCormick, who had gone to but did not graduate from college, was considered an educated, cultured man; there were not many like him. The curbstone brokers showed little interest in science, the arts, or society. Lou Teichman purchased a fairly expensive sailboat in 1909, and this was considered worthy of comment in the *Curb News*, a short-lived weekly devoted to community doings; neither he or any other curbstone broker would have dreamed of joining the New York Yacht Club.[1] Former Governor Roswell Flower was a member of the Stock Exchange; curbstone brokers were not involved in politics. Bird Coler, a prominent Brooklyn politician and a former comptroller of that city, was at the Big Board; his younger, less distinguished brother, was at the Curb. The Stock Exchange's Harry Content was a good friend of the Secretary of the Treasury, and was known as "the prince of brokers." His brother Wash did not move in such circles, and was known as "the old major." Both Stock Exchange and curbstone brokers played golf, but the former belonged to the better, more expensive clubs. Big Board members might take off early to witness a

[1] See Appendix VI.

polo match on Long Island and drink champagne afterwards at a North Shore club; curbstone brokers would travel to the Polo Grounds to see a baseball game and quaff beer.

It might be interesting to contrast the careers of Emanuel Mendels and Bernard Baruch. Mendels was a generation older, quickly rose to the top at the Curb, but was little known outside his own community. He testified before several state and federal commissions, received a brief obituary in the local newspapers, and has been all but forgotten. Like Mendels, Baruch was a southern Jew who relocated to the North and went to the financial district. He graduated from City College of New York, although this meant little at a time when only an Ivy League or foreign education counted for much at the Stock Exchange. Baruch worked for a respected firm, E. A. Houseman & Co., before going off on his own. At one time he went to J. P. Morgan with a proposition which interested the older man. But when Baruch said he was willing to "gamble" on the property, Morgan waved his hand to dismiss him; one did not discuss gambling with J. P. Morgan. Baruch was welcomed at the "Waldorf Crowd," and he ate strawberries and whipped cream with Diamond Jim Brady, Richard Harding Davis, Mark Twain, and Jim Corbett. He had a magnificent estate in South Carolina, a fine town house in New York, and for a while, an expensive yacht. Later on, Baruch became a major public figure, and in some respects was the most important man to come out of Wall Street in the twentieth century. He was never accepted into the Establishment however; his background, values, education, and attitude were not of the sort that was acceptable to Wall Street's blue bloods.

At this time Stock Exchange leaders lived on Park Avenue or in one of the more fashionable Westchester or Long Island suburbs; the town house and the country club were as much a part of their lives as membership in the Union League Club. Few curbstone brokers—even those who could have afforded it—lived in midtown Manhattan at this time. Instead, they had middle-class homes in the New Jersey towns of Nutley, the Oranges, Englewood, and Newark, older town houses in Brooklyn Heights, or small houses and apartments in Washington Heights and the Bronx. They went to work by one of the several Hudson and East River ferries, or the Brooklyn Bridge, by Broadway horsecar or automobile. After hours, when Stock Exchange leaders might go to the opera or concerts, their curbstone counterparts returned to the suburbs. A successful Stock Exchange broker might have a home in Newport and a chalet in the Alps; William Marko bred mules on a Long Island farm, Eddie Chartran had a modest summer cottage in Babylon, Long Island, John Curtis preferred fishing vacations in Canada, while Eddie Gonzales purchased undeveloped land in Middletown, New York, where he established a farm to which he hoped to retire after his curbstone career was over.

If the Stock Exchange had the district's aristocracy and the Consolidated its disreputable fringe, the Curb was imbued with middle class ethics and tastes. These men were Masons and joined the local churches or synagogues. They took pleasure in community sings and family picnics, and considered boat trips up the Hudson to Indian Point, followed by a good lunch and then games of baseball and bridge, to be a perfect way to spend a summer Sunday. They thought William McKinley the embodiment of all that was good in the nation, William Jennings Bryan a dangerous anarchist, and admired Theodore Roosevelt's style while fearing his rashness. They took pride in their flivvers, frequented the nickelodeons, and considered theirs the best of times. The curbstone brokers were, as a class, intensely patriotic and keenly aware that their good fortune could be traced in large part to the accidents of having been born at the right time and in the right place. They would compete with each other, but there was far more cooperation at the Curb than at any other market in the city, and nowhere else was a newcomer welcomed as genuinely, and helped with as much good will, as at that market. As much as any other institution in the city, the Curb provided a melting pot for newcomers and a ladder for the ambitious and intelligent young men of the district.

This difference in life styles, added to the fact that the Curb and the Stock Exchange complemented rather than competed with each other, further cemented the business alliance of the two markets. Not only were they separate aspects of the securities industry, but two different subcultures as well, with neither transgressing on the other's territory. Stock Exchange leaders tended to view their Curb counterparts in much the same way as a large, well-established manufacturer might consider an ambitious mechanic who opened a small shop that provided parts for the larger operation. There was a degree of respect between the two men; both were businessmen and had similar labor, governmental, and marketing problems; each man lived in comfort and considered himself a member of the "privileged class." They had no social contact; their children went to different schools, their churches were in different parts of town, and their interests were not at all the same. When they met on the street the mechanic would tip his derby and smile, while the manufacturer would touch the brim of his silk hat and nod slightly. So it was in the financial district.

If curbstone brokers resented this situation they gave little sign of discomfort or displeasure—even if they had, it would have done them little good. From time to time, some of their number would go over to the Big Board and purchase a seat, and on occasion unfortunate Stock Exchange members were obliged to leave their places at Wall and Broad, and would gravitate to the Curb. Neither fit in well at their new business homes. The former curbstone brokers could not readily break into the social life of the Stock Exchange; they could not join the right clubs and their wives were not invited to teas sponsored by the city's aristocrats. These men tended to retain old friendships, and would return to the Curb for frequent visits, telling their pals how things were done indoors, swapping tall tales, and accepting the admiration of those who remained outside. Those former Stock Exchange members who had joined the Curb were equally uneasy. Most if not all had never been too close to the Establishment, but they had been members of the greatest club in American finance, and now they were forced to trade in what they considered an inferior market. It was a hard blow to take. A few of these men retained an almost patrician bearing, or at least affected it. They were considered gentlemen by curbstone regulars, although never fully accepted, as were those who had begun at the Curb and remained there.

In 1906, the securities markets complex seemed fairly stable, with each exchange filling a specific function and attracting different types of clients. There was great prosperity for established brokers at all three exchanges, and certainly marked a pleasant change for those who remembered the dark days of the early 1890s. At this time, a series of events occurred that seemed of minor importance, but which would later spark a major attack from the outside and disturb this seeming harmony.

The New York Produce Exchange was the largest of the city's seven commodities markets, and until that time confined its business to grains, cottonseed oil, and a dozen or so other products. It had over two thousand members in 1906, some of whom also had seats at the Stock Exchange. Business was good that year; almost one half billion bushels of wheat were traded, a new record. Some Produce Exchange leaders talked of challenging Chicago for domination of the grain market; others had ambitions to replace the New York Stock Exchange.

On the surface at least this ambition seemed strange; the Produce Exchange was one of the leaders in its field; most of its members knew little of securities, and showed less interest in the venture. On the other hand, the Produce Exchange was a well-established organization, founded in 1862 by some of the city's leading merchants and boasting a membership as distinguished in its own field as the Stock Exchange was in securities. Until 1901 the commodities traders hadn't considered securities a proper field for investment. Then the Stock Exchange moved to 2 Broadway until its new building was completed, and commodities and securities traders were placed in close contact for the first time in a century. Seeing the great profits to be made in stocks and bonds, Produce Exchange leaders urged the membership to admit securities to trading. Early in 1907 they won an amendment to the charter authorizing such dealings.

The Stock Exchange ignored this challenge for the time being, but at the same time became increasingly aware of the dangers that might develop from such competition. As it happened, few Stock Exchange listed issues were traded in significant volume at the Produce Exchange. Instead, most of the securities business at 2 Broadway was in those mining shares that then comprised the bulk of the Curb's business.

The Curb itself was expanding around that time; several specialists had entered into the currency business, buying and selling moneys of countries not on the gold standard. In addition, the

Curb had become a gambling center; people could place bets on horse races, prize fights, elections, wars, etc., by going to the Curb to seek out brokers who handled such wagers as a sideline. Like the Produce Exchange's foray into securities, however, this did not represent a meaningful challenge to the Stock Exchange. Finally, business was good at the Consolidated. Although that market's records were poorly kept and highly suspect, million-share days were no longer unusual, and several Consolidated brokers had branch offices in different cities and were aggressively advertising their services to newcomers to stock speculation.

The Stock Exchange viewed all of these activities with alarm, probably overreacting to what it considered a threat to its position as the district's leading market and arbitor. The attacks on the Consolidated and the Produce exchanges were conventional and expected. When renegotiating its ticker contract with Western Union in 1900, the Stock Exchange inserted a clause forbidding that company from furnishing quotations "to organizations and exchanges in the City of New York competing with the New York Stock Exchange." Now the Big Board took Western Union to court to oblige it to withdraw tickers from the Consolidated, and that market promptly responded by obtaining a temporary injunction to prevent the move. At the same time, the Stock Exchange warned those members who had dealings with the Produce Exchange to withdraw from that organization, a request that was generally ignored.

The Stock Exchange's initial failures in these two cases indicated that it lacked the power to enforce rules in this area. Several leading brokers had seats at all three exchanges, and refused to relinquish any of them. As far as they could see, such business as they transacted at the Consolidated and the Produce exchanges did not harm the Big Board, and was none of its concern. The Curb represented another kind of problem. The Stock Exchange frowned on the gambling operations that had taken root there, but for the time being would do little to prevent it. Of greater interest was the huge volume of Curb trading in the new industrials and the growing mining stock list. On busy days the Curb traded in excess of two million shares, and although the greater part of this business was in low-priced stocks selling for less than $2 a share, it was evident that a great deal of money could be made there. Any Stock Exchange member who cared to walk to the Curb could see signs of this. Activity was high, the brokers obviously prosperous, and signs of growth abounded. In 1906 it was not unusual for a cubbyhole office to have dozens of telephones, one for each correspondent house, and a good location rented for $150 a month and more. Brokers with that kind of business, who could afford the overhead of four or five telephone clerks and three times that amount of runners, and still have funds for expansion, merited Stock Exchange interest. In 1906, the Big Board fought the Consolidated and the Produce exchanges to prevent them from taking their securities; in the same year, the senior market decided to acquire the cream of the Curb stocks.

Obtaining this business presented difficulties. Public interest in the industrials was high, and the Stock Exchange wanted to admit them to trading. But the new companies refused to make public the kind of information required for listing. Should the Stock Exchange lower its requirements, the regularly listed companies might react by withholding information, and a general deterioration might be started that could not easily be halted. There was, however, a back door to the Stock Exchange in the form of the Unlisted Department, which still existed from the time it had been used to combat the Consolidated. Frank Sturgis, a former Stock Exchange president, saw no reason why leading Curb stocks could not be admitted to the Unlisted Department. On March 21, 1906, he introduced a resolution asking the committee on unlisted securities to consider the possibility "of adding to the present list all the more important securities now dealt in upon the curb, with such regulations as they may deem for the best protection of the stock exchange, if any should be required, and that they report the result of their deliberation to the governing committee at the earliest possible date." The motion passed, and the idea underwent study.

Had the Stock Exchange decided to accept these securities to the Unlisted Department, it would have upset the balance between the two organizations in such a way as to cripple the Curb, and perhaps change the nature of the senior market as well.

In 1906 the relationship that had started two generations earlier was still intact; over 85 percent of all Curb transactions originated at the Stock Exchange, while the Curb concentrated on the wholesale side of the industry. In all probability volume in those Curb securities transplanted to the Big Board would have risen once they had achieved this new status. This would have been done without first obliging the industrials to release information on finances and operations, and so would have been considered a victory for those firms. In time, as interest turned to that section of the Stock Exchange, the Unlisted Department could have dwarfed the regular list.

The effect would have been greater at the Curb. That market could hardly survive should its standards for trading approximate those of the Unlisted Department. The Curb brokers might then have tried to sponsor lower-grade issues, in which case the outdoor market could have become a sleazy hangout for gamblers and confidence men. Unable to gain admittance to the Stock Exchange and unwilling to deal in such low-grade securities at the Curb, its most respected brokers would have been squeezed out of the financial district. Or they might have taken another way out, and entered the retail areas. Even then several curbstone brokers were beginning to concentrate on this market. Weir Brothers & Co. aggressively marketed copper mining stocks; Speyer & Babcock sold new industrials to the investing public. William S. Dugan & Co. specialized in mining securities, but was also an underwriter for such new industrial companies as De Forest Wireless and Marconi Electric, and had a string of offices for the general public. Morgan & Cole dealt in those rails and equipment stocks not listed at the Stock Exchange, and was interested in general brokerage as well. T. W. Stemmler, Jr., & Co. was already doing more business with the public than with the Stock Exchange. If these firms and others like them had lost their industrial securities to the Unlisted Department, and suffered a concommitant diminution of their commission business with Stock Exchange member firms, they might have been obliged to turn their attention to the general public. The Stock Exchange still showed little interest in the small investor in 1906; this slack might have been taken up by a new group of curbstone brokers, forced into that field by Stock Exchange actions. In such a case the Curb would have taken on an entirely different character. Having lost their stocks to the Big Board, the major specialists would have declined in number and power, while the commission brokers would no longer have had as many Stock Exchange orders. Their places would have been taken by a new group of retail brokers, dealing directly with the public and purchasing shares for clients wherever they could be had. The transition from this situation to one of direct competition with retail brokers at the Stock Exchange would not have been long in coming.

For the time being at least, the question remained academic; the Stock Exchange decided not to expand the Unlisted Department, in this way preserving not only its own reputation for high standards, but the very nature of the Curb. Although there is no indication that Wall Streeters of the time considered this problem, it seems clear today that the *raison d'être* of the Curb was its function as a proving ground for new securities, while that of the Stock Exchange was its willingness to concentrate on seasoned issues and maintain high standards for listing and trading. Should these two standards move closer together—should Stock Exchange and Curb securities be similar in quality—there would be little need for the outdoor market as it was then constituted.

The Stock Exchange refrained from action for reasons unrelated to its desire for expansion. In October of 1907, the nation was struck by the worst panic in its history, one that almost paralyzed the nation's economy and destroyed its international credit, and which in many ways was more severe than that of 1929. New York's major banks were obliged to shut down; insurance companies had to declare bankruptcy; volume reached new highs at all the city's markets, as prices plummeted in waves of selling. President Theodore Roosevelt did not know what to do in this situation; there was no precedent for federal action, even had he been able to marshal the government's powers to stop the crash. Only J. P. Morgan and the investment banking community that rallied behind him had the power and prestige to halt the crash, and after the rest of the nation's financial leaders joined in support, they were able to restore a semblance of calm.

Even the government cooperated, as Roosevelt placed the full resources of the Treasury at Morgan's disposal.

Although the speculative fever of the past decade had contributed to the crash, it was by no means its only cause. The nation had an unsatisfactory banking system at the time, one unsuited to the new industrial economy and the age of finance capitalism. There was no way to rally the community to prevent a series of runs on the banks, and no method of expanding or contracting the currency when the need arose.

The public was uninterested in lessons in economics or finance. It wanted a villain and one was at hand: Wall Street was to receive the blame for the disaster. For the past few years Roosevelt had attacked the trusts, and had even initiated prosecution under the Sherman and Interstate Commerce acts. Up to that time, however, most of the attention had been concentrated on the railroads and the new industrial companies. Now the public and its reformist leaders came to realize that these large firms would have been unable to combine and grow were it not for the financiers. After 1907 it seemed evident that the greatest trust of all was that of the bankers, and demands were heard to limit the powers of the "monied interests."

Most of those who used this term had little knowledge of American business and less of the financial community, while those who investigated Wall Street in the next few years were determined to "break up the monster" without first understanding its anatomy. It was possible to consider Standard Oil or United States Steel a trust, and treat them as monoliths, for each company had its own objectives, interests, and programs. It was equally evident that there was no such thing as a petroleum or steel trust at that time, for although the other companies in these industries were dwarfed by the giants and at times obliged to cooperate with them, their interests and markets were oftentimes different. Similarly, the Wall Street community was led by firms such as Morgan & Co. and Kuhn, Loeb, each of which competed with the other, and vied with a dozen other large investment banks for business. Several years later Louis Brandeis would observe that "the Morgan-Rockefeller interests" had "341 directorships in 112 corporations having aggregate resources or capitalizations of $22,245,000,000." Such a statement was misleading, for more often than not the Morgan and Rockefeller interests did not coincide, and the two groups were usually on opposite sides of any given issue.

The situation appeared somewhat simpler insofar as the securities markets were concerned. Clearly the New York Stock Exchange was the dominant factor, competing with some rivals, at times cooperating with others; if there was anything like a trust anywhere in the financial community, the Stock Exchange came closest to filling the description. Even here there were nuances. Prior to 1906 the Stock Exchange and Curb were on the best of terms, and despite the abortive attempt to expand the Unlisted Department these two markets continued to function well together. The same might be said regarding the Produce Exchange, which in the main coexisted with the Big Board. The Consolidated presented another situation. That organization came out of the 1907 panic without too much difficulty, and remained the Stock Exchange's chief rival. The fact that the Stock Exchange did not deal in odd lots, pipeline certificates and the like, banned bucket shops, and had far higher standards both for securities and brokers, indicated that the two exchanges were not competitors in all areas. For the most part, however, these distinctions evaded the reformers, at least at first. What they saw was a giant Stock Exchange allied with the biggest banks and most powerful trust companies in the nation, dominating a market and refusing to allow the Consolidated and Curb (which at times they lumped together) to compete on an equal basis. None of the reformers seemed to understand that the Curb accepted and was generally content with its role; in effect they tried to encourage the curbstone brokers to compete with the Big Board. For their part, the men of the Curb were unwilling to cooperate in making the financial district a more competitive market place; they had no desire to anger the Stock Exchange Establishment. Smarting under the attacks, the senior market became more opposed to reforms at the Curb than it had been in the past.

The 1907 panic marked the beginning of a new period in financial district history, one in which the combination of an outside reform impulse, together with the Mendels Circle's desire to further regularize trading at the Curb, would enable that community to make its first important step toward formal organization. Although the Stock Exchange was bound to look upon such moves with heightened suspicion, the Establishment could do little about it since government now was assuming a new role in the market place. This period also marked the decline of the Consolidated, for any attacks on shady dealings in the district, though aimed at the Stock Exchange, were bound to hurt the Consolidated to a greater degree. In the end, the attempt to "break up Wall Street" would result in the Stock Exchange becoming more of a monolith than ever.

VII

Mendels and the Establishment

THE PANIC OF 1907 and the public outcry for reform that followed led to a series of state and federal investigations. These in turn resulted in new legislation and spurred the securities community to undertake major revisions in its institutional structure. For the time being, however, little in the way of leadership could be expected from Theodore Roosevelt. Shocked by the panic and aware that the nation had been saved by Morgan and his group, the President abruptly ended his well-advertised antitrust campaign. The Justice Department did not enter into new prosecutions for the rest of the Roosevelt Administration, and several cases that had already been initiated were quietly withdrawn. United States Steel was allowed to merge with Tennessee Coal & Iron, a clear violation of the Sherman Act, but Roosevelt said nothing; this was part of the price he paid for Morgan's help.

The New York Stock Exchange was an unincorporated body, as were all the city's major markets, and therefore did not come under the purview of the antitrust and other regulatory acts. In theory it was a club, and the governing bodies could do what they wished without becoming liable to legal actions. State and federal governments could declare certain of its activities to be of a criminal nature, however, and new legislation along this line could easily have been introduced and passed. Roosevelt certainly never considered proceeding along this line but Governor Charles Evans Hughes of New York, elected on a reform platform, felt no such compunctions. Hughes had been one of the city's leading corporation lawyers and afterwards a professor of law at Cornell. In 1905 he had become counsel for the Stevens Gas Commission which investigated utilities practices in the state, and later in the year was counsel for the Armstrong Commission, which exposed abuses in the life insurance industry. When Hughes ran for the governorship on the Republican ticket in 1906 he was considered a vigorous reformer, and in fact was more conversant with business practices and the securities industry than any other political figure in the nation. Since his Democratic opponent, publisher William Randolph Hearst, was equally anti-Wall Street, it seemed clear that whoever won, the district was in for an investigation. Hughes defeated Hearst, and was preparing for just such an inquiry when the panic struck. Now his reform programs were backed by a newly angered public, pressures from which were soon felt in Albany. Even before the Governor could name a panel to investigate the Wall Street community, the legislature struck the first blow. Late that summer it discussed and passed an anti-bucket shop law, which was aimed at the gaming rooms but not the marginal brokerages then operating in the district. The law, which went into effect on September 1, made the operation of such a business a felony, punishable by fine or imprisonment.

The first indictments were filed within weeks, and in the case of *Hurd* vs. *Taylor* the State Court of Appeals declared that although such devices as short sales and options were within the law, the broker must actually buy or sell securities to complete the transaction, and could no longer function as though he were a bookmaker. "If the intention is that the so-called broker shall pay his customer the difference between the market price at which the stocks were ordered purchased and that at which they were ordered sold, in case such fluctuation is in favor of the customer, or that in case it is against the customer, the customer shall pay the broker that difference, no purchase or sales being made, the transaction is a wager and therefore illegal."

The law and the *Hurd* vs. *Taylor* decision effectively closed down most of the city's gaming rooms. They did not affect the true bucket shops, where brokers actually purchased securities and then immediately sold them, in effect making the transaction a wager. Indeed, several large gaming rooms soon reappeared in the guise of seemingly legitimate brokerages when in fact they were bucket shops. The purpose of the law was to clean up Wall Street; its effect was to drive gambling underground and enlarge the bucket shop community.

The Consolidated launched a campaign against bucket shops in the early summer of 1908; this was a regular occurrence, and by that time surprised no one. The financial community expected neither an investigation nor the expulsion of any member, and was not disappointed when the entire affair fizzled out. Similarly, the Stock Exchange proclaimed a large-scale investigation of its membership, and promised to root out wrongdoers if any were there. Here, too, little was expected in the way of actual reform.

The situation was different at the Curb. For years Mendels and his friends had tried to cleanse the Curb of those marginal brokers and securities which not only gave the outdoor market a bad name, but harmed the respectable element as well. Mendels believed that reform could be accomplished only through regulation; the Curb needed an organization that had the power to expel members for wrongdoing and ban securities that were fraudulently issued, represented, or traded. Such an organization need not compete with the Stock Exchange. Mendels went to great lengths to observe that the Curb required no new business to prosper, but rather a regularization of the old. Still, the evident desire to raise standards would seem to indicate that the Curb wanted to move closer to the Stock Exchange in stature, and this could lead to troubles in the future. Stock Exchange suspicions were further heightened when curbstone brokers spoke of moving indoors. The reason given was the desire to avoid the police and the elements, but in the past a move indoors had always marked the appearance of a rival exchange, and the Establishment was wary of such talk.

So long as Mendels favored and talked of reform but did nothing about it, the Stock Exchange ignored him. Now he had a strong though unsolicited ally—the reformist element of New York. Mendels could announce a program to clean up the Curb and say it was in response to public demands, and not merely his old ambitions. He believed that the Stock Exchange, which itself had made similar statements in favor of honesty and against evil, could not comfortably oppose his plan. Mendels was basically correct.

What happened next is not completely clear, and must be reconstructed from old memories, fragments in newspapers, and allusions in proposed legislation. It would appear that in the late summer of 1908 the Stock Exchange decided to sponsor reform at the Curb and at the same time take control of that market. If Mendels wanted standards he could have them; independence was another matter. The Stock Exchange would meet with Curb leaders to organize a committee that would work for the incorporation of the outdoor market into the Stock Exchange nexus. At the time there was a vacant room—actually a large lobby—at the New Street entrance to the Stock Exchange building. The Big Board would permit acceptable curbstone brokers to trade approved securities in that room, while rejected men and securities would remain outdoors. Then the Unlisted Department would merge with the "indoor Curb," thus creating a second market at Wall and Broad. Since the Stock Exchange would control all committees and retain a major voice in all affairs, the new indoor Curb would, in effect, become the stepchild of the Big Board. At the same time, of course, the remaining brokers—those not permitted indoors—would be condemned by the Stock Exchange members and cut off from all commission business. How such a program was to be enforced, and how the Stock Exchange could prevent its members from dealings in those securities that remained outdoors, was not indicated.

Apparently some of the smaller specialists and large commission brokers thought well of the plan and urged its acceptance. These men relied heavily on the Stock Exchange, and hadn't the resources to refuse it anything it wanted. But the larger specialists, who were more self-reliant and tended to view themselves as the Curb's natural aristocracy, joined with the smaller commission brokers and independent traders to politely reject the Stock Exchange proposal, and were able to prevail. Thus, in 1908 the Curb turned down its first opportunity to go indoors.

The problem of regulation remained; if the Curb were to

avoid restrictive legislation, something along these lines would be needed. This presented both the Curb and the Stock Exchange with a dilemma. Article XVII, Section 4 of the Stock Exchange Constitution stated that "Any member who shall be connected directly, or by partner, or otherwise, with any organization in the city of New York which permits dealings in any securities or other property, admitted to dealing in any department of this exchange, shall be liable to suspension for a period not exceeding one year, or to expulsion, as the governing committee may determine." This section had been directed at those members who had dealings with the Consolidated, and although it had never been strictly enforced, it could be construed in such a way as to be used against the Curb. At that time several prominent Consolidated houses were also trading at the Curb and a few of them such as M.E. & J.W. De Aguero and Orlin Kyle & Co., were even listed in the Curb Directory. If the Stock Exchange desired, this could be interpreted as a violation of Article XVII, Section 4, and used as an excuse for an attack on any formal market Mendels might organize. As usual, however, there was a way out. The Article stipulated a ban against Stock Exchange members who traded at rival *organizations*. What if the Curb did not actually form an organization but functioned as though one existed? This seemed the best way out of the dilemma, and one Mendels brought to the Stock Exchange for its approval. The Big Board must have accepted this distinction, for in late autumn of 1908, Mendels presided over the birth of the New York Curb Market Agency.

Mendels went to great pains to avoid antagonizing the Stock Exchange. The first official manual had, as its heading, the words, "New York Curb Market Manual, containing general information regarding contracts, deliveries, listing, transfers, directory, etc. of the New York Curb Market which has no organization whatever." Four pages later we find a statement of its functions, which ends with the affirmation that the Agency "has NO ORGANIZATION WHATEVER but for the comfort and convenience of all interested." There can be no doubt that Mendels went out of his way to avoid misunderstandings about this. And as though to underline his intent, the regulations began with a "Special Notice," which stated that "TRADING OR

QUOTING STOCKS LISTED ON NEW YORK STOCK EXCHANGE ABSOLUTELY PROHIBITED, AND EXCLUDED FROM CURB QUOTATION AND SALE LIST."

The new organization had no officers or committees, but simply a solitary unpaid official with the title of "agent." As might be expected, Mendels was the first man to fill this office. The method by which he was selected is unclear; the Manual offers no clues. But then, Mendels wrote most of that document. In fact, the Curb Agency was really a semiofficial extension of what the Mendels Circle had been trying to do at the Curb for the past decade and more. The Agency's office was in rooms 51 and 52 at 6 Wall Street, adjacent to E.S. Mendels & Co. By this time Mendels' sons, William and Walter, had taken over most of the firm's work and were doing quite well at it, having become specialists in Cities Service and several other important Curb securities. Thus "Pop" Mendels was free to devote most of his time to Agency duties. In 1908 these were simple and few. According to the Manual,

This Agency attends to all the following detail matters of the New York Curb Market: Street sprinkling and cleaning, repairs, extra labor, supplies, snow removal, keeping electric clocks in repair and connecting same with the Western Union Time Service, furnishing free badges for employees, keeping record of same, also for Public Messengers, regulating charges of same, and keeping a record of their names and addresses, gratuities, office expenses, clerks, free blanks for Curb use, issuing Curb directory, correspondence, telegrams, blackboard notices, circulars, postage, telephone, maintaining a Bureau of Statistics and a record of Transfer and Registry offices for general information, also forms and application blanks for listing new securities, and keeping a record of same. . . .

All of these services were provided for a charge of $25 a year, payable in advance and in semiannual installments. The Manual apologized for this high cost by noting, for the third time in four pages, that "The New York Curb Market not being an organization and having no fund to draw upon . . ." would have to rely upon voluntary subscriptions from its members, the names of whom would be inscribed in the Manual.

Some of the services were self-explanatory. Although the sanitation department kept the Broad Street area fairly clean, snow removal was another matter; the Agency would hire groups of boys and men to make the trading area more habitable after a severe storm. Similarly, the street was sprinkled with water during hot, dusty summer days. All members of the Agency had to wear badges for identification purposes; since there were some five hundred brokers, traders, clerks, and runners at the Curb in those days, and no single man could know them all, trades were often concluded by glancing at the badges and taking down names as well as prices and quantities of securities. The public messengers were also required to wear badges, which told their employer's name as well as their own. These were clipped to special caps which each messenger received along with his job. In 1909 a messenger would be paid 5 cents for each trip in the area bounded by Broadway, William, Cedar, and Beaver streets, and was permitted to negotiate charges for deliveries outside the area, although these were usually 10 cents plus carfare. In addition, messengers were allowed to charge an additional 5 cents for each ten minutes they were required to wait for answers, and there was a schedule of charges for certifying checks and the like.

Since at times a messenger would carry thousands of dollars in negotiable securities, it was important that he could be identified by number and employer, and so the badges were a necessity. Similarly, rapid identification would act as a deterrent to overcharges, a violation that was both common and annoying to Mendels, who would discipline such offenders personally. There were more serious problems which the badges were supposed to prevent or mitigate. The Agency roped off the Curb trading area and was on good terms with the local police, who helped Mendels guard against the criminal element. However, messengers were in constant danger from thieves who would waylay them and take their securities. A wise messenger soon learned to avoid individuals without caps and badges, and this cut down somewhat on the robberies.

Finally, the badges helped eliminate dangers faced by the younger boys from the older and stronger messengers, who would bully them into turning over their messages and so collect the fees themselves. In such a case the attacked boy might take down the badge number and report the bully to Mendels, who would call him in and give him a tongue lashing or in serious cases banish him from the Curb. More often, the young messenger would tell his employer, who would argue the matter out with the broker who had hired the older boy, or as was sometimes the case, invite the bully to a fistfight behind the Stock Exchange building.

Most of the Agency's rules merely codified practices long prevalent at the Curb, such as methods for delivering securities, hours of trading, and bidding procedures. The Agency printed several forms for use in trading, but these too did not represent a new departure. What was different were the first regulations regarding listing of securities and the acceptance of members.

In the past, the Curb would trade any security that had buyers and sellers, and admit any person who happened to come along, with the stipulation that he be recognized by those with whom he did business. Starting in September of 1908, the Curb had a means of listing securities. Should a specialist or anyone else wish to make a market in a new stock or bond, he would write its name on a blackboard provided for that purpose. During the next five working days the curbstone brokers would be given an opportunity to investigate and learn more about the security, and in this period it was not to be traded. At the same time, the would-be specialist would fill out a one-page form and file it with the Agent. On it were spaces for the company's business, the names of its officers, and place of incorporation. There were questions regarding capitalization and dividends, but none for earnings. The security would have a transfer agent, and promises would be made regarding the sending of reports to the Agency. In the case of mining stocks, the Agency was to receive relevant maps, assay reports, etc. Should there be no objections, the security would be admitted to trading on the sixth day. Although it was not a rule, the curbstone community generally recognized that the man who had brought the security to the market would become its specialist. Mendels kept a file on all "listed" securities, so that any time a broker wanted information on its transfer office, dividends, capitalization, and the like, he could go to 6 Wall Street and look up the figures and names.

The system had many flaws. There was no means of learning whether or not the reports were accurate, and many phoney securities appeared on the list in the next few years, to be un-masked only after the company failed. The Agency had no power to enforce rules, so that most unlisted mining stocks were traded without benefit of blackboard and forms. Finally, the Agency lacked the power to delist a security. It should be noted, however, that the new organization had only as much power and authority as its members desired it to possess, and at the time this was precious little.

Similarly, the Agency had an informal method of admitting "members" to the community. The Curb Directory of January 1, 1909, listed 314 brokers and firms who were Agency members. Theoretically, this meant they had accepted the market's rules and regulations, but in practice it merely indicated they had paid the Agent their $25; most of them transacted business pretty much the same way as they had in the past. There is no way of knowing how many unlisted brokers traded at the Curb in 1909, or for that matter how many of the listed members were "regulars." Those few men still alive who were clerks and runners in those days indicate that about half the listed members were either unknown to them or were rarely in the district, while they can name others who were trading fairly regularly but did not appear in the Directory. The continuing informality of the Curb may be seen in a paragraph entitled, "Contracts With Strangers."

The New York Curb Market is open to all who wish to trade there, but no one is obliged to accept any contract which is not acceptable. Strangers must be properly identified, in justice to themselves and those they attempt to trade with, and they may be called upon to give up acceptable persons before the contract is closed. This is for the safety of all concerned.

The Agency did have a form to be used for members' applications. It asked only the name, address, business, and references. There is no record of any broker having been turned down at that time, although Mendels obviously hoped that eventually disreputable brokers could be barred from the Curb. For the time being, however, this rule, like most of the others, only codified previous practices.

In its 1908 formulation, the Agency represented a compromise between the strong organization Mendels had projected for the Curb and the rather nebulous structure preferred by the Stock Exchange. It was cohesive enough so as to provide a foundation for future growth, but not so strong as to indicate a threat to the Establishment.

Satisfying the state's reformers was another matter. On December 14, 1908, two years after the state legislature passed its anti-bucket shop law, Governor Hughes appointed a committee to investigate further the securities markets and report back on "what changes, if any, are advisable in the laws of the State bearing upon speculation in securities and commodities, or relating to the protection of investors, or with regard to the instrumentalities and organizations used in dealings in securities and commodities which are the subject of speculation." The so-called "Hughes Committee"—more properly known as the Committee on Speculation in Securities and Commodities—was composed of prominent political and academic figures, but contained no member of the securities professions. Its chairman, Horace White, was a former businessman and although considered an authority on banking, had never been engaged in the securities business. John Clark of Columbia University was a leading academic economist; Charles Schieren was a former mayor of Brooklyn; Clark Williams was the State Superintendent of Banking, and the others were of similar backgrounds. The Committee held meetings in the early part of 1909, and issued its report on June 7 of that year. It was a short document —only forty-three pages—but was well considered, carefully written, and a work of no little sophistication.

The Hughes Committee findings and recommendations covered a broad range of subjects, from atttacking the Stock Exchange's unincorporated status which freed it from state and federal regulations, to a criticism of the practice of serving liquor and providing free lunches and space for card games at brokerages. The report had little to say about the Consolidated, and devoted more space to the Curb than to the Stock Exchange itself.

Ignoring the weak Agency except to allude to Mendels as "an individual who, through his long association with the curb, is tacitly accepted as arbiter," the Hughes Committee recommended the transformation of the Curb into an incorporated market. It criticized its listing methods and observed that there were greater possibilities for fraud there than at the Stock Exchange. The fault for this, however, was not to be found at the Curb, but was due rather to Stock Exchange refusals to allow that market to organize. "The attitude of the Stock Exchange is, therefore, largely responsible for the existence of such abuses as result from the want of organization of the curb market. The brokers dealing on the latter do not wish to lose their best customers, and hence they submit to these irregularities and inconveniences." Indeed, the Big Board was responsible for many of the worst abuses to be found at the Curb. "We are informed that some of the most flagrant cases of discreditable enterprises finding dealings on the curb were promoted by members of the New York Stock Exchange." As far as the Hughes Committee was concerned, the Big Board had failed in its "moral obligations to the community at large" in so acting. Since the Stock Exchange had the power to act in the matter, it should have assisted the curbstone brokers in setting down stricter standards for listing and membership. As part of this program, the Stock Exchange could have helped the outdoor market seek a permanent home; "under such regulation, the curb market might be decently housed to the relief of its members and the general public." Only Stock Exchange opposition had prevented such a move; "the Exchange itself keeps the curb market in the street, since it forbids its own members [from] engaging in any transaction in any other security exchange in New York. If the curb were put under a roof and organized, this trading could not be maintained."

The Hughes Committee Report made little impact on the nation or even the state. The inquiry had begun at the end of the great reaction that had followed the 1907 panic; the report was made public at the beginning of the Taft Administration, when the hulabaloo of the Roosevelt era was being replaced by the comparative calm of his successor's term. In some respects Taft was more vigorous in the antitrust field than Roosevelt, but his accomplishments there and in other areas were overshadowed by political infighting between progressive factions, the debate on the tariff, and programs for governmental

reform. The Aldrich-Vreeland Act, passed in 1908, had authorized national banks to issue circulating notes on commercial
paper. Under this act, the banks could borrow from the federal
government up to 90 percent of their pooled assets. The federal
government's power was placed behind the banks, in this way
making the effort to prevent another rash of failures such as that
which had taken place during the 1907 panic. More importantly,
the Act established a National Monetary Commission, which was
given a mandate to draw up plans for a central bank, one that
would replace the Money Trust in power and influence. E. H.
Harriman died in 1909; Morgan was in a state of physical and
mental decline that year.

With the passage of this legislation and the fading of men
who symbolized Big Money, the great anti-Wall Street crusade
left center stage for the time being, to remain a comparatively
minor issue for the rest of the Taft years. Hughes left the
governorship in 1910 to assume the post of associate justice of
the Supreme Court. The Report of the Committee on Speculation in Securities and Commodities had seemingly been forgotten by the national progressives within a few months of its
release, although it remained a topic of interest on Wall Street.

The release of the Hughes Committee Report was one of three
important events of 1909 which taken together would change
the financial district's institutional structure and determine its
direction for the next decade. The second was the impact of the
Report at the Curb, where Mendels prepared for another try at
an indoor, organized market. Finally, the nine-year-old court
struggle between the Stock Exchange and the Consolidated
regarding the Western Union tickers came to an end, with the
State Supreme Court deciding in favor of the Consolidated.
Realizing that legal recourses had been exhausted, the Stock
Exchange leaders now initiated a direct assault on their chief
rival, aiming to crush it swiftly through a strict ban on trading
as well as any other means as were available. The Big Board
would later claim that this attack was prompted by a desire to
implement the Hughes Committee's findings and recommendations, by cleansing the district of bucket shops. In fact the first
assault came three weeks prior to the Report's release.

The Stock Exchange announced the beginning of a new

crusade against the Consolidated on May 19. The resolution passed by the Board of Governors could not have been more explicit:

Resolved: That any connection, direct or indirect, by means of public or private telephone, telegraph wire, or any electrical or other contrivance or device or pneumatic tube or other apparatus or device whatsoever, or any communication by means of messengers or clerks, or in any other manner, direct or indirect, between the New York Stock Exchange Building or any part thereof, or any office of any member of said New York Stock Exchange, and, any building of the Consolidated Stock Exchange, or any part thereof, or any room, place, hallway, or space occupied or controlled by said Consolidated Stock Exchange, or any office of any member of said Consolidated Stock Exchange, or any transmission, direct or indirect, of information from said New York Stock Exchange Building, or from the office of any member of said New York Stock Exchange, to the said Consolidated Stock Exchange, through any means, apparatus, device, or contrivance as above mentioned, is detrimental to the interest and welfare of this exchange and is hereby prohibited.

Thus, the Big Board issued a direct challenge in the form of a 169-word sentence. The statement continued:

Resolved: That any member of this exchange who transacts any business, directly or indirectly, with or for any member of said Consolidated Stock Exchange, which is engaged in business upon said Consolidated Stock Exchange, shall, on conviction thereof, be deemed to have committed an act or acts detrimental to the interest and welfare of this exchange.

In the past the Stock Exchange had warned its members against dealings with the Consolidated, although little had been done to enforce such rulings. This time, however, the Board of Governors passed the word that violators would be dealt with severely.[1]

At the time, the Consolidated had a membership of 1,200, about half of whom were active, and in 1909 would report a volume of trading approximately one-quarter that of the Stock Exchange. In addition, the Consolidated did a lively arbitrage business with out-of-town exchanges, and handled a smattering of commodities trading. Even though pipeline certificates were

[1] See Appendix III.

no longer as important as they were earlier, the Consolidated had better relations with small petroleum companies than did the Big Board or the Curb. To outsiders, it would seem that the Consolidated had become as permanent a part of the financial scene as the Curb or the Produce Exchange. The newspapers referred to it as the "little board," and its recent presidents, Mortimer Wager, Lewis Randolph, and Ogden Budd, were considered on a par with such Curb luminaries as Mendels and Pforzheimer. As recently as 1906 the Consolidated had constructed a handsome new building at the southeast corner of Broad and Beaver, for which it paid $1.2 million. William Curtis, head of the law firm of Sullivan & Cromwell, congratulated the members on April 17, 1907, as he presided over ceremonies marking the building's official opening. "You have been successful in the past," he said, "and greater success awaits you—greater than even you now anticipate."

The Stock Exchange's move to crush its rival came little more than two years later, in 1909. Within months it was evident the ban was being enforced. Stock Exchange firms which for years had had profitable and friendly relations with leading Consolidated brokers now informed them that their contacts had ended. Within two years the membership was down to fewer than eight hundred, and only a quarter of them were active. By that time, too, the Stock Exchange had been able to convince the presidents and boards of directors of leading listed companies to refuse to register shares purchased at the Consolidated.[2] The Little Board was being choked to death, and some of its members might have recalled, with irony, the words used by William Curtis in his 1907 dedication speech: "The institution well illustrates in its history the theory of survival of the fittest. . . ."

Concommitant with its attack on the Consolidated, the Stock Exchange considered new means of eliminating the Curb. On May 12, 1909—a week before the Stock Exchange would declare war on the Consolidated—Frank Sturgis, both Chairman of the Stock Exchange and head of the law committee, recommended and the Board of Governors approved a special study regarding Stock Exchange-Curb relations. Specifically, he wished the

[2] See Appendix IV.

committee to consider "the matter of adopting a quotation in this exchange of securities traded in on the curb. . . ." During the past two years Sturgis had established himself as the Stock Exchange's champion in its anti-bucket shop crusade. At the same time, he made no secret of his belief that both the Curb and the Consolidated were dens of thieves, to be hounded from the district by whatever means were necessary. With public interest on his side, he hoped now to obtain a full monopoly of securities trading for the Stock Exchange.

On May 19, after having passed the resolution condemning dealings with the Consolidated, the special committee presented its report, in which it recommended consideration of the following questions: "Shall the members of the New York Stock Exchange be prohibited, after a certain date, say December 31, 1909, from dealing, directly or indirectly, in the market known as the curb? And further, shall said special committee consider and report upon any and all matters connected with this subject?" The committee voted unanimously to consider these questions.

Mendels was notified of this decision which, if carried out, could have destroyed not only his young organization, but the Curb itself. Always the realist, Mendels knew he had no chance of winning any fight he might enter into against Sturgis; should Stock Exchange-Curb Agency relations deteriorate—should the Curb anger its potential allies at the Big Board—it would suffer the same difficulties as the Consolidated. But while the Little Board had a hope of surviving such a blow, by continuing to specialize in those areas (such as odd lots and commodities) not covered in Big Board trading, the Curb as it was then constituted could be snuffed out in a matter of weeks.

Mendels informed his members of the Stock Exchange resolution, and brought some of the Curb leaders into the Agent's office. In the next month he established the positions of "agent's advisers," the first of whom being such leading specialists and commission brokers as his son William Mendels, John L. McCormack, Carl Pforzheimer, Edward Chartran, Frederick Ackerman, and Washington Content. Franklin Leonard, Jr., a respected curbstone broker who had a law degree as well as friendships at the Stock Exchange, was also named to the post, as were three other men. Together they would attempt to unite the membership, present their case to the Stock Exchange, and try to defeat Sturgis' plan.

At this point Mendels initiated a correspondence with Sturgis. The letters that passed between the two men have been lost, but apparently Mendels tried to convince Sturgis that a healthy, honest Curb was in the best interests of the Stock Exchange and the financial community. Should the resolution be passed, and Stock Exchange members be forbidden from Curb dealings, the out-of-doors market's respectable element would be destroyed, but the bucket shops would remain and take control. Whether or not this argument led Sturgis to reconsider his resolution is unknown; considering the Chairman's earlier and later stands regarding the Curb, it is highly unlikely that he was open to Mendels' plans.

In any event, the Stock Exchange dropped the idea of isolating its own members from the Club. In all probability this was due in part to Mendels' good relations with other Stock Exchange leaders and his success in winning them to his cause. It is possible that leading Curb commission brokers had been able to gain support from their Stock Exchange correspondents; Pforzheimer and Content in particular were well known and respected by several important Big Board houses. More likely, however, the plan was allowed to die in the wake of the Hughes Committee Report, which was released three weeks after the Sturgis-sponsored resolution.

Following the death of that resolution, Mendels moved again to consolidate and organize the outdoor market. Using the Hughes Committee Report as his text, he renewed his campaign for an indoor market. If one were constructed or rented, the bucket shops and unscrupulous brokers could more easily be excluded; those who remained out-of-doors would be avoided by both the Stock Exchange and the New York Curb Market (the name Mendels had selected for his new exchange). This would satisfy the state's reformers as well as raise the tone at the Curb. Should the Stock Exchange oppose this plan, it would seem that no matter what its official explanations, it was deliberately aiding the Curb's shady element. Of course, a move indoors would be costly; considering real estate prices and construction costs, a building would require a fund of at least a million dollars; even with a high mortgage, the members would be required to pay at least $500 a man for necessary costs and the down payment. A rental would be less expensive, but in the past Mendels had pressed for full ownership, and there is no reason to believe he had changed his mind on the subject.

On November 26, 1909, Mendels wrote Sturgis of his plans for an indoor market, assuring him that "all the rules and regulations which now exist by common consent be the government thereof." In other words, the indoor Curb would continue to work in harmony with the Stock Exchange, and refuse to deal in securities listed on the Big Board. Observing that action was necessary before December 31 in order to facilitate planning for the 1910 budget, Mendels urged Sturgis to give the matter "prompt attention."

There is no indication Sturgis answered this letter, or that if he did, he approved of the plan. The fact that Mendels quickly dropped the matter suggests that Sturgis had made it clear he would not stand still in the face of what he deemed to be pressures and threats. Furthermore, the Chairman renewed his attacks on the Curb, switching from a frontal assault to one directed against the Curb's flanks. On January 19, the Stock Exchange recommended what amounted to a revival of the 1906 plan to expand the Unlisted Department, by admitting to trading shares of mining companies then active at the Curb. In order to prevent Mendels from fighting this action, the Stock Exchange suggested these companies' shares be traded without the firm's having made application "of their own accord." In other words, the companies would have no choice in the matter; Stock Exchange specialists would register their shares with or without permission. Thus, the Big Board would combat the Curb by using the out-of-door market's own methods. Furthermore, the Stock Exchange commissions on all Unlisted Department trades would be lowered so as to correspond to those of the Curb; the Big Board and the Curb would be in competition for the heart of the latter market's business. Somewhat sanctimoniously, the resolution concluded by stating:

Your committee realize that an open curb market in some form will always exist, but they think the course which they have recommended will gradually minimize the evil and convince the community that the governing committee of the stock exchange are determined to give at all securities as open a market as may be permissible, or consistent with proper precaution and due security. The committee believe that there are many securities, both of mining and other nature, that, by a modification of the commission law in so far as they are concerned, will seek the exchange floor of their own accord for the transaction of business.

Thus, while the Stock Exchange castigated the Consolidated for having stolen its business, it prepared to do the same against the Curb. All of this, of course, was justified by the need for greater honesty in the financial district.[3]

Fortunately for the Curb, Mendels had sufficient friends at the Stock Exchange to prevent passage of this resolution, and once again he was able to repulse a Sturgis attack. The victory was incomplete, however, for during the next few months several leading mine stocks were admitted to trading at the Unlisted Department, and the commissions on these stocks were lower than those of the others. Thus, the Stock Exchange was in fact in competition with the Curb. As had always been the case, curbstone brokers stopped trading in these securities; to do otherwise would have been to polarize opinion at the Stock Exchange, which then would have supported the Sturgis position. Recognizing this, Mendels bowed to greater strength. He had won his point, but Sturgis had not lost everything.

As had been so often the case in the past, Mendels used the power of others to obtain changes he himself could not accomplish. The Hughes Committee Report had criticized the Unlisted Department; it had urged legislation to oblige the Stock Exchange to discontinue its operations and merge its securities with those of the regular list or banish them from trading. In so doing, it would set an example for higher financial district standards. Early in 1910, there was talk in Albany of passing legislation for this purpose. At the same time, the industrial stocks were becoming favorites of investors and speculators alike, replacing the rails for the first time. Hoping to feature this business, Stock Exchange members asked the committee on stock list to switch industrials from the Unlisted Department to the regular board.

[3] See Appendix II.

If this were done, the Unlisted Department would have been left with a few rails and utilities, but the majority of its stocks would have been marginal issues (such as the newly acquired mines) that traded at reduced commission rates, and this would have presented the state's reformers with an even more inviting target.

Accordingly, the members asked the committee to eliminate the Unlisted Department by requiring all companies with securities to apply for regular status. Despite strong objections, the suggestion carried. The Unlisted Department was eliminated in 1910, with most of its stocks going to the regular board, while the mining shares returned to the Curb, along with a handful of speculative issues that had left the out-of-doors market years earlier. The net result was to enlarge the scope of Curb operations. By recognizing the political atmosphere at the Stock Exchange and keeping informed of developments in Albany, Mendels had been able to obtain the substance as well as the form of victory over Sturgis. At that time, the best action for him to have taken was no action at all.

The decision to close the Unlisted Department was reported in the press, but it made no great stir on Wall Street. For that matter, not many curbstone brokers appeared to have been elated at the news, even though it meant they would have more business than before. At the time it was presented as simply another Stock Exchange attempt to please the state's reformers, in much the same vein as an attack on bucket shops or promises for higher standards. But it was far more than that, and its implications were of vital importance to Mendels and his advisers. For years the Unlisted Department had been the chief threat to the Curb; whenever the out-of-doors brokers had attempted to better themselves as a group, they had to face the possibility of Stock Exchange retaliation in the form of Unlisted Department expansion. Now this threat was gone. By ending unlisted trading, the Big Board had widened the gap between its own securities and those traded out-of-doors, and, generally speaking, the larger the differences in standards, the better business at the Curb would be. Furthermore, in continuing its crusade against the Consolidated and coming to terms with the Curb, the Stock Exchange indicated that the latter market would receive its imprimatur—albeit reluctantly bestowed—as the city's second securities market. More than any institutional change since the organization of the Consolidated in 1886, the death of the Unlisted Department helped shape the Stock Exchange's future development.

Mendels was well aware of the implications of this move, and believed the time right for a switch in tactics. Now he went on the offensive, and began to press the Stock Exchange for concessions. He asked the Big Board whether it would object to the formation of a regulated association at the Curb, and did so without raising the question of an indoor market. This was still a touchy matter, for the Stock Exchange Constitution still forbade dealings with members of other associations within the city. What Mendels wanted at this time were assurances that the old relationships between the two markets would continue, even though the Curb would now be an organized body and not a mere agency. Sturgis' answer of January 6, 1911, was short and to the point:

Dear Sir: I beg to state that while the law committee of the stock exchange assume no authority or supervision over the members of the curb market or their transactions, they are of the opinion that so long as no dealings are had in securities listed at the stock exchange, the curb is justified in making all necessary rulings and laws for their own protection.

Yours truly,
F. K. STURGIS, *Chairman*

Mendels now felt free to further organize the Curb. A few weeks later he and his advisers met to draw up the constitution for the New York Curb Market.

VIII

The New York Curb Market

I N FEBRUARY OF 1911 the city's newspapers carried stories
regarding the formation of the New York Curb Market,[1] and
on March 17 reports of its initiation the previous day. Actually,
there was little reason for more than a slight stir on Wall Street,
for the new organization was essentially a continuation of the
old. Article I of the Constitution read that the Curb Market
would "take over all archives or other assets held or owned by
the New York Curb Market Agency." The Agency's rules became part of the Constitution, and all those brokers who had
been members of the earlier organization automatically belonged
to the new one. Significantly, no provision was made for ratifica-
tion of the document; the Mendels Circle naturally assumed its
acceptance.

Had he so desired, Mendels easily could have won designation as the Curb Market's first chairman, but he declined the
honor because of age. Instead, he supported and the brokers
selected John L. McCormack for the post. Mendels went into
semiretirement, as his sons carried on the firm's business. In late
summer he left the Curb due to illness. Mendels went to California on a business trip-vacation in September. He returned to
his Newark home in early October, and was sent to a local

[1] The new organization was also known as the "New York Curb Market
Association," but the last word was used rarely, and so will be omitted in
this narrative.

hospital, where he died on October 18, 1911, at the age of sixty-one.

John L. McCormack then was forty-five years old. He was born, raised, and lived in Brooklyn. Mendels' successor was a family man, who spent more time with his wife and eight children than with financial affairs. In fact, contemporaries remember McCormack as a rather bland individual, who had many friends and no enemies; perhaps this was his major qualification for the post.

McCormack's career was typical of those of his generation. He had left school at the age of nine to take a job as messenger boy for Western Union. In 1880, at the age of thirteen, he became a clerk for Kiernan Publishing Company, a job printer with offices on New Street. McCormack probably wandered down to the Curb from time to time, and became interested in its activities. He left Kiernan in 1887 to take a job as clerk for Moore & Schley, then a major Stock Exchange house.

The firms's senior partner, Grant B. Schley, was a former mining engineer with interests in western copper mines. Since most of the mining securities were traded at the Curb, he had several representatives there to take care of his orders. McCormack started as clerk for one of these men, and in a few years had risen to the post of chief Moore & Schley Curb representative. He left the firm in 1898 to open his own office, and soon earned the reputation for honesty and intelligence so necessary for a career at the open air market. Since McCormack retained his Moore & Schley connections, and was well liked by other Stock Exchange houses, he was able to fill a useful function for the Mendels Circle when its relations at the Big Board were strained. His selection for the chairmanship indicated that his major task would be to further cement good relations between the two markets.

It soon became evident that John McCormack lacked Mendels' organizational skills and political astuteness. Affairs at the Club tended to drift during his almost three years as chairman. McCormack would meet problems as they arose, but would not press ahead for such goals as the indoor market when the time was ripe. Nor would he work for higher standards for both brokers and securities. Almost to the end, McCormack retained the friendship and affection of his fellow-brokers, but his easy-going nature led other, stronger men, to take advantage of him, and this eventually led to his downfall.

McCormack's most important contribution was in setting into motion the machinery established under the new constitution. Almost all power was in the hands of a board of representatives, drawn from the membership and elected on a staggered basis every three years. The Chairman presided over its meetings, and was an ex-officio member of all committees, of which there were originally eight. It was here that the Curb Market was most strikingly different from the Agency, for two of these committees were to deal with membership and listing.

There had been no formal membership requirements at the Agency; anyone who so wished could trade at the Curb. This condition changed only slightly under the new constitution. The membership committee, consisting of five men, passed on all applications, and a majority vote was necessary to obtain admission. In addition, the applicant had to be over twenty-one years of age, as were all representatives of listed brokerages. This provision was needed to assure the legal liability of new members. Finally, the applicant had to be free of debts at the time of his admission. There was a method by which a member could be suspended, but this was rarely used. For that matter, the admissions requirements were among the lowest for any exchange in the nation, and few men who desired to join were turned away. As before, membership was not necessary for those who operated at the Curb, although in time it came to be expected.

Of greater importance, and the true heart of the new Curb Market, was the committee on listing, comprised of three members. The old methods used at the Agency were added to and enlarged. As before, the Curb pledged itself to delist any security accepted for trading at the Stock Exchange. The usual documents were still required—assay reports, maps, charters, leases, etc. for mining companies and balance sheets, officers' names, and registrars' offices, for these and the industrials. But most important, each application had to be accompanied by a $100 listing fee.

The money itself was of no consequence, and in fact was

usually paid by the specialist who brought the issue to the Curb. Whenever one of these men came across a promising company, he would contact its officers and ask if they were interested in having their securities listed at the Curb. The potential specialist would then assist in the procedures, and subsequently try to control the stock's trading. Should the company refuse the request, it was not unusual for the specialist to purchase a few hundred shares and then pay the fee himself as a "part owner." In addition, he might obtain the necessary documents from government offices and place them on file at the Chairman's desk. Then the stock would be traded, despite the fact that none of the company's officers had authorized its listing. In practice company officers usually did nothing to prevent this procedure, but in theory at least they might have blocked it by instructing the company's registrar to complicate matters for those new stockholders who had purchased shares at the Curb.

Initially, the new listing requirements served to further divide Curb stocks into two groups.[2] Members were strongly urged to avoid trading in unlisted securities. This half-hearted ban had little meaning, since it was so easy for almost any security to obtain listing. Later on, however, it would come to have great significance. Those securities refused admission—usually the most speculative mining shares—would be traded by some Curb Market members, but there was a stigma attached to such business that was more social than financial, for it stamped these men as second-class Curb citizens, whose wares were not of the best quality. Thus, as the more substantial brokers concentrated on listed securities, the marginal men dealt in marginal stocks. This meant that there were three classes of securities that could be purchased by investors and speculators. The highest quality stocks and bonds were usually found at the Big Board; less seasoned issues and securities of those companies unwilling to release sufficient information to receive Stock Exchange acceptance found their way to the Curb list. Now there was another

---

[2] The first stock list contained several companies that would be familiar to today's investors, such as E. I. DuPont, International Salt, Otis Elevator, and Sears-Roebuck. American Tobacco, which traded in the 450 range, and Standard Oil of New Jersey, which was in the 600s, were the Curb aristocrats, the first being dominated by Oscar Bamberger, the second by Carl Pforzheimer.

category: those securities rejected by the Curb. Of course, the out-of-doors market had always avoided certain types of stocks, in particular those of thinly capitalized and closely held banks and insurance companies. Now these were joined by the most speculative securities of the most questionable companies. In time these stocks and bonds and the brokers who specialized in them would become the core of the embryonic over-the-counter market, a nebulous institution with no organization at that time, no specific trading area or requirements of any kind, much of whose business was done over the telephone. But this development would not take place until the Curb Market raised its listing requirements and enforced them. Just as the Curb gained additional securities each time the Stock Exchange raised its standards, so the over-the-counter market would have additional marginal mine stocks and industrial securities whenever the Curb followed suit.

By mid-1912 the financial district had taken on the appearance of stability once more. The Stock Exchange attacks on the Consolidated and Produce markets had proven effective; the latter exchange now traded only in banks and insurances and a mere handful of unimportant issues, while the Consolidated, having lost its Stock Exchange correspondents, was reduced to odd lots and non-Exchange securities, in addition to some commodities. The Curb Market had proven itself, and was a thriving institution. It seemed that in a few years the Stock Exchange-Curb nexus would dominate and control all securities trading in the city.

At this point government once again intervened in the financial district. President Taft had proven an ineffectual politician, and a struggle for power erupted in the Republican Party early in his administration. The Democrats were able to take advantage of this division, and won sweeping victories in the 1910 congressional elections. For the first time since 1896, they took control of both the House of Representatives and the Senate, and with it were able to name their own men to head important committees.

In the past, the Committee on Banking and Currency of the House of Representatives had been both the source for criticism and defense of Wall Street. So long as the Republicans controlled the Committee, the critics were powerless; during the first two years of the Taft Administration, it was relatively unimportant. When Democratic Representative Arsène Pujo attempted to mount an investigation of the financial district, Taft and the Committee's Republican majority were able to block him easily. Now that the Democrats controlled the Committee, Pujo was free to procede with his investigation; in mid-1911 he received permission to head a special subcommittee, with a mandate to probe American finance.

Pujo was a rather obscure figure at the time. The fifty-year-old Louisiana congressman knew little of Wall Street and less of the complexities of American business. He had been elected for his first term in 1902 and would leave Washington for good in 1913, after having failed in a bid for a Senate seat. Pujo then returned to his rural home parish to practice law, and live in relative obscurity until his death a quarter of a century later. The other subcommittee members were also undistinguished at the time, although thirty-two-year-old Representative James Byrnes of South Carolina, then a congressional freshman, would later become a national and world figure. From the first, however, the congressmen were content to remain in the background, leaving most of the work to their chief counsel, Samuel Untermyer, who was then at the peak of his career.

Untermyer was one of the most important and colorful figures in the reform movement. He had been born in Virginia three years before the Civil War, and in 1866 his family moved to New York. At a time when some others with his background were going down to the financial district to seek jobs as runners, Untermyer found employment as a law clerk and attended City College of New York at night. From there he went to Columbia Law School, which granted his degree in 1878, a few months after his twenty-first birthday. Untermyer was admitted to the bar, and soon after set up his own office, where he specialized in corporation law. He was quite successful; Untermyer was earning $50,000 a year before he was twenty-five, and was a millionaire within five years. By that time he was recognized as an expert on mergers—at the beginning of the merger movement. Untermyer operated in real estate, construction, steel, and whatever else came along. He asked for and received a $775,000 fee for bringing together Utah Copper, Boston Consolidated, and Nevada Copper. Later on he dueled with and bested the Rockefeller interests, which were then expanding into Nevada and other copper areas.

By 1911 Untermyer, then fifty-three years old, was considered one of the nation's leading authorities on corporation finance. Had he allied himself with one or another Wall Street firms or industrial combines, he might have become a prominent figure in business circles. But from the first, Untermyer had an interest in social justice and reform which took him along other paths. His contacts with the business community sharpened these proclivities and led him to conclude that concentration of wealth posed a serious threat to the nation. In December, 1911, he delivered an address entitled: "Is there a Money Trust?" before the Finance Forum in New York. The speech indicated that big money on Wall Street controlled big business throughout the nation, and that unless halted by the power of government, the financiers would transform American democracy into something resembling fascism. The speech caused a great stir, and made Untermyer a well-known figure in the national reform movement, while the term "money trust" passed into the vocabulary. When Pujo asked for recommendations for the post of chief counsel, Untermyer was the natural selection.

The hearings began in the summer of 1912 and ended nine months later. During this time the subcommittee heard testimony from many Wall Street figures, from J. P. Morgan down to marginal brokers at the Consolidated. Untermyer dominated the hearings, which came to be known as the "Money Trust Investigation."

As the investigation progressed and Untermyer challenged witness after witness to expain and defend the methods used by banks, brokerages, and other financial institutions, the public received an important glimpse into the mechanisms of Wall Street. Many Americans were shocked by what was disclosed. They learned how the power of a Morgan or a Rockefeller could permeate many parts of the country far from New York. To these people Wall Street had always appeared a rather exotic place, where fortunes could be made and lost in a wink. Now they came to realize that the financial nexus centered at Wall and Broad could also make or break large companies, determine the rates of interest to be charged farmers and homeowners, and —in the opinion of a few—whether the United States would enter a war. The general reaction was one of shock and bewilderment at the seemingly vast concentration of power accumulated by the Money Trust.

The investigation concentrated on the investment banking community and industry, but several sessions were devoted to the operations of New York's securities exchanges. Most of those called were members and officers of the New York Stock Exchange. The average American who followed the hearings read of George Ely's defense of the Big Board's war against the Consolidated; the Stock Exchange's Secretary clearly saw nothing wrong in using pressures to defeat a smaller rival, and this seemed a vindication of every charge made against big business by progressive reformers.[3] James Mabon, the Stock Exchange President, testified on relations with the Curb Market, an organization only two city blocks from his office. Mabon had purchased his seat in 1891, at a time when the Curb functioned outside the Mill Building, almost directly across the way from the Stock Exchange. Yet, he swore that he had never seen it in operation.[4] In testifying on relations with the Consolidated, Frank Sturgis claimed, "I am not familiar with what occurred in 1909," insofar as the struggle was concerned. Sometimes sarcastically, but more often in anger, Untermyer introduced documents and other testimony to demonstrate that such statements and answers were either evasions or outright falsehoods.

There was a second level to the testimony that escaped most observers. Untermyer on the one hand and the Stock Exchange witnesses on the other represented differing standards of values and ethics. This was most clearly demonstrated during J. P. Morgan's testimony, which came late in the hearings. To most this was the climax of the investigation, the clash between the nation's leading progressive critic of Wall Street and its most powerful financier. Morgan was wary but direct, while Untermyer chose his questions and comments more carefully than previously. When the chief counsel asked Morgan if his in-

[3] See Appendix I.
[4] See Appendix II.

fluence was as great as it seemed, the banker indicated that it was. Untermyer asked if it were true that Morgan had representation on the boards of over one hundred large corporations, and here too Morgan agreed with the figure. Untermyer appeared surprised at Morgan's candor; the banker may have been puzzled by the questions. To Untermyer, such great concentration of power was an abomination, no matter how it had been arrived at, or how it was used. Morgan saw nothing wrong with great power so long as it was not abused. Indeed, the nation as a whole was far better off having men like him as trustees of its large industries than they would be under intensive competitive conditions, in which disreputable men might rob and hoodwink the public. There was little disagreement on the facts, but the two men were poles apart in their interpretations of them. The greatest surprise of all came toward the end of the testimony, when Untermyer asked how Morgan selected his associates and the companies he would back. Morgan indicated that a man's character and sense of honor were of prime importance. Untermyer seemed shocked, and wanted to know whether economic power and connections were not of greater importance, to which the financier responded with vigor that such was not the case; a man's word and respect for it were the most important recommendations in the financial district. This brief interchange served to further indicate the differences between Wall Street and Main Street at that time. Morgan was puzzled by the question while Untermyer—and most of the nation with him—was amazed at the response.

Both aspects of the testimony—the evasions of men like Sturgis and Mabon and Morgan's show of raw power—resulted in a further determination on the part of reformers to crush the Money Trust.[5] Since the New York Stock Exchange was supposed to be part of it, the reformers naturally talked of measures to assist such markets as the Consolidated and the Curb. As for

[5] It should be noted that the reformers as a group generally ignored the securities markets when talking of reform, but tended to include them as part of the Money Trust when discussing legislation. See Louis Brandeis, *Other People's Money* (New York, 1913) for an example of this. Brandeis' book, based on a series of magazine articles, hardly mentions the Big Board and completely ignores the Consolidated and Curb in this most famous attack on the Money Trust.

the Little Board, it meant a new lease on life, supported by both legislation and voluntary restraints on the part of the Stock Exchange. Insofar as the Curb was concerned, the implication was that the Stock Exchange would probably not attempt to block a move indoors, due to fears of government intervention. Although 1913 was not a particularly good business year, Mc-Cormack might have made some effort in that direction. Occupied with other matters and never very enthusiastic about such a move, he allowed the opportunity to pass.

The situation was different at the Consolidated, which at the time was being led by Miguel E. De Aguero, an able broker who well understood the financial district's politics and was determined to press for every advantage he could obtain while memories of the Money Trust Investigation were still fresh. De Aguero was renominated for a second term as president on April 16, 1913, and was elected the following week. His testimony at the hearings had been most effective, and had earned him the respect of many at the Stock Exchange as well as the admiration of the average newspaper reader.[6] Soon after his reelection, De Aguero went to Albany to testify on proposed legislation regarding the securities industry. He strongly urged the Assembly to consider a new law that would prevent the Stock Exchange from conducting its crusades against the Consolidated, while at the same time convincing them the Little Board's current anti-bucket shop drive had been successful. The combination of such testimony, Big Board refusals to respond, and the public interest aroused by the investigations, resulted in a new law, passed on May 10 and signed by the Governor four days later. It now was a misdemeanor for officers of any exchange to enforce rules discriminating against any other exchange. This law, which would take effect on September 1, meant the Stock Exchange could no longer demand that its member firms have no dealings at the Consolidated.

De Aguero was jubilant; as far as he could see, that day marked the beginning of a new order in the financial district, one in which "a good deal of business for the Consolidated [would be] transacted upon the Big Board." Soon after the bill was signed, Consolidated brokers called their former correspond-

[6] See Appendix IV.

ents at the Stock Exchange and attempted to renew contracts, and they found among some of them at least a willingness to cooperate. Others, however, while agreeing the law superceded the Stock Exchange Constitution, still felt morally bound not to accept Little Board business. The atmosphere was tense at the Stock Exchange during the next few months, as those who still boycotted the Consolidated refused to speak with others who were accepting orders. But this "gentleman's ban" was ineffectual, for volume began to soar at the Little Board while it leveled off and actually declined somewhat at the Stock Exchange.

The Consolidated's revival could also be seen in the price of its seats. On July 18, 1913, one sold for $700 which, with the transfer charge of $500, brought the total cost to $1,200, a new high for the year. Two days earlier a Stock Exchange seat was sold for $37,000; this represented a new low. Emboldened by success and the clear evidence of the Little Board's popularity, De Aguero announced plans for the establishment in Chicago of a Consolidated branch office, to be opened sometime in 1914. "Chicago is entitled to a branch of the Consolidated Stock Exchange," he told the press, "and we are going to provide one." Nor would this be the only such move; De Aguero spoke of affiliates in cities across the nation, all interconnected by Western Union wires and tickers. In the past, Wall Street had ignored the small investor and trader, who looked upon the financial district as a den of mysteries. Now the Consolidated would strip away all of this; it would bring Wall Street to the country, and do so in a matter of a few years. According to him, the Consolidated would actively solicit business, through advertisements and telephone calls, a practice frowned upon by the Stock Exchange. Acting with a vigor rare for the financial district, De Aguero reduced the transfer charge for seats from $500 to $250, and initiated a campaign to recruit new members who would presumably operate from the regional offices.

De Aguero's plans were both bold and imaginative, perhaps too much so for the limited resources at his disposal. The Consolidated had won victories, to be sure, but was still no match for the more powerful Stock Exchange, and to declare war in this fashion was to prove a mistake. De Aguero compounded the error by announcing his expansion plans in such a way as to worry progressive reformers, who had no desire to help create another giant market while limiting the first of them. Finally, he angered both securities and commodities traders in those cities scheduled to be "invaded" by the Consolidated's branches. In late 1913 the Pujo Committee met to frame legislation to correct the abuses uncovered during its investigations. The hearing had covered three broad areas, and it was expected the proposed laws would do the same. Untermyer wanted a new national banking system, under the control of the government, which would take such powers from New York's private bankers. He asked for a law to provide for full disclosure by corporations of earnings and finances to those exchanges which listed their securities. Finally, he wanted laws to protect the minor exchanges from Big Board power.

The first of Untermyer's recommendations was embodied in the Federal Reserve Act of 1913, which established the first viable national banking system since the closing down of the Second Bank of the United States. Then came the Pujo Stock Exchange Bill, sponsored by Senator Robert Owen of Oklahoma, a section of which provided for the incorporation of all securities markets, and the regular reporting of pertinent information by those companies whose securities were listed. On the surface this seemed reasonable enough, but De Aguero realized immediately that its passage could harm his organization. Incorporation, he claimed, would limit the Consolidated's powers over its own members. In the past, the various committees could punish a member for acting in any way contrary to the Consolidated's interests; now the specific prohibitions would have to be spelled out in the constitution, and any member who felt wronged could appeal to the courts for a redress of grievances. In De Aguero's opinion, this would cripple his campaign to upgrade the Consolidated.

The reformers saw matters differently; to them it appeared that De Aguero had come out in opposition to Wall Street reform. The Consolidated's leader decried the disclosure provisions, arguing that corporations might interprete them as meaning they had to provide the Stock Exchange with information, but could safely ignore the Little Board, since few of them had ever attempted to seek listing there. In such a case the

Consolidated would be forced to operate at a serious disadvantage, said De Aguero, but the reformers read his statement as meaning he was opposed to open disclosure. In time parts of the Pujo Stock Exchange Bill were passed, but not before the Consolidated had lost some of the good will it had earlier accumulated in reform circles.

As a result of these and other factors, the Committee did not frame a bill to protect the minor exchanges; the reform impulse was soon to go into hibernation. By the time De Aguero had won reelection to a new term in 1915, the public had forgotten Wall Street's problems, and the reformers had turned to other issues, most notably World War I. Thus, when the open warfare between the Stock Exchange and the Consolidated erupted once more in November, it was scarcely noted in the newspapers.

This time the battle began in Chicago, where De Aguero continued to work for a regional branch. Since the Consolidated traded commodities as well as securities, he soon clashed with the leaders of the Chicago Board of Trade. In the past, the Consolidated had received grain quotations from Chicago by wire. On November 9, without warning, the Board of Trade discontinued this service. The move was carried out in great secrecy, and surprised Little Board brokers when they arrived at work the next morning to find the wires had been removed the night before. De Aguero attacked the move and sought an injunction against the Board of Trade, which on its part stated it had no obligation to continue doing business with a disreputable organization.

De Aguero expressed surprise at the action and subsequent statements from Chicago. He told reporters his members wouldn't suffer from the move, since they hadn't dealt in grains for a long time. "The business simply died out when trading in stocks became so much more important. It will not make a bit of difference, since there is no business in grain anyway." De Aguero was essentially correct, and this would seem to indicate the Board of Trade had not acted so as to prevent commodities dealings at the Consolidated, but rather in retaliation against the Little Board's move to its city.

For the next week charges were hurled back and forth between New York and Chicago. The Board of Trade called the

Consolidated a bucket shop operation, to which De Aguero responded by asking the attackers to make specific charges or shut up. The actual fight was of little moment, since the Consolidated's New York business wasn't harmed by the removal of the wires and the plans for a regional branch never matured. What was significant, however, was the fact that the Consolidated was unable to obtain an injunction against the removal of the wires. In the past, the courts had decided that Western Union's tickers were, in effect, common carriers, and the company or its customers could not prevent others from using them. Now a federal district court decided that the grain quotations were the property of the Chicago Board of Trade, which could prevent their use by other organizations.

Leaders of the Big Board showed great interest at this decision. The New York State Supreme Court had earlier ruled in favor of the Consolidated insofar as stock ticker services were concerned. Attempts at removing stock tickers from the Little Board had been abandoned, but now the idea was revived; in 1916 the Stock Exchange began a series of new court confrontations with the Consolidated.

De Aguero did not run for a new term in 1917. During his term as president the Consolidated had fought off serious challenges from the Stock Exchange and had gone on to enjoy a brief period of relative respectability, made possible by reformist actions and threats and his own strong leadership. During his last few years, however, De Aguero had made several tactical mistakes, any one of which would have been serious, and which taken together had led to a new decline at the Little Board.

The outgoing president selected J. Frank Howell as his successor, and his choice was ratified by the board of governors. Howell had been born in Kentucky, and although of humble origins had acquired an air of gentility which at that time was associated with "Kentucky colonels," and was considered quite charming. He had earlier been a railroad telegrapher, and in 1897 had come to New York to join the Consolidated. Howell won election to the board of governors in 1910, and was able to win De Aguero's confidence as his right hand man. But Howell was the wrong selection for the presidency. He was unable to deal successfully with the Stock Exchange and proved incapable of continuing De Aguero's anti-bucket shop campaign. During the next two years the marginal operators and bucket shop operators expanded their powers and number. In April of 1919 one of their group, the then-notorious but now-forgotten William Silkworth, challenged Howell for the presidency, and after a bitter contest, Silkworth won by a substantial majority. With this, the Consolidated's last hope for respectability and survival vanished.

The dissension and clashes at the Consolidated bore some resemblance to a separate and unrelated power struggle which had taken place five years earlier at the Curb Market. In both cases the exchanges divided into two factions, and the fight ended in the exit of an incumbent president and the victory of his opposition. There the similarities ended, for while the Howell-Silkworth contest ended in the decline of the Little Board, the differences between Curb factions were resolved in such a way as to enable that market to go on to increased power and prestige.

It began in 1904, when several states initiated antitrust actions against Standard Oil of New Jersey. In that year the giant firm controlled about 85 percent of domestic and 90 percent of the export trade in petroleum. The firm would earn $57.5 million the following year, a more than 700 percent increase over the 1885 figure. Standard's great power had been derived in part from the industry's growth, but was also won at the expense of rivals, after successful and bitter struggles in which no holds were barred. More than any other company, with the possible exception of U.S. Steel, Standard symbolized monopoly capitalism. Reformers had attacked the company, and legislators called for its dissolution under the terms of the Sherman Antitrust Act. President Roosevelt was uncertain about the election that year and unwilling to anger the powerful Rockefeller interests, and so he took no action. Instead, the governors of several midwestern states brought suits against Standard Oil's affiliates under state laws. Tennessee initiated an action against Standard Oil of Kentucky in April, 1904, and Illinois followed in September. Kansas brought its action against Standard of Kansas in March, 1905, and this was quickly followed by Missouri's suit against Standard of Indiana, Republic Oil Company, and Waters-Pierce Oil Company. During the 1904–06 period twenty-one such actions were filed, directed against the most important links in the Standard Oil complex. This was followed by an Interstate Commerce Commission investigation of the trust, the results of which were released in 1907. Commissioner Herbert K. Smith asserted the report showed that throughout "the past thirty-five years a substantial monopolization of the petroleum industry of the country, a deliberate destruction of competition, and a consequent control of that industry by less than a dozen men" had taken place. President Roosevelt, who was soon to leave the White House and no longer had to worry about political considerations, joined the attack by charging that "every measure for honesty in business that has been passed during the last six years has been opposed by these men . . . with every resource that bitter and unscrupulous craft could suggest and the command of almost unlimited money secure." It remained for his successor, William Howard Taft, to initiate an antitrust action against the giant firm, and on May 15, 1911, the Supreme Court ruled that the company would have to be dissolved within a six-month period. Attorney General Wickersham said that "substantially every proposition contended for by the government is affirmed," while Alfred D. Eddy, the Standard Oil counsel, remarked that "the business of the Standard Oil Company will go on as usual, although changes will be made."

The most important of these were the disaffiliations of the member companies of the Standard Oil complex. Where there had previously been a single giant holding company, there would now be thirty-three major producing, refining, marketing, and pipeline companies, each with its own charter and—most importantly for the New York financial district—with its own securities. Insofar as the "new issues" market was concerned, the Standard Oil divestiture was the most exciting news on Wall Street since the 1901 U.S. Steel flotation.

Standard Oil of New Jersey's stock register was closed on September 1, and during the next three months owners of the old shares received certificates for their new holdings. This was a complex and to the uninitiated, a baffling procedure. At the time there were some six thousand shareholders in Standard of

Jersey, of which there were 983,383 shares outstanding. Each of these shares was exchanged for a bundle of securities, and in some cases these were fractional; for example, Jersey shareholders would receive 0.054 shares of Eureka Pipe Line for each Jersey Standard share owned on September 1.

Although the Rockefeller interests had complied with the terms of the decision, the group still hoped to keep its empire intact. It soon became evident that the descendent companies were connected in much the same way as they had been when under the old corporate umbrella. Standard of New York continued to purchase refined products from Standard of Jersey, which in turn used the same pipeline companies, now independent, as it had in the past. Furthermore, some of the new companies continued to maintain offices at 26 Broadway, Standard's New York headquarters. Some of this was necessary and should have been expected; Standard of Jersey had been a highly integrated company, and the successor firms would have had to continue along the old lines even had they desired to do otherwise. The refining companies were natural customers for the pipeline firms, for example, no matter what legislation would have been passed in 1911. To the public, however, it seemed as though the successor companies were conspiring to defeat the spirit of the Supreme Court ruling. This suspicion appeared to be confirmed by the new companies' relations with their stockholders. Standard of Jersey had always refused to release information to stockholders, and so its stock had been traded at the Curb rather than the Stock Exchange. The successor companies were even more secretive. Colonial Oil refused to provide its new shareholders with information as to the methods by which they could purchase fractional shares to even out their holdings. Standard of Indiana and the Prairie Oil & Gas Company declared abnormally high dividends, sparking rumors of insider manipulation and causing their shares to fluctuate widely. So suspect were these and related activities that *Financial World* had to advise its readers that the purchase of successor company stocks were in the category of blind speculation.

All of these activities had their repercussions at the Curb Market, where Standard of Jersey had long been the bluest chip traded. Of course, the Rockefellers took no notice of the Curb Market's formation, and did not attempt to have Standard's stock added to the list by filing papers and paying the $100 fee. Still, the curbstone brokers handled orders for this and other securities whose companies took the same position toward the listing requirement.

It would have been difficult to act otherwise, for in 1912 the larger part of the industrials still were not on the list, which at the time of the divestiture consisted of 198 different securities in 187 companies, all but twenty-two of which were mines. On any given day, however, the Curb Market would trade in only a fraction of them, with fifty being considered a broad market and a volume of seventy thousand on a slow day not thought unusual. Had the Curb published a "most active list" in those days, it would have been led by such low-priced stocks as Bovard Consolidated Mines, C.O.D. Consolidated Mines, Cobalt Central Mines, Diamondfield Daisy Gold Mining, Eureka Mines Co., Greenwater Copper Mining & Smelting, and Jumbo Extension Mining Co. The Curb also listed such foreign stocks as Montezuma Mines of Costa Rica, Cuban Telephone, Giant Banana, Mexican Milagros Mining & Smelting, and Oil Fields of Mexico. Almost all the stocks on the 1912 list would either go out of business or become parts of larger firms within the next decade; only a handful survived to advance to the Big Board. Miami Copper, International Rubber, and Guggenheim Exploration were among these. The few listed industrials were low-priced and thinly capitalized. New York Engine Company, with 35,000 shares outstanding, traded below $10; Michigan-Pacific Lumber was a penny stock with 150,000 shares outstanding; Georgia Development Company would not trade for weeks on end, and had only 20,000 shares listed at the Curb Market. On the other hand, the unlisted Curb securities included not only Standard of New Jersey, but also American Tobacco and other large firms unwilling to submit information to the Stock Exchange, much less the Curb Market.

McCormack had no choice but to look the other way and allow this trading to continue. According to the Constitution, members were supposed to deal in those securities on the list and exclude all others, but in practice to do so would have been impossible, since there was far more money to be made in handling unlisted securities. Brokers like Carl Pforzheimer, Tom Marsalis, and Oscar Bamberger, who were leaders on "millionaires' row," the high tone section of the Curb, would hardly stand for a ban on trading in such unlisted favorites as Standard of New Jersey, U.S. Tobacco, and U.S. Sugar.

They had another, even more important reason to ignore the constitution. The practice of the time was for the Bennett Press representative to gather trading information for listed and unlisted stocks at the close of each business day. Brokers were supposed to report on the day's high and low sales prices as well as the closing quotations, and the volume, and submit a list of each transaction along with the price. The other brokers had access to all this information, although the transaction lists were not printed in the press sheets. Bennett Press would also publish the opening, high, low, and closing prices for the unlisted securities. Pforzheimer and others who dominated trading in high-priced unlisted stocks had no desire to have the commission brokers know too much about the drift of trading, for if they did, they might conclude that millionaires' row was charging too high a price to purchasers, and paying too low a price to the sellers.

At the time of the divestiture, Pforzheimer and his circle effectively controlled trading in Standard of New Jersey. This meant that should any Stock Exchange house receive an order for the security, its Curb representative or commission broker would take it to the specialist and ask for quotes, after which he would place the order. Not many shares were traded, since the stock was so closely held. In 1911 slightly more than one hundred people owned more than 70 percent of the shares, and these were hardly ever traded, while the rest were almost as tightly owned. This meant that Pforzheimer and his associates had to have a stock reserve in order to maintain their positions. Since Standard of New Jersey (old) had not traded below $390 a share since 1900, and was well over $1,000 in 1911, it meant that this group had to maintain a large investment.

Generally speaking, the thinner and higher-priced the security, the greater the "spread" between the bid and ask prices. In other words, Pforzheimer might on a given day offer to buy Standard Oil of New Jersey (old) at $1,050 and sell at $1,200.

Since he was the only major specialist in the stock, the buyer or seller would have to accept the offer if he wanted to complete the transaction. From time to time some other specialist would attempt to challenge him. To do so required a sizable amount of capital, and this eliminated almost all the curbstone brokers. But those who tried would appear in millionaires' row and offer slightly higher bids and lower asks to potential customers. As might be expected, millionaires' row did not look kindly at such activities, and it took a great deal of courage as well as capital to attempt such a challenge. By 1911 all had been beaten back, and Pforzheimer reigned supreme over Standard Oil trades, as well as being the Curb's foremost copper specialist.

The divestiture upset this situation. Active markets developed in dealings for stock in each of the successor companies, which were first traded on a "when, as, and if" basis, meaning that although the new securities were not as yet issued, they would be delivered to the purchaser when available to the seller. At the same time some arbitrageurs, most notably Ackerman & Coles, began buying and selling Standard of New Jersey (old) in an attempt to make money that way. Needless to say, all of this upset millionaires' row, but activity was so large, and interest so high, that even had the challengers the power to dominate all the new issues, they lacked the capital. Even after Pforzheimer cut back on his positions in the copper stocks he could not control all trading in subsidiary company stocks.

The struggle over the Standard Oil successor securities continued throughout 1912, and by the end of the year, the distribution among the specialists was completed. The older, richer, and more secure firms maintained control over the higher-priced issues, such as Waters-Pierce common, which sold for over $2,000 a share, Standard of Indiana common, and the securities of other producing companies whose quotations ranged between $300 and $1,500, as well as Chesebrough Manufacturing, which was quoted around $700. The lower-priced issues were left to others. One young broker put a sign around his neck which read, "Anglo-American, Odd Lots at the Market." Within a short time he managed to become the leading specialist in that security, which sold at around $10 a share.

McCormack and other Curb Market officers were now presented with a most difficult situation. If the Curb Market was to survive and grow, listing standards would have to be maintained. But the most powerful and prestigious members, who specialized in the most popular securities, had refused to comply with the rules. The Standard Oil brokers in particular argued that in fact they were not disobeying the Constitution. As they saw it, the old Standard Oil stock had an established position at the Curb prior to the dissolution, and its component companies automatically inherited that place. The officers had never protested against the old stock, these specialists seemed to be saying, and so had no right to try to place restrictions on its successors. The Standard Oil crowd wanted Bennett Press to print the usual quotations, but not each individual transaction, for this might affect their "spreads," and encourage others to compete with them. Thus, Pforzheimer wanted some of the privileges that went with listing, but not the others.

McCormack and the Curb's counsel and secretary, Franklin Leonard, Jr., took the position that unless the rules were obeyed the Curb Market might as well be dissolved; since the key rule was that of listing, something had to be done about the Standard Oil stocks. They were supported by many commission brokers, who believed that listing would close the bid-ask spread appreciably, and make their jobs easier. Should other specialists come to handle the Standard Oil stocks as a result of listing, millionaires' row would no longer be able to dictate prices. McCormack was also backed by those younger brokers who were prepared to issue such a challenge. According to their plan, some of their number would purchase shares in each of the successor companies and then pay the $100 listing fee themselves. The committee on listing would then conveniently ignore the documents requirements and admit the stocks to authorized trading and status. Then the Curb Market would establish a transfer agency, and the younger specialists would pool their resources to make markets in the stocks, being certain their bid-ask spreads were lower than those at millionaires' row. In such a way, they would wrest control of the securities from their present specialists. Had this happened, there might have been two curb markets in the city, each attempting to destroy the other.

The matter came to a head in December of 1913. Trading had been heavy at the Curb that year, with the Standard Oil stocks leading the way. As of yet, only Standard of New Jersey (new) and Anglo-American were on the Curb's list. Seeking a compromise, McCormack recommended the establishment of a separate list for the Standard Oil stocks, which would be traded "at the Curb but not on it." The Bennett Press representative would gather and report on individual transactions, and make this information available to all brokers. There was a precedent for such action in the earlier formation of American Tobacco and U.S. Sugar lists, which contained these companies' successor stocks. The separate list would be a victory for the older specialists, while the availability of information would assist those who challenged them as well as the commission brokers. For the moment, the older men had the power to block the proposal for full information; that resolution was defeated by a vote of 123-78 on December 18. The Curb did decide to establish a Standard Oil list, however, which was reported upon soon after.

The 1912–13 struggles had their repercussions the following year. Having been defeated in the vote, the younger specialists and the commission brokers went ahead with the rest of their plan, and tried to win control of the higher-priced issues from millionaires' row. Although they attempted at first to remain aloof, McCormack and Leonard were drawn into the struggle, and they aligned themselves with the younger men.

One of their number, L. D. Ketcham, attempted to win Standard of California from Pforzheimer. Ketcham had been a marginal operator until 1911, when he had joined with Louis Cartier to become a prime specialist in Miami Copper, at a time when it was an active and top-rated security. Ketcham made a killing in Miami, and his association with the respected Cartier firm gave him increased stature. Now he became the commission brokers' hero in the fight against Pforzheimer, and in the process won McCormack's tacit support.

At the same time as these two specialists struggled for control of California Standard common, McCormack prepared for the coming Curb election, at which time millionaires' row was expected to back a rival candidate. Still, it appeared Pforzheimer had made many enemies, and that McCormack would have little difficulty winning reelection.

Then, on June 15, L. D. Ketcham & Co. was suspended from membership for having failed to deliver California Standard shares. The Curb subsequently learned that Ketcham had been bucketing the stock for the past month, and that the first complaints had reached McCormack's office in late May. This inactivity could not be explained; curbstone brokers tended to assume the worst when McCormack resigned from his post at the board of representatives on June 19. The outdoor market buzzed with rumors, the most persistent of which was that Pforzheimer had been preparing charges against McCormack, who had stepped down to avoid any unpleasantness. Leonard was accused of malfeasance, but the grievance committee quickly cleared the Secretary of any wrongdoing. The bitterness remained, as both sides prepared for the coming election.

At this point tensions were suddenly dissipated, although it is impossible to discover the reasons. Perhaps both sides realized that to continue the fight would mean the destruction of the organization; maybe they agreed to a mutual withdrawal. All that is clear is that those members of the board of representatives involved in the struggle submitted their resignations, and announced they would not stand for reelection. Thus, McCormack and Leonard, as well as Pforzheimer and his allies, Dudley Gray and George Taylor, left the Curb Market's leadership, not to run for office again. Leonard retained his position as Curb Market counsel, but withdrew from the Secretary's office. All of these men retained their memberships, however, and would from time to time serve in other capacities.

In late June, 1914, the Curb Market's reins passed into the hands of experienced brokers but inexperienced administrators. Such younger men as Alfred B. Sturges, Samuel Wood, and Louis Teichman now took places on the board of representatives, while old-timers like Andre Jacobi, E. M. Buchanan, and Washington Content were drawn into other, less important committees, along with newcomers to Curb politics like Spencer

Koch, William Gallagher, John Slattery, and George Fanning. Content was elected Treasurer, while Sturges took Leonard's place as Secretary, with Eugene R. Tappen as his assistant.

The new Chairman was Edward R. McCormick. Without the struggle over Standard Oil, he would probably have remained in the background, but now he came forth as leader of harmony forces at the Curb. Although a few years later the factional struggle at the Consolidated would end with that organization's being led by the disreputable William Silkworth, the conflict at the Curb Market was resolved by the selection of McCormick, who in the next seven years would prove the most important figure in the Curb's long history.

IX

The Boom Years

O<small>N JUNE</small> 5, 1915, the Curb Market Association released
the following memorandum:

The undersigned as Chairman and Secretary of the New York Curb
Market Association request the privilege of stating for the information
of the public the following:

The New York Curb Market is a public market and therefore may
be used by brokers not members of the association for flotation and
trading of securities not listed with the association and over which
the association has no jurisdiction.

Therefore the public are advised that if they will confine their
trading to listed stocks and their orders in same to brokers that are
registered members of the association, the association desires to state
that it will gladly extend to the public its good offices for the reception and investigation of any complaints that may be filed against any
of its members.

The New York Curb Market Association

by   E. R. M<small>c</small>C<small>ORMICK</small>, *Chairman*

A. B. S<small>TURGES</small>, *Secretary*

Thus, McCormick disposed of the question of unlisted securities, while at the same time strengthening the Curb Market.
This statement, worked out by members of the board of representatives and other interested parties, indicated a victory for
millionaire's row; the Standard Oil successor stocks would remain on their own list. The Curb Market itself gained power,

however, by indicating it would investigate complaints from the public regarding transactions in listed securities, but had no responsibility regarding unlisted stocks. During the next four years McCormick would spend a good deal of his time upgrading the list and investigating complaints. His vigorous work in this area made listing a status symbol of some importance, one to be desired rather than ignored, as had previously been the case. McCormick also conducted a quiet but effective campaign against the bucket shops and marginal brokers, maintained friendly relations with the Stock Exchange while steering an independent course, and piloted the Curb Market through an exciting period of expansion and prosperity. During his first two terms he was able to give substance to the constitution, and helped make the organization more respectable and honest than even Mendels might have dreamed possible.

McCormick presented a striking contrast to his two predecessors. Mendels was a man of stern morality who took a paternalistic attitude toward the curbstone brokers. Like most of his contemporaries, he had little in the way of formal education, and rose at the Curb through hard work, honesty, and native intelligence. John McCormack was a gregarious broker, one with many friends and few enemies, who enjoyed fraternization and comradeship with the men of the Curb. Edward McCormick, on the other hand, was aloof, rarely engaged in horseplay, and tended to ignore the behavior of other brokers so long as it did not affect the Curb Market organization. He was far more efficient and knowledgeable of Wall Street and national happenings than were Mendels and McCormack, who tended to act subservient to Stock Exchange leaders. Edward McCormick was every bit as able and sophisticated as his Big Board counterparts, and he knew it. Where Mendels acted as a father to the curbstone brokers and John McCormack a friend, Edward McCormick was a leader, who demanded respect. When necessary he could talk with the curbstone brokers, individually and as a group, to plead with them to accept changes, and he could participate in their social functions, of which there were many at this time. There was no doubt, however, that he considered his information and political abilities to be superior to theirs. Mendels would develop his programs together with his friends, while John McCormack often allowed other men to do his thinking for him. Edward McCormick would inform the Curb of his intentions and activities after they had been formulated and carried through, and at times would lead the membership into paths they had either not previously considered or actually opposed. McCormick consulted few men for their advice; Alfred Sturges was the only one whose opinions carried much weight on their own merit, and even he was never allowed to forget that the final decisions were up to the Chairman and no one else.

McCormick was only thirty-six years old when he took office. He was born in Philadelphia in 1878, of a middle-class family. In 1892, at the age of fourteen, he entered the freshman class at La Salle College. The following year he transferred to St. Francis College in Brooklyn, but apparently found little of interest at either school. McCormick was concerned with the theater and the arts, and from time to time he would go into Manhattan for shows and exhibits. In one way or another he learned of the financial district, and found it more exciting than his studies. He left St. Francis in 1894 to take a clerk's job at the Stock Exchange house of H. M. Hume & Co. During the next ten years he worked for several other brokerages, learning about the financial world and apparently doing fairly well at it. Where Mendels was happiest in Newark, and John McCormack in his family circle in Brooklyn, Edward McCormick preferred Manhattan. He rented an apartment on Fifth Avenue and spent as much time at literary and artistic gatherings as he did in business affairs. Contemporaries indicate that McCormick was not a particularly original, powerful, or prominent broker; perhaps this was because his interests were diffuse, or it may have been due to a lack of temperament. In any case, he went to the Curb in 1905 as a commission broker, where he did a good though not spectacular business.

There was always something of the patrician about McCormick. He was a man of medium height with a wiry figure. McCormick was a strikingly handsome man, with sharp features, a firm, square chin, and a strong, almost hard mouth. Contemporaries remember his eyes, which were piercing and transfixed those with whom he spoke. He had the intelligence, background, looks, and manners of his counterparts at the Big

Board. One might have expected him to seek a seat there, but for some reason, perhaps the lack of money, he remained at the Curb. McCormick was not *of* the Curb, however. He did not participate in the organization of the Curb Market, was not involved in the various investigations, had not been called upon by Mendels or McCormack to serve on committees, and had not taken sides in the Standard Oil controversies. Perhaps this was why he appeared a perfect candidate for the chairmanship in 1914.

McCormick's first priority was the indoor market; thus, he revived the old idea first put forth by Mendels before the turn of the century. Unlike Mendels, McCormick did not consult the Stock Exchange prior to acting, indicating he would take a more independent line than his predecessors. Instead, he polled the membership informally, trying to discover how far they would go in order to have their own building. For example, the Curb Market would need a fund to pay for the site and construction charges. The Chairman thought this would have to be in the neighborhood of $600,000; since there were some three hundred Curb Market members in mid-1914, the building would require an assessment of approximately $2,000 a man. Few brokers were able to afford such a fee, while many of those who could considered the benefits of indoor trading not worth the price. In this period most curbstone brokers had their own little niche in the out-of-doors market, and seemed unwilling to exchange it for uncertainty indoors. No amount of recitations regarding the benefits of a building could convince them otherwise. When McCormick and Sturges observed that an indoor market could bar non-members effectively, regulate listing and trading, and offer Curb securities enhanced status, they met with shrugs and negative comments. Not even the knowledge that a building would protect them from the elements could convince them otherwise. So long as the police left them alone, and the Stock Exchange did not protest their existence on Broad Street, the large majority of brokers seemed willing to stay where they were.

Within a month the question was academic. By late July it appeared that a large-scale European war could not be avoided. Volume rose and prices fell at all American exchanges, as foreigners sold their holdings and put their funds into gold; almost $13 million of American gold went to Europe in the week ending July 27, and much of this came from the sale of American securities. This was a world-wide phenomenon, and one not confined to the United States. Selling intensified on July 28, as Austria-Hungary declared war on Serbia. Fears of imminent economic collapse led to the closing down of the Montreal, Toronto, and Madrid securities exchanges that day, with the Vienna, Budapest, Brussels, Antwerp, Berlin, and Rome exchanges following suit on July 29. The next day Wall Street suffered its worst decline since the 1907 panic, and all the Latin American exchanges as well as the young St. Petersburg securities market shut their doors. On Friday morning, July 31, the London Stock Exchange was officially closed for the first time in its history; not even during the Napoleonic period had such action been deemed necessary.

News of the London closing reached New York before dawn. The New York Stock Exchange called a hurried meeting, as the streets filled with anxious sellers. Curb brokers arriving for work found Broad Street lined with customers; had the market opened as usual, the Curb could not have functioned. But the Stock Exchange decided to halt all trading; a few minutes before ten o'clock, the crowd learned the Big Board would be closed for an indefinite period. The next day Germany declared war on Russia, and by week's end, almost all the major European powers had taken sides in the struggle.

The Curb Market and the Consolidated shut down in the wake of the Big Board's closing. Not until November 12 were some Stock Exchange issues traded on a limited basis, and full trading did not commence until December 14, although minor restrictions remained for another three and a half months. The ban on trading only affected the markets themselves, however. Theoretically, it bound the members as well, since they were not supposed to deal at other exchanges. Non-Exchange members were not bound by the rule and some who belonged to one or another of the city's organized markets chose to ignore the ban.

On August 3, John H. Crockett, who owned a seat at the Consolidated, advertised his willingness to buy and sell securities from his office in the Continental Hotel on 41st Street. S. H. O.

Pell & Co., of the New York Stock Exchange, petitioned for permission to sell those securities it held as collateral for loans, and was allowed to do so. Such advertisements and requests were rare, however. For the most part, brokers who wanted to deal in securities merely did so without bothering to ask permission. There was an active, outlaw market in the city during the period of the ban, which resembled the pre-1790s, before the first organized auctions.

The curbstone brokers did a thriving business. More than any other group in the nation, they were used to informal trading. Of course, they could not operate from their old stands on Broad Street; to do so would be to unnecessarily earn the Big Board's wrath. Instead, they transferred operations to New Street, behind the Stock Exchange building. There they would meet from ten o'clock in the morning to three o'clock in the afternoon, buying and selling securities in full sight of all who cared to investigate. Not all the brokers participated in this market, and not all Curb issues were traded. On the other hand, a few Stock Exchange members joined them in the open air, and both they and the Curb brokers dealt in Stock Exchange listed securities. For the first time since the unification of the Open Board and the Stock and Exchange Board in 1869, curbstone brokers dared trespass into the forbidden realm.

McCormick said and did nothing about this; to attempt action and then fail—as he inevitably would have done—would have solved no problems and helped create new ones. Nor did the Stock Exchange try to deal with the surreptitious market, even after it began printing daily quotation sheets that were available to all in the financial district. The Stock Exchange did send some of its members to investigate reports of a New Street market, but they returned with tales of knots of men talking about business, without mentioning the trading which undoubtedly was going on at the time. Another member sent to investigate found nothing but "four boys and a dog," at a time when there must have been dozens of brokers trading openly. What the Stock Exchange did not wish to see, it ignored.

McCormick worked in harmony with Big Board leaders during the period of the ban, and although he took no steps to prevent the New Street trading, his willingness to suspend operations officially sat well with Establishment leaders. The Consolidated's officers took a different course. Although Howell thought it wise to remain closed, the majority of Little Board members pressed for a resumption of trading. The Consolidated reopened for dealings in pipeline certificates on September 1, and business was so good the leaders made plans for full trading two days later. Only the greatest pressures from the Stock Exchange and leading banks were able to prevent this move. During the next two months the Consolidated considered reopening several times, and on each occasion the action was blocked. In the end, the Little Board followed Establishment leadership, but not before further ascerbating the differences between the two exchanges.

The war had a transfiguring effect on the United States. From 1914 to April, 1917, when President Wilson asked for and received a declaration of war against the Central Powers, the nation experienced one of its strongest economic booms. Iron ore production rose from 41.9 million to 75.3 million long tons; the export balance of trade, which was $435.8 million in 1914, rose to $3.6 billion in 1917. In the earlier year the United States exported $6.3 million worth of explosives to Europe; in 1917 the figure was $803 million. By December 1, 1916, the Allied powers had floated almost $2 billion worth of bonds in the United States, most of which went to pay for war materials purchased here. To this was added the $8.2 billion loaned the Allies after April, 1917. At the same time, Europe's private investors rushed to the American securities markets to place their holdings in "safe" hands. The more than $200 million per annum gold production of British South and West African mines came to the United States, and this was only one-fifth the total sent by Paris and London alone. It was in this period that Wall Street in New York replaced Lombard Street in London as the center of the world's money market. Quite naturally, the change had its impact on American securities; from August 1, 1915 to April 1, 1917, the Dow-Jones Industrial Average more than doubled, in a great upward surge more astounding and breathtaking than that of the century's early years.

The Curb securities participated in the bull market, with mining shares in particular leading the market. More important insofar as the curbstone brokers were concerned were the volume figures. In 1913, the last peacetime year, Bennett Press reported a total of $2.3 billion worth of listed industrial stocks traded at the Curb, and only slightly less in 1914. Industrial volume in 1915, the first full wartime year, was substantially over $20 billion worth of these securities. Net worth of mining issues rose in a similar fashion, from $10.5 billion in 1913 to $41.2 billion in 1915. Volume for petroleum stocks doubled in the same period. Curbstone brokers, who had suffered through days in 1913 when volume in listed securities fell as low as fifty thousand shares a day, enjoyed million-share sessions regularly in 1915. Never before had the curbstone brokers been so prosperous; not even during the wild years of the late 1920s would so much money be made so quickly by so many brokers.

This sudden, unexpected prosperity was bound to have institutional effects at the Curb, and these were not long in coming. The first and most obvious of these was a rapid expansion of the stock list.[1]

Prior to the war many industrial and mining companies that could easily have qualified for listing didn't bother to file papers and pay the fee, since they saw no benefits to be derived from such a status. Now conditions were different; as trading expanded and many new securities came to the market, investors and speculators found it difficult to keep up with the changes. One way to distinguish an honest firm from one that was merely paper would be to consult the stock lists at the Big Board and the Curb Market, since securities on these rosters had at least made some open disclosures and had passed listing committees. Knowing this, many companies rushed to have their securities listed and approved by the Curb Market. This movement intensified when it was noted that quotations usually rose dramatically after a stock joined the list. The fee—$100—and the documents seemed a small price to pay for such benefits, and the young, unseasoned mining and industrial companies soon came to realize this.

Never one to allow an opportunity to pass without taking

---

[1] In 1913, the list contained 124 mining issues, 34 industrials, and 8 petroleum stocks; in 1916 it had 184 mining stocks, 86 industrials, and 19 petroleums.

The Tontine Coffee House (extreme left) was located in the wharf area at Wall Street's East River end. It was the first home of the Merchants' Exchange, which in 1817 became the New York Stock and Exchange Board. In addition to providing facilities for members, the Tontine had boarding facilities, an inn, and meeting rooms. It was the first symbol of the Establishment, and closed to members of the Curb community. *(Photograph courtesy of the New York Public Library)*

Wall Street during the Civil War still retained much of its earlier qualities. The Street was still the address of several private families, and there were small shops, store-front brokerages, and boarding houses there as well as banks and federal buildings. *(Photograph courtesy of the New York Public Library)*

This drawing of curbstone brokers published sometime in the 1870s indicates the public view of them at that time. According to contemporary reports, one could find silk-hatted gentlemen, farmers newly arrived from the countryside, and immigrants. This mixture would continue for the next half century. (*Photograph courtesy of the New York Public Library*)

The Curb Agency was organized in 1904, the year of this photograph. The man on the left with the watch chain across his vest is believed to be Emanuel S. Mendels, Jr., the founder of the organization and its first agent. (*Photograph courtesy of the American Stock Exchange*)

Youth and vigor were important in the outdoor market where brokers traded regardless of weather. Several of these confident young men, posing on Broad Street prior to World War I, were still active at the American Stock Exchange a half century later. *(Photograph courtesy of the American Stock Exchange)*

Lower Broadway, near Battery Park, was the home of the bucket shops at the turn of the century. The Consolidated Stock Exchange's old building (lower right) was their focal point, but bucket shops could be found as far north as City Hall. *(Photograph courtesy of the New York Public Library)*

The Consolidated Stock Exchange occupied the first two floors of this building at Broadway and Exchange Place from 1888 to 1906. The offices above the Exchange proper were occupied by the bucket-shop operators, many of whom had seats on the Consolidated. *(Photograph courtesy of the New York Public Library)*

An architect's conception of the Consolidated Stock Exchange Building, which was completed and occupied in 1909. At the time of its opening, the Consolidated was at the height of its power and prestige and seemed as permanent a part of the financial community as the Big Board itself. *(Photograph courtesy of the New York Public Library)*

Emanuel S. Mendels, Jr., posed for this photograph around the time he was organizing the Curb Agency. A talented and respected leader, Mendels was able to win Establishment support for the new organization. *(Photograph courtesy of the American Stock Exchange)*

Frank Knight Sturgis, who was among most powerful men at the New York St Exchange in the early twentieth centu opposed both the Curb and Consolida Exchanges. His attempt to engulf the mer while destroying the latter was unc ered during the Pujo Investigations. *(F tograph courtesy of the New York Pu Library)*

John L. McCormack, who was the first chairman of the New York Curb Market, served in that post from 1911 to 1914. Less aggressive than Mendels, he did not press for either an indoor market or higher standards, and would leave office after a bitter factional dispute. *(Photograph courtesy of the American Stock Exchange)*

Edward R. McCormick served as chairman of the Curb Market and then its president from 1914 to 1923. An ambitious and able man, he fought off challenges from the Big Board, raised standards, and led the movement indoors. McCormick was generally conceded to be one of the giants in Curb history. *(Photograph courtesy of the American Stock Exchange)*

The Curb Market building site at Trinity Place and Broadway in the winter of 1920. Note Trinity Churchyard in the background and the elevated lines in front of the site. *(Photograph courtesy of the American Stock Exchange)*

The exterior of the New York Curb Market in 1921, shortly after the building was opened for trading. The present American Stock Exchange was constructed in 1929-30 on top of this building. (*Photograph courtesy of the American Stock Exchange*)

The trading floor at the indoor market was designed to resemble that of the outdoor area as much as possible, and at first it appeared a successful transplant, with the outdoor spirit being retained indoors. The hand signals, shouting, and horseplay remained, and traces still linger at today's American Stock Exchange. (*Photograph courtesy of the American Stock Exchange*)

advantage of it, McCormick pressed the committee on listing to raise requirements while the demand continued. The committee acted on the matter early in 1917. Beginning on March 1, mining and petroleum companies were obliged to deposit additional information at the Curb Market office before being considered for listing. Among other things, they had to indicate whether theirs was a developed or undeveloped property and to make such information a matter of public record. The Curb was empowered to remove a security from the list should it fall below the minimum requirements, and this power was used on several occasions in 1918. To ease the transition from unlisted to listed status, the committee could recommend that while the application was being considered, the security be placed on the list for temporary trading on a when, as, and if basis. Finally, the listing fee was raised from $100 to $200. Transfer charges and arbitration fees were also raised.

McCormick asked for and received an amendment making it a punishable offense to misuse transfer tax stamps. The Chairman's boldest move, however, was to ask for an end to the practice of making rebates to those Stock Exchange firms doing business at the Curb. He also wanted higher qualifications for membership, a corollary of which was the exclusion of all non-members from Curb Market dealings. The members balked at these drastic suggestions which, if carried through successfully, would have made the Curb Market more independent of the Stock Exchange than had ever been the case, and would have given the officers powers to decide who could and could not trade at the outdoor market. McCormick was ahead of his time with these requests; they would not be accepted until 1920.

Of equal interest though not as long-lived was the appearance of a group of brokerage firms more interested in the retail than the wholesale aspect of the Curb business. In the past, over 85 percent of all Curb transactions had their origins at Stock Exchange houses, with the rest being handled by a variety of marginal brokers, bucket shops and the like. These firms hadn't amounted to much prior to the war; interest in curbstone securities was never so high as to justify an elaborate sales effort directed at the general public. All of this changed in 1915. During the war years as before, the vast majority of Curb transactions were for and with Stock Exchange houses, but now some of the marginal brokers and bucket shops expanded their operations and facilities, concentrating on the small investor and speculator who liked to dabble in penny stocks. Most of these firms were poorly financed and shabbily run, and did not last for more than a few months after the boom had ended. Two of them, however, became major organizations, and were larger in terms of offices and customers than any Stock Exchange member firm prior to the mid-1920s.

The first of these was L. L. Winkelman & Co. Winkelman had arrived at the Curb in 1910 as a commission broker. He was always a loner and had few friends, but was respected as a daring and innovative speculator. Winkelman joined the Curb Market in 1911, and soon after took out membership in the Consolidated as well. All attempts by McCormack and others to oblige him to leave the Little Board failed; Winkelman was a law unto himself. He was accused of bucketing, but these charges were never proved. His firm dealt in Big Board securities, and would not stop the practice even when it was observed he was harming the Curb by so acting. By 1914 Winkelman and his associate, A. K. Nicholson, had a large and impressive office at 44 Broad Street, where they entertained clients with food and drink, traded in all kinds of securities, and in general prospered as the Curb's major general brokerage house.

Winkelman was quick to realize the nature of the wartime prosperity and the opportunities presented by the increased interest in securities. In 1915 he established a branch office in Philadelphia, which did very well. Thus encouraged, Winkelman & Co. offices were opened in Chicago, Milwaukee, and Akron, and soon became the leading investment houses in the last two cities. Winkelman then turned to the smaller cities, which never before had seen a major brokerage office; by war's end he was in Findlay, Zanesville, Parkersburgh, Marietta, Uniontown, and Wheeling. Winkelman now dominated trading in many parts of the lower Midwest. In 1918 he employed 150 clerks in his New York offices alone, and 200 more in the field. Later on, Winkelman & Co. would move to sumptuous offices at 62 Broad, to accommodate its more than four thousand New York clients.

The Curb Market failed in repeated attempts to force Winkelman to leave the Consolidated, and his activities were a constant source of embarrassment to the leaders. He finally quit the Little Board in 1921, but only because he no longer saw the need for such an affiliation. By then he was a major force in the retailing of securities, and would remain so until the firm's failure in 1923.

Despite this impressive record, Winkelman & Co. was not the largest of the Curb's new retail operations, for another, similar firm appeared that surpassed it in size, power, and innovation. Jones & Baker, a midwestern firm that arrived in New York in 1912, soon transferred all activities to the Curb Market and quickly became a leader there. Nothing is known of Baker, but William Jones was generally considered a "go-getter" who would not hesitate to bend the rules to make an extra dollar. His associate, Jackson Sells, was acknowledged as the brains of the organization, while Jones was charged with taking care of clients who dealt in what was generally believed to be a huge bucket shop operation. Like Winkelman, Jones & Baker had large, ornate offices; the first of these was at 50 Broad Street. And just as Winkelman had expanded with the war, so did Jones & Baker. There the similarities ended. Jones & Baker concentrated on the large cities and ignored the small towns. In 1918 the firm had offices in Chicago, Pittsburgh, Philadelphia, and Boston. Two additional rooms were opened in New York, both of them uptown, to serve those clients who preferred to watch the tickers and meet with brokers during their lunch hours. The New York staff alone numbered four hundred, making it larger than Winkelman & Co. Where Winkelman employed brokers, clerks, runners, and secretaries, Jones & Baker offered a full line of positions to its employees and services to clients.

The firm had seven departments—an information bureau, a statistical department, an investor and trades department, a telephone and services division, a small staff that handled the private wires that went to important clients' homes and offices, a correspondence division, and a staff to take care of all needs clients might express in the offices. All of this, of course, was in addition to the usual complement of brokers, clerks, runners, etc. It was, in effect, the first full-line brokerage the district had ever known. The *Jones & Baker Curb News*, which was distributed to clients weekly, was the first important market letter on the

Street, and soon had a host of imitators, none of which was as complete, factual, and informative as the original. This newspaper was usually four pages an issue, each larger than today's tabloid page. On special occasions Jones & Baker would print an eight-page edition. The newsletter contained assay reports on new mines which were obviously written by engineers rather than stockbrokers, registration and securities information, and similar reports of value to investors in Curb securities. Never before or since has the financial district seen such complete financial reporting in a publication of this kind, for many of the items in the *Jones & Baker Curb News* required a greater knowledge of mining techniques than that possessed by most of today's investors. What is more, the information was accurate; although most curbstone brokers continued to consider the firm a bucket shop, its information bureau and statistical department were clearly first rate.

Jones & Baker also published a full line of pamphlets aimed at educating the general public as to the nature of the Curb Market and the potential of its securities. Although some of these were crude by today's standards, better ones would not be produced at the financial district until the 1950s. Sells appears to have been a believer in "people's capitalism" two generations before the term appeared, and his advertisements—most of them flashy and exaggerated—anticipated Stock Exchange techniques of the late 1920s. The company particularly liked to use slogans in its advertising messages. "It's no use waiting for your ship to come in unless you have sent one out," was one of these, and "While money can be earned by labor, it can be *multiplied* only by investment" was another.

Jones & Baker passed Winkelman in size by 1917, and a year later advertised itself as "the largest brokerage in North America." Like Winkelman, Jones & Baker went bankrupt in 1923. But its nine thousand creditors received full payment, and no one lost a cent when this pioneering organization went out of business. By that time, too, its methods were being adopted by other, similar houses, like Ira Haupt & Co. of the Consolidated and the Curb's Horace Stoneham & Co., as well as many Stock Exchange firms of the wild 1920s. Such retailing operations had little place at the Curb, however. This business had never been an important part of the out-of-doors market's business, and after the war, with these two notable exceptions, the others who attempted to sell Curb securities to the general public returned to specialization and the commission business. McCormick took advantage of the unexpected boom to push ahead with plans for the indoor market. His failure to win support for the move in 1914 had taught him to lay a proper groundwork before raising the question a second time. During his first year in office, he cultivated both the Pforzheimer and Leonard factions, winning their confidence and support. By that time the major specialists had rallied behind Pforzheimer, while most commission brokers tended to side with Leonard. Realizing that he lacked the kind of personality needed to affect a reconciliation, and that both groups would prefer the intervention of a more mature broker to that of the brash young chairman in so sensitive a matter, McCormick turned increasingly to Alfred Sturges, the Curb Market's Secretary, for assistance.

Sturges was forty-six years old in 1916, and although a Curb veteran, was still considered one of the "younger crowd." He had come to the Curb from Danbury, Connecticut, in 1883, at the age of fourteen. After the usual jobs as runner and clerk, he became a commission broker and, finally, a specialist. Sturges was one of the bright young men Mendels considered his friends, a charter member of the Curb Agency and Curb Market, and a man trusted by all in the district. Furthermore, he had a home in and was a leading citizen of Nutley, New Jersey, close to many of the Curb leaders' residences; Sturges knew most of them socially as well as professionally. From time to time he would invite a carefully selected group of specialists and commission brokers, together with their wives, to his home for social evenings, where old animosities were dissolved in the retelling of anecdotes. Sturges' young assistant, Eugene Tappen, who was then a salaried Curb employee but before that Franklin Leonard's clerk, was often at these gatherings. A frustrated opera singer, Tappen would entertain the groups with a medley of old songs, after which all would join in the singing. From time to time, the men would talk of the future over cigars and brandy. In 1916, they agreed the Curb needed a permanent new indoor home, and were united behind McCormick and Sturges.

The Curb set up an *ad hoc* special committee to seek a site for such a building in mid-January of that year. Sturges met with the press to tell them of the plan a month later. He spoke of the organization's background and present problems, the need for an indoor market to protect brokers from the elements and eliminate the fringe of unethical bucketeers, and the Curb's bright future. Sturges took care not to mention the Stock Exchange; nor did he indicate in any way the Big Board had been consulted as to the move. The Secretary was deliberately evasive. "When we will move or where we will move I do not know, nor does any one else. Some of the brokers wish to get inside and some wish to stay on the curb, and the question must be decided by a vote. I cannot predict which way that vote will go. All I know and all any one else knows is that it had been suggested that the Curb Market move from its old place." In the past, Carl Pforzheimer had shown little interest in such a move; now he endorsed the search. Pforzheimer told reporters that Broad Street was too narrow and confined for the burgeoning Curb Market. The police were already complaining traffic could not move during busy sessions. Thus, relocation would be necessary in the near future, and should one be made, Pforzheimer firmly believed it should be indoors. Then he added, somewhat cryptically, that he was of the opinion that the indoor market should not be affiliated with any other exchange. Since there was no possibility of working with the Consolidated, it was evident Pforzheimer was referring to the Big Board. The Stock Exchange had from time to time during the past decade discussed the possibility of bringing the more acceptable curbstone brokers into the Establishment through the back door, both literally and figuratively. The earlier suggestion that these men be allowed to trade in the New Street lobby may have been revived at this time, or perhaps some other plan was being discussed in the boardrooms at Wall and Broad. Whatever the case, it was clear that Pforzheimer, one of the Curb's most powerful men and a broker with excellent Big Board connections, would have none of it. It was also evident that McCormick and Sturges had unified the Curb community by 1916. The old bitterness had faded; the drive for the indoor market, independent of the Big Board, would continue.

As expected, the Stock Exchange was quick to react to this news. In early February the city's newspapers carried stories of Stock Exchange members who had complained of irregularities at the Curb. Bucketing, poor deliveries, overcharges, and other old grievances were mentioned, as the Big Board demanded a thorough investigation of wrongdoing at the out-of-doors market. None of the newspapers thought it strange that these complaints should come less than a month after the Curb had announced its search for an indoor market. The Stock Exchange also observed that under its rules, no member could be connected in any way with any other exchange, implying the proposed indoor Curb would be considered such an organization. Since the Curb could not survive without Stock Exchange business, the meaning of this observation was clear and could not be misunderstood.

The Big Board's most subtle attack was also the most unexpected. All at once the Curb Market received dozens of applications for membership from commission brokers, most of whom in the past had indicated an unwillingness to join. The Curb leadership was quick to grasp the meaning of this sudden change in attitude; McCormick, Sturges, and others believed the Stock Exchange was encouraging those commission brokers not yet members but who were closely tied to Big Board firms to join the Curb Market, after which they would oppose the move indoors with their voices and votes. In this way, the feared relocation would have been prevented by Curb Market members themselves, while the Stock Exchange could claim to have done nothing to prevent the move.

McCormick and Sturges sidestepped this thrust. On March 9, they introduced a resolution, which in part read, ". . . in view of important steps being taken for the reorganization of the New York Curb Association, the Special Committee recommends to the Board of Representatives that in fairness to the present members, no new applications for members be considered by the Membership Committee of the New York Curb Market Association until such time as plans now pending are matured." The motion passed, but even then it was obvious that some curbstone brokers allied to important Big Board houses were organizing to oppose the move indoors.

The Curb Directory had two separate but overlapping lists in 1916. The first consisted of members of the Curb Market, while the second was of registered firms. Those whose names appeared on the first list, and who were members of firms, were also listed under the firm name on the second roster. In addition to these, the Stock Exchange houses with large Curb interests were also on the registered firms' roster. Needless to say, such individuals and firms exercized great power at the Curb. As it happened, the fight against the indoor market was led by those individuals and houses which had important connections at both markets.

The newspapers carried reports of Big Board opposition to the indoor market on June 1. Furthermore, there would be an "inquiry" into the situation at the Curb, to be headed by Stanley D. McGraw, who was a member of the Stock Exchange, but whose firm, McGraw, Blagden & Draper, had an affiliation at the Curb as well. Two days later McGraw announced the formation of a committee to assist in this work. Its members were George T. Adee of Batchellor & Adee, Henry E. Butler of Charles D. Barney & Co., W. Fraser Gibson of Foster & Lounsbery, and George L. Weinn, Jr., of Weinn Brothers & Co. Adee and Gibson belonged to the Curb Market although their firms were of the Big Board, and while Butler was not a Curb member, his firm was a major force there. Weinn was not a Curb member, nor was Weinn Brothers & Co. a Curb house. The makeup of the committee, and the timing of its announcements, would appear to indicate that the Stock Exchange was prepared to use as much leverage from within as was necessary to prevent any action which it might find distasteful.

For the next four months the investigation and maneuverings took place with little publicity. Then, on October 1, 1916, the Curb was rocked by news of the Rice scandal.

George Graham Rice first gained prominence as a marginal broker for a marginal firm. In 1910 he had worked for B. H. Scheftels & Co.; neither man nor firm belonged to the Curb Agency or Curb Market. Scheftels was involved in the bucketing of several mining securities, and when forced to the wall by sellers, had been obliged to close down. A subsequent investigation determined that Rice was guilty of fraud and so, late in the year, he went to jail. While there he wrote a book about his adventures, which exposed the corruption of bucket shops at the Curb and Consolidated. Rice left jail in 1912, to return to the Curb. Needless to say, he was most unpopular with the regulars, but this didn't seem to bother him in the least. He opened a bucket shop, specialized in shady mining stocks, and apparently did fairly well.

Rice was in his element during the bull market that began in 1915. He pushed several bogus mining stocks, whose companies had charters but whose securities were of little value. Of course, all of these were unlisted, but in the wild days of 1915–16, even the most suspect of securities could find buyers. Two of the Rice stocks, Old Emma Leasing and Emma Copper, were particular favorites that autumn. By manipulating prices in various ways, Rice was able to boost the former's price from 10 to 85 cents, while Emma Copper rose from 60 cents to $4. All the while, Rice was issuing false quotations to stimulate buying, and then unloading the worthless paper on unsuspecting lambs.

The prices of both securities broke downward on October 4, as it became evident that Rice had been manipulating the stocks. Other brokers learned of Rice's double-dealings, and demanded he make good their losses. When Rice refused, they attacked him, and the bucketeer was engaged in a series of running fist fights on October 6 and 7. In the end, Rice wound up in jail once again, and the work of the Curb continued.

The Stock Exchange saw in the Rice affair a weapon to use against the Curb. McGraw and others charged the Curb with being infiltrated with disreputable types. Surely such a market should be cleaned up and investigated before being permitted to make the move indoors. As McGraw saw it, the enhanced status of an indoor market would lead clients to be less wary of the Curb than they should be, and so he demanded the organization remain in the streets for the time being.

As was his wont, McCormick rolled with the punch and was even able to use the Rice affair to his own advantage. First of all, he admitted the worst; Rice was indeed guilty of grave offenses, and had to be punished. Furthermore, there were others like him at the Curb, and they too deserved to be expelled from the community of honest men. How better to do this, he asked, than to establish an indoor market? The corrupt element would be left in the streets, where they would soon wither and die, leaving the honest brokers to handle business indoors. McCormick observed that Rice had not been a member of the Curb Market, and could not have qualified for the list had he made application. Unwary dealers could not have known this, for he traded side by side with the Curb's honest men. Had the Curb been indoors in 1916, he argued, Rice would have remained on the outside, and this would have warned the unsuspecting from dealings with him. McCormick's arguments made sense, especially when several other brokers were indicted along with Rice, all of whom were nonlisted dealers. By the end of the year, the Curb was closer to an indoor move than it had been before. The McGraw investigation fizzled out; the Stock Exchange seemed to have accepted the inevitable.

The inevitable would have to await the end of the war, however. So long as the nation was fighting in France, there would be no time or money to spend on a new building in the financial district. This meant that almost all parts of the community, including the Stock Exchange, would be obliged to operate in close quarters for the war's duration, as Wall Street obeyed the admonition against nonessential construction. Space was at a premium from 1917 to 1919. Rents soared and clerks worked in double shifts so as to maximize the use of available offices and desks. As might be expected, the various brokerages had to compete with each other in bidding for whatever offices fell vacant. J. P. Morgan & Co. in particular felt the squeeze, and in 1917 put in a bid for the entire Mills Building which was rejected, not so much because of price as to the fact that the building was fully occupied at the time and could not be easily vacated without court actions. Morgan and others then looked south of Exchange Place for offices, but all the buildings there were occupied. What is more, the lessees of these buildings themselves were expanding, and challenging established Wall Street firms for offices north of the financial district. Morgan realized, of course, that many Mills Building offices were still being rented by curbstone brokers, and the other Stock Exchange firms in the process of expansion quickly learned that the Curb Market dominated the area south of Exchange Place. If the Stock Exchange were to expand, the natural direction would be to the south, and this would mean the displacement of the Curb community. Of course, all of this was in the realm of speculation; should trading volume decline after the war, as many expected it would, then both organizations might shrink to their prewar sizes. Should business remain good, and the pressures of war cease, then the Stock Exchange firms would use all their influence and power to cause the curbstone brokers to vacate their offices and seek a new trading area. In this way, they would prove useful allies for McCormick in his drive for an indoor market elsewhere in the financial district. Thus, just as the Stock Exchange leaders had their allies at the Curb, who had worked against the indoor market, so McCormick could count on support at the Big Board when he tied together the move indoors and the removal of curbstone brokers from prime Broad Street offices.

X

The Move Indoors

ONE OF THE MORE unexpected results of the wartime boom was the relative decline of the Consolidated. Before the war the Little Board had been a haven for small gamblers and odd-lot speculators. Now such individuals were wealthier than ever before, and they tended to transfer operations to the Stock Exchange. Earlier they had dealt in odd lots, usually paying cash for purchases. Now these same men seemed to prefer using margin to buy round lots at the Big Board. This not only increased the chances for profit in a bull market, but enhanced the prestige of these formerly small traders. After more than thirty years of existence and victories over the Stock Exchange in the early twentieth century, the Consolidated still could not escape its reputation for sleaziness and shady dealings. The Little Board's trading volume actually declined in 1918, while the Stock Exchange's showed impressive advances and the Curb's soared. The Consolidated's leadership would make bold claims of progress in the months to follow, but scandals, mismanagement, and the increasing challenges not only from the Stock Exchange but the Curb Market as well, would lead to further declines in the postwar years. Not even the great bull market of the 1920s was able to save it from ruin. In 1927, after losing its building, and with its officers either in jail or disgraced, the Consolidated "faded away," not even bothering to formally announce its demise.

The Stock Exchange reported a volume of over 191 million shares in 1918, while the Consolidated handled little more than 20 million. This was a far cry from the situation in the century's early years, when the Consolidated had boasted that in a short time it would overtake the Big Board. Equally dramatic, however, was the Curb volume which, according to Jones & Baker, was over 167 million shares, and rising at a more rapid rate than the Big Board. Had the wartime boom continued for another year, it is likely the Curb Market would have passed the Stock Exchange in terms of volume in 1919.

Of course, these figures are suspect; neither the Stock Exchange nor the Curb Market were as accurate then as they should have been. Furthermore, the Stock Exchange list was dominated by the higher-priced, more seasoned issues, which were purchased on margin, while the Curb's most active stocks were usually quoted as below $5 a share. During a fairly typical week in May, 1918, the volume leader on the Curb was Aetna Explosives, which traded 148,000 shares and closed at $8.50; Aetna was also the highest-priced security on the ten most active list. It was followed by Nixon-Nevada Mines (128,000 shares closing at $1.68¾); Jerome Verde Mining Co. (70,500 shares closing at $.50); U.S. Steamship (52,700 shares closing at $5.87½); and Green Monster Mines (32,800 shares closing at $.62½). To be sure, not much in the way of commissions could be made on such low-priced securities, and although the Curb Market was neck-and-neck with the Big Board in terms of volume, it was far behind in total earnings from commissions. Still, when the war ended, many men who had been hand-to-mouth brokers in 1914 were able to purchase their own homes, take vacations in Cuba, and in other ways enjoy lives of relative affluence.

The good times attracted more than the usual number of newcomers to the Curb, and in 1918 and 1919, they were joined by returning veterans, eager to make up for their lost year or two. Fortunately, volume remained high and commissions good; there was sufficient business for all. Like most of the nation, the financial district was in a state of euphoria during the first postwar year. The war to end wars had concluded with a glorious victory, one that many Americans were convinced they had made possible. President Wilson was clearly the most popular man in the nation, if not the world; he was greeted enthusiastically wherever he went in Europe, as he prepared to meet with other victorious statesmen at Versailles to discuss peace terms. And Wall Street remained the center of world capitalism, a status tacitly acknowledged by both London bankers and the Bolsheviks, who were then attempting to consolidate their power in Russia.

The Curb Market leaders saw in this atmosphere of confidence and wealth a good opportunity to press ahead with plans for an indoor market. The times could not have been better. Volume was high and Broad Street clogged with brokers; the police, once polite and willing to work with the Curb Market, by now were pressing it to make a move to a different location. Doubtless they were inspired by some Stock Exchange leaders who still wanted the office space in the Mills and Broad Exchange buildings then occupied by curbstone brokers. There were rumors of a new investigation of the Curb, which the district attorney's office was then charging with the usual crimes of bucketing and misrepresentation, and this added impetus to the drive for an indoor market, which supposedly would solve these and related problems. In the past, many outdoor traders had refused to support such a move, pleading lack of funds. This could no longer be an excuse, since they had never done so well in their lives as they had in the past five years. By 1919 it was possible to contemplate a new building, since the wartime restrictions were quickly ended. Finally, there seemed to be less opposition by the Big Board to a move indoors than had previously been the case. The great prosperity at the Stock Exchange, the Consolidated's decline, and the harmonious atmosphere of the period combined to soften the old rigidity at Wall and Broad.

Accordingly, McCormick scouted the membership to ascertain whether or not a suggestion for a new market would be well received. Apparently enough brokers indicated support for the move to encourage him to pursue the matter. McCormick called a meeting of the board of representatives, augmented by several respected curbstone brokers not then on the board, to convene in a private dining room at the Hotel Commodore on June 6, 1919. Naturally, McCormick and Sturges were there, but so were Leonard, John McCormack, Carl Pforzheimer, and Dudley Gray; the old wounds were completely healed by that time. The minutes of the meeting were either not kept or have been lost. Apparently the men had a good meal and then discussed the Curb's future over brandy and cigars until late at night. During the next few days McCormick and Sturges sounded out opinion at the Curb as to the matters discussed at the Commodore.

Meanwhile, news of the meeting was leaked to the press, and reporters asked McCormick why he was pressing for a move at that time. The most obvious reason seemed to be the threat of an investigation by the District Attorney sometime the following autumn. McCormick did not deny this had something to do with the move. An indoor Curb, he said, "will eliminate fakers from the market." Thus, McCormick could silence some critics by intimating the move had become a necessity, and not an object of his vanity as some were then charging it to be. The Chairman told reporters that there was widespread support for the organization of a new market, which he believed would cost from $750,000 to $1 million, including land and building. He claimed that Curb Market members had already pledged from $400,000 to $500,000 for shares in a building fund, plans for which would soon be made public. McCormick announced that a committee of distinguished brokers, headed by John McCormack and including George Winchell, Herbert Einstein, and William Hoffman, would solicit funds and would release regular progress reports. When asked about the role the Stock Exchange would play in the organization of the new market, the Chairman remained silent.

McCormick told reporters of the formation of the New York Curb Market Realty Associates, Inc. on June 10. This group, headed by John McCormack, was to take up the work of the earlier committee, find a site for the indoor market, arrange for its construction, and in other ways help prepare the way for the move. Although John McCormack was the Realty Associates' titular head, McCormick and Sturges retained control of most of its powers, especially those regarding the site. The Realty Associates was to be capitalized at $750,000, the money to be raised by selling 7,500 shares at $100 apiece to curbstone brokers who wished membership privileges at the new exchange. Despite the initial enthusiasm for the project, the curbstone brokers were in no hurry to purchase shares. This was not due to Stock Exchange pressures, for during the first week at least the Establishment took no position toward the move. Rather, the majority of brokers seemed reluctant to accept the innovation, although they and their predecessors had been talking about just such a move for the past half-century. On June 21, Mc-Cormick announced that membership would be restricted to five hundred; this meant that each member would be expected to purchase fifteen shares in the Realty Associates, which would come to $1,500 a man. At the time the Curb Market had only slightly more than three hundred dues paying members. Where would the additional two hundred members come from? And what if insufficient members joined, or if the $750,000 proved inadequate for both building and site? Would this mean further assessments? The majority of Curb Market members could have afforded the $1,500 fee, but these men could still remember the days when they had struggled for existence at the Curb, and they feared a return of bad times. Thus, they were reluctant to join, and the money was slow in coming.

Almost a score of men who purchased shares in the Realty Associates are alive today and remember their responses and reactions to the indoor market. Some indicate they had faith in the plan, and were almost certain of its success. The $1,500 was a lot of money, they said, but the risk seemed worthwhile. In some cases, however, memories may have been short. One broker tells of trying unsuccessfully to talk his partner into joining. The partner refused, since he had no confidence in the new organization. While he was gone on vacation, the broker went to John McCormack and purchased two seats for a total price of $3,000. Not all of this money was paid out at once, to be sure, and for a while the broker was able to keep his secret. But when the partner found out what had happened, he was livid; to him, the money was thrown away, as good as lost. Another broker, a rather reckless type, purchased a seat but didn't really believe the building would ever be constructed. He was worried about the police, however, and thought the least the Realty Associates would do would be to purchase a vacant lot. There, away from the police, the curbstone brokers could continue to trade in the open air, and this privilege, he thought, merited a subscription. A third broker purchased a seat because all his friends did, and he didn't want to be left alone and thought a slacker. So it went. By the end of June, McCormick was able to announce that $470,000 had been pledged. Only a small fraction of this money had been actually received; it seemed the curbstone brokers thought they were buying seats on margin. And although McCormick denied it, the flow of new memberships had declined in the last few days to a trickle. It appears most out-of-doors brokers who were members of the Curb Market had pledged to join the new venture, even though their $1,500 had not yet been deposited at the offices. Sturges was still obliged to go into the street to collar those whose pledges had not been acted upon. (Of course, these men could have had no idea of what would happen in the financial district during the great bull market of the 1920s; nor could any of them, in their wildest dreams, have believed a seat at the Curb Market would sell for as high as $350,000 in 1969.)

The reasons for sluggishness on the part of many members came out into the open in early July; after waiting for almost a month, the Stock Exchange took a stand which seemed opposed to the indoor market. The statement itself was more sophisticated and indirect than had been previous blows directed against the Curb and the Consolidated. The Big Board merely announced that in the future it would require its members to report all dealings they had at the Curb to the Secretary's office. These transactions would be gathered and sent to a printer, who would release them the following day prior to the start of trading. The implication was clear enough: the Stock Exchange was saying the Curb Market had been manipulating its quotations for the sake of its brokers and against the public interest. Thus, the Big Board indicated the Curb Market was not as honest as it might be. The Stock Exchange went on to note that some 80 percent of all Curb transactions originated at the Big Board. This statement appeared strangely out of place in the context of the news release, but its meaning could not be missed. The Stock Exchange could, if it so desired, dominate the Curb through pressures on those members who had interests in both markets. Although it was an unspoken suspicion at the time, the Stock Exchange might have noted that one reason McCormick was having difficulties in selling memberships was the refusal of Big Board houses to purchase seats, even though many were long-time members of the Curb Market. Finally, the Stock Exchange claimed to have had conferences with Curb leaders regarding these matters, implying that a significant part of the Curb supported its actions.

McCormick responded quickly. First, he denied that any important Curb official or member had been present at Stock Exchange meetings where the indoor market had been discussed; the Curb was sufficiently independent, he indicated, to act without approval, and strong enough to deal with opposition from within. As though to underscore this, he claimed the Stock Exchange initiated only 60 percent of the Curb's business, and not the 80 percent as previously believed. Then he announced that his office, and not the Stock Exchange, would regulate Curb activities. "We are going to attempt to regulate the Curb. Among other things, we are going to force all of our members to report all Curb transactions daily. The plan is new and details must be worked out, but we have decided on the general policy. Of course, we will not be able to force brokers who are members of the New York Stock Exchange to report their curb dealings with us, but so far as our own members are concerned, they will be forced to report." In this way, McCormick implied that he accepted the principle of official reporting of all transactions, and this would replace the rather informal and unsatisfactory work of the Bennett Press. Also, he believed his methods would be equally effective if not more so than those of the Stock Exchange.

Clearly, Edward McCormick would not be intimidated by such attacks which in the past had worried John McCormack and Mendels. Thus, on July 9, the Stock Exchange abandoned the idea of transactions reports and revived the old idea of joining the two markets in some kind of close relationship. The Big Board made no announcement, but the following day's newspapers reported a plan afoot to bring Curb brokers to the

Stock Exchange, where they could trade on their own floor, and enjoy the facilities and status of some kind of associate membership at the Big Board. It was believed the board of governors' meeting room, perhaps expanded somewhat, would be cleared for that purpose.

Although the room in question was quite large as such rooms go, it could scarcely have accommodated more than a few dozen brokers; even when expanded it would have been insufficient for the Curb Market's 1919 membership, much less the five hundred brokers McCormick hoped would purchase seats. Thus, the offer's meaning seemed clear: the Stock Exchange would take in those Curb brokers it approved of, and leave the rest to their own devices. If this plan had carried through, it would have meant the death of the Realty Associates and the severe crippling of the Curb itself. On the other hand, it would have brought new men to the Stock Exchange, and had an effect on that organization similar to that which had taken place in 1869, when the Open Board merged with the Stock and Exchange Board.

The jockeying for position continued throughout the late summer and early autumn of 1919, but it was evident the Stock Exchange's offer had no appeal to Curb Market members, who may have resented the attempt to place them in a small cubbyhole of the Big Board. McCormick played upon the members' opposition to the offer, and protested the Stock Exchange's actions in attempting to take the Curb under its wing. At the same time, he dropped hints of sites, building plans, facilities, etc., calculated to give the impression of great progress and a vision of the blessings awaiting those who came indoors. Whatever the reason, subscriptions continued to come in, and most of those who had earlier pledged the $1,500 eventually deposited their checks with the Realty Associates. The Stock Exchange was forced to admit defeat on November 19, when it withdrew its offer for a Curb home at the Big Board. The Establishment had hoped to foil the move indoors by first regulating the Curb, and that had failed. So did attempts at taking the "respectable" Curb elements to its bosom as stepchildren. For the moment at least, the attack abated, as the Stock Exchange awaited new developments.

Wall Street did not have long to wait. In November, McCormick announced that the Realty Associates had sufficient funds to begin the site search in earnest. The Chairman implied but did not specifically state that the membership drive had been successful, but he did note that "only a few more seats" were available. Actually, there were more than one hundred unfilled subscriptions at the time, and it appeared that all who had wanted to join had already indicated their desires to John McCormack. The Realty Associates had enough money to purchase a site, but certainly could not have thought of a building until more money was forthcoming. McCormick's statements to the press and his conversations with curbstone brokers were probably designed to encourage Stock Exchange member firms and others to buy seats before there were none left. It was a calculated and daring gamble, for had it failed the Curb would have had a vacant lot but little else; McCormick would have been made to appear a bumbler, and the dream of an indoor market might have been crushed for another generation.

Still, the Realty Associates did conduct a thorough site search. It is difficult to discover which plots were considered, and for what reasons. Obviously, price had a lot to do with the final decision; the Curb could hardly have expected to buy a plot anywhere within one city block of the Stock Exchange; such land was costly and, besides, was occupied by buildings in demand by Big Board member firms. Still, one might have expected the Curb Market to find a home within a reasonable distance of Wall and Broad, since the close relationship with the Stock Exchange was still of primary importance to the out-of-doors brokers. There were some old buildings on Broad Street below Beaver, not too far from the Produce Exchange, which might have been demolished to make room for a Curb building. South William Street was another possibility, and land could have been had east of William Street for a price the Realty Associates could have afforded. The Curb could have found a home two blocks to the north of Wall Street, on Pine. Lower Broadway was out of the question; the Curb would not have wanted to be too close to the bucket shops. Land was available on Broadway near Cedar Street, a short walk from the Stock Exchange. When one considers all of these possibilities, the final choice seems rather strange. On December 18, the Realty Associates announced it had purchased a site on Trinity Place, just west of the Trinity Church graveyard, the view of which would be blocked by the elevated train lines that then ran along Trinity Place. The old American Bank Note Company had previously occupied the site, which measured little more than forty thousand square feet. The cost was $1 million, far more than the Realty Associates had in its coffers, but McCormick said that negotiations for a large mortgage had also begun. Later on, the Curb Market announced its hopes of raising $250,000 of the land price through such a loan.

Why did the Curb select such an out of the way site? It was certainly a distance from Wall and Broad, and the price was not much lower than a similar plot on the east side of Broadway would have been. To get from the Trinity Place site to the Stock Exchange one would have to take the winding path through the graveyard, or detour through Thames or Rector streets. The elevated trains would be noisy and mar the new building's appearance. In fact, there seems to have been many reasons to go elsewhere and none to recommend Trinity Place. For this reason, one may assume that McCormick and Sturges did not see some of these problems as liabilities, but rather as advantages.

During the past year relations with the Stock Exchange had deteriorated, as it seemed the Big Board wanted to dominate any new indoor market that might appear. By locating the site close enough to Wall Street to remain part of the financial community, but sufficiently distant so as to have an independent existence, McCormick might have been pointing the way for the Curb Market's future. Of course, he could not have planned the placement of Trinity Church between the two exchanges, but this was a nice touch and the symbolism might have crossed his mind.

News of the site's selection was considered an encouraging sign by the curbstone brokers, and even the doubters were coming to believe the building might yet be constructed. In late December, John McCormack received a veritable flood of new applications, the majority of which came from men who already had seats at the Stock Exchange. Clearly, the Big

Board by this time considered the indoor market an inevitability. On January 1, McCormack was able to report that only a handful of seats remained unsold, with 380 applicants for these. By month's end, the Realty Associates had taken title to the land, paying for it with $750,000 in cash and assuming a $250,000 mortgage.

At this time the Stock Exchange made yet another effort at controlling the Curb. Sometime in February it began a secret investigation of the outdoor market, concentrating on those members who were suspected of illegal activities. Such practices were neither new or unusual; the Stock Exchange had often investigated both the Consolidated and the Curb. But coming when it did, and under cover of secrecy, it appeared the Big Board was still engaged in an attempt to master the new exchange. The story broke in mid-June, and was printed in most of the city's newspapers.

At first the Stock Exchange attempted to deny the reports. Then it admitted that it had indeed sponsored an investigation, but not of the Curb Market itself; instead, it was attempting to uncover irregularities of specific curbstone brokers, who went unnamed. There was some talk of these men's wire privileges being revoked, and in other ways having them punished by the Big Board. This too was not unusual; in the past the Stock Exchange had made similar threats. This time the reaction was different. McCormick said nothing of the incident, but a group of leading curbstone specialists, including Pforzheimer and Gray, sent a letter of protest to the Stock Exchange, attacking the investigation and demanding pledges of an end to such undercover inquiries. In the future, they said, any Stock Exchange questions involving the out-of-doors market should be addressed to the Curb Market, which was well able to enforce rules of honesty and good conduct. This marked a new feeling of independence that came with the site acquisition. As though to underscore this, the board of representatives released a new resolution, passed on July 2, "that hereinafter no member or firm of which such member is a partner shall clear or cause to be cleared, directly or indirectly, any transaction made on the New York Curb Market by non-members." This resolution was aimed primarily at those curbstone brokers who had not joined the indoor market, but it could also be used against enemies at the Stock Exchange if necessary. In the past the Big Board had acted as though the Curb existed on its sufferance. The Curb Market now indicated that it realized this close relationship did exist, but that it benefited both exchanges, and in the future it expected to be treated with more respect.

McCormick knew that a declaration of independence from the Big Board would be a gratuitous insult which could do the Curb Market great harm. In the 1919-20 period, however, the outdoor market did move toward greater autonomy. It did not hope to be treated as an equal; clearly the Curb was in no position to challenge the Big Board even had it so desired. But the curbstone brokers, buoyed by the promise of an indoor market, now came to expect a certain amount of courtesy from the Stock Exchange which previously had been lacking in their relations. They received it, not so much in a direct statement or action, as in the absence of them. Never again would the Big Board attempt to so dominate the Curb Market.

If the Realty Associates had no future fears from the Stock Exchange, it did have to cope with an even more worrisome problem, that of money. In the summer of 1919, McCormick had thought the site and building would require no more than $1 million. Now, he had paid that much for the site alone, and had nothing left for the building. Originally, it was believed a modest but handsome structure could be erected for around $500,000; in 1920 the architects indicated that the minimum price for the building would be twice that amount. Of course, the Curb had always planned to take a large mortgage on the structure, but such funds were hard to come by that summer, and negotiations ground to a halt. On July 12, Herbert Einstein, the Realty Associates' secretary, told the press that all plans had been temporarily suspended until additional financing could be arranged. Einstein added that the builders would not begin work until granted a cost-plus contract, which would guarantee them the return of their original costs plus a percentage for profits. Under such a contract, the Realty Associates would have no clear idea as to total costs, and with a near-empty exchequer they could not proceed.

McCormick was too close to his goal to give up. The five

hundred seats had already been sold, and those who had waited too long before applying were bidding for them. A handful had already been sold by brokers who had paid the original $1,500, and one was transferred for a price of $10,000. On each sale, the Curb Market received a $500 initiation and transfer fee, which helped replenish the fast-dwindling treasury. Clearly such individuals would be willing to pay a premium price for seats, and there seemed no reason for the Realty Associates not to profit therefrom. Accordingly, McCormick announced that an additional fifty seats would be put on sale at a price of $6,500. These were quickly taken, and brought the Realty Associates an additional $325,000. Then, to raise more money and at the same time placate those Stock Exchange member firms which had not purchased seats, McCormick announced the creation of associate memberships, which could be obtained for a $250 initiation and transfer fee for those who would later purchase them from the original subscribers. Associate members would be permitted to use all Curb facilities and trade with regular members, thus deriving savings on commissions. Such members would not be allowed a vote at the new exchange, and would not own stock in the Realty Associates. Thus, those Stock Exchange firms who purchased associate memberships would not be able to direct Curb Market affairs, but would be obliged to hew to the rules of the indoor market. Of course, McCormick could not make such a statement publicly. Instead, he justified associate memberships by telling the press they would "make it possible for banking and brokerage firms throughout the country to become identified with the association with special privileges." By the time the new building was ready for occupancy, 320 associate memberships had been sold, bringing the Realty Associates an additional $80,000.

The Curb Market was ready to proceed with the building in late September of 1920. The Realty Associates selected Starrett & Van Vleck as the architect, while the construction contract went to Thompson-Starrett, with W. A. Hathaway Company as interior decorators. The contract called for construction of a three-level building, with an exterior of light gray brick with a limestone base and copper cornices. It was to be fronted by a lawn, the only one south of City Hall. The first floor would be taken up by a restaurant, cloak room, lobby, and entrances, while the main trading floor would occupy the second. This was to be the heart of the building. The ceiling would be highly ornamental, with elaborate chandeliers, while large windows would occupy the east and west walls. The north and south ends of the floors were taken up by banks of desks, where clerks would sit, sending and receiving orders as they had from the windows on Broad Street. The floor itself would resemble a cross between the London Exchange and the trading area on Broad Street. Like the former, there were stations with seats (though rarely occupied) where the brokers would congregate, each specialist going to his own area. Each circular station was topped by a device that looked suspiciously like a street lamp, such as those on Broad Street. The trading floor would be new, but contain enough of the old to make the curbstone brokers comfortable. Executive offices were to be on the third floor. The building would cost about $1.2 million, and the New York Title and Mortgage Company agreed to take an $800,000 mortgage on the structure. This meant, in effect, that if all went well, the Curb Market would be able to open its doors with a large debt but money in the bank when the building was completed and ready for occupancy.

The groundbreaking ceremony took place on December 5, 1920, and construction proceeded without a hitch throughout the winter. The curbstone brokers remained on Broad Street while their new home was being erected, but after hours many would cross Broadway to view the building as it went up. Those who remember that period describe the sensations they had. One considered it more important than the building of his own home; a second awaited the opening as a child counted the days till Christmas; a third compared it to waiting out the birth of a new child. The exteriors were completed in early May, and the interior portions a month later. By that time the Curb Market memberships were being bid at $8,000 apiece, with no takers. On June 4, McCormick announced the building would be ready for use on Monday, June 27, which would also be the first trading day indoors.

The few desks and papers belonging to the Curb Market were moved to the new third-floor offices at 86 Trinity Place on

June 24, so that all would be in readiness for Monday morning. The brokers came to work early that day, wearing their usual colorful garb, but acting somewhat like seniors preparing for commencement ceremonies. At 9:00 McCormick went to the head of the group and announced they would take the walk to Trinity Place. The curbstone brokers fell in behind him, joking nervously as they went. They arrived in front of the new building by 9:30, at which time John McCormack presented the Chairman with the keys to the building. The brokers crowded onto the lawn, passed the iron gates and fence that surrounded their new business home, and shoved against the old New York University Wall Street Division building to the north.

Their new building had two imposing entrances, with three windows between them. The second-floor windows were quite large and impressive, and a few feet above, carved in stone, were the words, "NEW YORK CURB MARKET," while over them was the third floor façade. McCormick called for silence and addressed the members. "The die is cast," he said. "The old order is gone forever." After he finished speaking, Eugene Tappan led the members in singing the "Star Spangled Banner." But not all the brokers joined in. Most were looking up at the third floor, as though expecting to see a clerk, telephone in one hand, the other waving an order to buy or sell a security. McCormick opened the doors and the brokers entered. They had finally ended their stay out of doors, begun almost one hundred and eighty years earlier.

Postscript

NOT ALL the curbstone brokers were in a carnival mood that June 27, 1921, morning. When Edward McCormick announced the march to Trinity Place, a handful stood on the sidelines and watched, remaining there even after the crowd had gone. As McCormick received the keys to the new building on the far side of Trinity Church, those who stayed behind were joined by others, and on Broad Street at 10:00 they began trading in the open air. As had been the case in 1792, when a group of brokers who had formed the predecessor of the New York Stock Exchange had gone indoors, so it was in 1921, when the curbstone brokers went to Trinity Place as a major step in the formation of today's American Stock Exchange: some stayed behind.

These men—there were fewer than fifty of them that day—were an oddly assorted lot of very old and very young men, with only a few in between. The older group was led by Thomas Cook, a marginal broker who had always refused to join any organization, all of which he considered infringements on his freedom. Cook had been on the curb since the turn of the century, specializing in low-grade mining issues and living a rather poor existence. Others, most of them of a similar background but some of whom were important bucket shop operators, joined him in opposing first the Curb Agency, then the Curb Market, and finally, the move indoors. As early as November 18, 1920, Cook had proclaimed his little war against the indoor market. He and some of his friends formed a committee to lead the opposition. The new market was too exclusive, they claimed; by raising standards it would exclude many men as well as securities then being traded at the outdoor market. Those who remained at Broad Street would specialize in these, and so fill an important function. Cook's group told those brokers uncertain as whether or not to join the move indoors that after the mass of traders had left, there would be less business at Broad Street, but far fewer brokers to carve it up. Thus, while fighting the move, they also seemed to welcome it.

At first blush Cook's position seemed to make sense. In 1921 the Curb stock list was quite small, with the brokers still doing a larger business in unlisted than in listed securities; although none could know it at the time, such would be the case for another quarter of a century. Those who remained outdoors would make markets in these stocks and bonds, and attempt to keep them from the Curb Market, while at the same time the Curb's more seasoned securities would eventually move to the Big Board. In this way, the new indoor market would be faced by pressures from above and below, and soon disintegrate. This, at least, was the reasoning of Cook and others who had refused to join the new organization.

There were two flaws in this argument. In the first place, the Stock Exchange and the Curb Market had retained their business connections even when tensions arose between them in 1919 and 1920. As had been the case for generations, the Curb would drop a stock once it went to the Big Board, and the Stock Exchange gave its business in nonlisted securities to the curbstone brokers. Cook and others in the street could hope for none of this, and so were obliged to deal only in those securities rejected both exchanges (including the Curb's unlisted section) and find means of expansion in the retailing of stocks and bonds. These men lacked the wherewithal for the latter, and business in those securities unacceptable to both exchanges was so small as to offer only the meagerest existence. And if this were not enough, they were faced with competition from below, in the form of the growing over-the-counter market. Between this "telephone bourse" and the Curb lay the remaining out-of-doors brokers, and they, rather than the men who went indoors, were to feel the squeeze. Nor could they hope to make money by pandering to the gambling instincts of the more daring speculators. Low-priced Curb issues had always appealed to this group, but there were still plenty of them who traded at the indoor Curb Market; and what was more, the stricter rules enforced by McCormick and other officers seemed to offer the kind of honesty and safety lacking on the street. Finally, the growing popularity of margin buying made the Stock Exchange too a place for gamblers, few of whom frequented the remaining out-of-doors brokers.

More interesting than the old-timers who remained were the very young brokers who stayed outside. Some were there because they agreed with Cook's reasoning, but most either could not afford the fees or were below the twenty-one-year age requirement set by Curb Market regulations. Unlike the older men, they were aggressive and ambitious brokers, who hoped to rise rapidly through hard work and skill. McCormick and other Curb officers realized this, and so treated them differently than they did the older men. That summer Eugene Tappen and Alfred Sturges made a point of going to Broad Street to speak with the young men. They told them that while the Curb Market could understand why they were trading out of doors, such activity would jeopardize their chances of obtaining a Curb seat once they had the money for one or were of age. Many of these men then took clerk's jobs at Trinity Place, or simply left the district until they had the money or reached twenty-one, at which time they would purchase seats.

Cook applied for a charter for his new outdoor market, and received one on December 8, 1920, even while the Curb Market remained at Broad Street. The new organization was to be called the Curb Stock and Bond Market, but for the moment had no regulations or members. Cook charged the Curb Market with attempting to destroy his group before they could start operating. Later on, he would lay claim to the title of "Curb Market," saying the new indoor organization was a social club, and not a bona fide organization. Franklin Leonard investigated both charges and termed them unsupportable. There is no indication that either the Curb Market or the Stock Exchange bothered to oppose the Curb Stock and Bond Market; it simply was not important enough to bother with. In any case, the new organization never amounted to much. By early autumn the police were asking the remaining outside brokers to move on, and before the end of the year, Broad Street was clear of traders.

In this way, the last of the curbstone brokers left the financial district. They had arrived sometime around 1790. No one knows the exact date, or who the first of them was, or how he decided to trade in securities. He probably came because there was a need for his services and the possibilities for profit. The last of his tribe left the district late in 1921. Again, we do not know who he was, or when he ceased trading in the open air, or where he went. But the need for his services had ceased to exist, as did profits from such trading. And so he went, ending the history of outdoor trading in New York's financial district.

An Essay on Sources and Methodology

IN PLACE of the usual bibliography, I have written an informal essay on sources and methodology, which I believe will give the reader a clearer idea of the problems and possibilities faced in the preparation of this book than would the usual list of works consulted. Writing the history of the curbstone brokers was a difficult task for reason of the sources. It is unfortunate that a work such as this could not have been undertaken a generation earlier, for then men like McCormick, Sturges, Tappan, and Pforzheimer could have given the historian the benefit of their recollections and observations. As it is, I had to learn of these men and their activities second-hand. It seems clear that the bulk of the information to be found in this book would have been completely lost had the project been undertaken a decade or so from now. Thus, this is not solely a bibliography or notes on sources, but also an explanation of the problems faced by all historians of the financial district.

Wall Street in general and the outside markets in particular offer little in the way of raw material for historians interested in the pre-New Deal era. Some investment banks, brokerages, and related institutions have preserved their records, especially those relating to current business in one way or another. Generally speaking, however, they periodically discard papers and ledgers no one at the firm believes worthy of keeping. From time to time these will be overlooked, but space in financial district offices tends to be at a premium, and those individuals charged with weeding out old correspondence and business papers have been most thorough.

Both the New York and American Stock Exchanges maintain fine libraries, which are most useful for brokers and other district workers interested in the kind of information that will assist them in their work. Papers relating to Securities and Exchange Commission requirements, for example, are preserved with great care. The rest are discarded as being of no use, and since this book deals exclusively with the pre-S.E.C. period, the exchanges' libraries were of little help (with one notable exception discussed below).

Member firms maintained few records prior to the 1930s, so there is no way to discover through the use of the written word how they functioned in the out-of-doors period. Firms that went out of business merely sold their papers for junk or called the garbage collector. Even now, valuable records are being destroyed by men who are unaware of their historical worth. For example, both exchanges get rid of specialists' books a few years after they are handed in. These books, which contain notations regarding the dealings of key men on the exchange floors, would provide a prime source of information for historians of the future who may wish to discover how the financial community operated in the 1970s. But they will not be available. The exchanges are not attempting to hide anything in so acting, and they are surprised "outsiders" would be interested in such things; sometimes, frankly, they are suspicious of the motives of such people. Both the New York and American Stock Exchanges would probably be pleased to deposit their records at some respected library under proper safeguards as to use, but as of yet, no library has approached them. Readers of historical journals know that libraries often receive rather odd collections, which they accept with gratitude. (Several years ago a large midwestern university library announced with pride that the head of the state's Boy Scouts in the 1930s had bequeathed his papers to their manuscript collection.) No library has the papers of the New York and American Stock Exchanges. Nothing better illustrates the "cultural gap" between American business and the academic world than this sad situation, which could probably be easily remedied, but of which neither is aware.

As a result, it is most difficult to write historical monographs in the field of financial district history. The historian is obliged to rely heavily upon memoirs, newspapers, the few old treatises in existence, government publications, a mere handful of documents, and interviewees. The situation is even more difficult when one approaches the outdoor market, for there is absolutely nothing in the way of primary sources remaining for the pre-1903 period. The old Curb was considered of minor importance by outsiders; they wrote little of the institution in the nineteenth century, except to note its color and strangeness. After that time both the Curb itself and others showed some interest in the historical record, and the closer one gets to the present, the more information may be found. Even here there are wide gaps, for the field is still largely unexplored. The literature is bare of historical treatments of the Curb and its successors. George Garvy's short survey, "Rivals and Interlopers in the New York Security Market," *The Journal of Political Economy* (June, 1944), LII, 128-143, is drawn from some mining journals, testimony before government investigating committees, and some of the more familiar secondary sources. It remains a good introduction to the subject, but no more than that. His was the last significant article on the subject to be printed in a scholarly journal.

As a result of the problem of sources, research for this book was often frustrating. On several occasions I was faced with what appeared to be dead ends and contradictory evidence, which had to be handled with greater than usual care. Most of the time the problems were resolvable through the use of indirect evidence, such as newspapers and contemporary journals. At times I was obliged to abandon the search when no new information appeared, and I have indicated such occasions in the book. On other occasions I felt able to make calculated and guarded statements, and come to tentative conclusions based on spotty evidence; these were also indicated as such. Fortunately, there were few of these.

The book may best be divided into two sections. The first deals with the pre-1900 period and is covered in the first three chapters and parts of the next two, all of which were drawn exclusively from written records. Since I had covered this period from a different perspective in two earlier books (*The Big Board* and *Panic on Wall Street*), I was able to draw upon a framework of knowledge that was filled in through a careful analysis of fairly familiar works, which may be found in the bibliographies of these two books. Such newspapers as the *New York Journal and Patriotic Register*, Niles' *Weekly Register*, *The New York Times*, and the *New York Evening Sun* were most useful, but the New York *Herald* had the best financial page of the period, and was the most frequently consulted. Among the more important works used in this section were:

Andreades, Andreas. *History of the Bank of England, 1640–1903*. London, 1909.

Barrett, Walter. *Old Merchants of New York*. Five volumes. New York, 1870.

Clews, Henry. *Fifty Years in Wall Street*. New York, 1908.

Dayton, Abram. *Last Days of Knickerbocker Life in New York*. New York, 1880.

Domett, Henry. *A History of the Bank of New York, 1784–1884*. New York, 1898.

Dos Passos, John. *A Treatise on the Law of Stock-Brokers and Stock-Exchanges*. New York, 1882.

Eames, Francis. *The New York Stock Exchange*. New York, 1894.

Ewan, C. L. *Lotteries and Sweepstakes*. London, 1932.

Ezell, John. *Fortune's Merry Wheel*. Cambridge, 1960.

Fowler, W. Worthington. *Twenty Years of Inside Life in Wall Street*. New York, 1880.

Gibb, George and Knowlton, Evelyn. *History of Standard Oil (New Jersey), The Resurgent Years, 1911–1927*. New York, 1956.

Harrington, Virginia. *The New York Merchants on the Eve of the Revolution*. New York, 1935.

Harris, Charles. *Memories of Manhattan in the Sixties and Seventies*. New York, 1884.

Hill, Frederick. *The Story of a Street*. New York, 1908.

Hinkling, John & Co. *Men and Idioms of Wall Street*. New York, 1875.

Hunt, Freeman. *Lives of American Merchants*. New York, 1858.

Lamb, Martha and Harrison, Mrs. Burton. *History of the City of New York*. Two volumes. New York, 1896.

Lefevre, Edwin. *Reminiscences of a Stock Operator*. New York, 1923.
———. *Wall Street Stories*. New York, 1901.
Medbury, James. *Men and Mysteries of Wall Street*. New York, 1870.
Meeker, J. Edward. *The Work of the Stock Exchange*. New York, 1922.
Myers, Margaret. *The New York Money Market*. New York, 1939.
New York. *Report of Committee on Speculation in Securities and Commodities, June 7, 1909*. Albany, 1910.
Pomerantz, Sidney. *New York: An American City, 1783–1803*. New York, 1938.
Smith, Matthew. *Sunshine and Shadow in New York*. Hartford, 1893.
Stedman, E. C. *The New York Stock Exchange*. New York, 1905.
United States, Congress, House of Representatives, 62nd Congress, 3rd Session, *Report of the Committee Appointed Pursuant to House Resolutions 429 and 504, To Investigate the Concentration of Control of Money and Credit*. Washington, 1913.
Wilson, Rufus. *New York Old and New*. New York, 1909.
Wycoff, Richard. *Wall Street Ventures and Adventures through Forty Years*. New York, 1930.

Chapters four through ten were based on a wider variety of sources, the most important of these being interviews with those members of the outdoor Curb Market who survive. Most were willing to speak openly of their experiences and memories. As might be expected, a few of their reminiscences were exaggerated or cloudy, and no statement given me on these occasions was used until it was independently corroborated by others or by the written record. There was a near-universal agreement on trading methods of the period, inter- and intra-Curb relationships, the social aspects of the curbstone brokers, characterizations of important individuals, and who and why certain men rose to the top of their professions. On the other hand, these men knew little of the fights with the Stock Exchange, political maneuverings, and the reasons why changes occurred. Nor were they able to enlighten me on the reasons why the various ethnic groups got along with each other so well at the Curb. Indeed, they seemed surprised to hear such questions, as though they had no idea it might have been otherwise. The most important of these interviewees, and the years in which they took out Curb Market membership, follows. It should be noted that most of these men worked on the Curb in various capacities for several years prior to actually joining the association:

MEMBER	YEAR ADMITTED
Jacob Feinstein	1919
Samuel Frank	1911
Victor Grande	1920
Louis Herman	1921
David Jackson	1934
R. W. Kerpen	1920
Julius Leff	1917
Charles Leichner	1920
Edward O'Brien	1920
Edwin Posner	1921
Herbert Tully	1917

In addition, I was able to speak at length with Edwin D. Etherington, who was president of the American Stock Exchange from 1962 to 1966, and left to become president of Wesleyan University. Mr. Sol Langel of the American Stock Exchange firm of M. L. Weiss & Co. (who became a member of the Curb after the move indoors) also gave generously of his time, as did Mr. James DuHamel, the American Stock Exchange's cashier, who probably knows more about the "old-timers" than anyone else. Mr. DuHamel also located many of the rare photographs included in this book, literally "dug out" old, faded copies of the *Curb News*, excerpts from which appear in the appendix, and waded through whatever old files remained to find pertinent historical information helpful in my work. Most important, he verified my suspicions that the old Curb Market records no longer exist.

The American Stock Exchange Library has an incomplete collection of manuals, stock lists, membership rolls, and other such rosters which date back to 1903. These enabled me to find out who belonged to the Curb Agency and Curb Market, although the actual number of brokers involved at the Curb was usually larger than the rosters would indicate. In addition, the Library has copies of three old memorial volumes, which contain some information about the early days and historical sketches of the outdoor market. The earliest of these, published in 1928, is entitled *The New York Curb Market*. The others, dated 1937 and 1938 respectively, are entitled *The New York Curb Exchange*, and both were clearly based on material in the 1928 volume. There is no indication as to the authors, although Mr. DuHamel believes Charles Murphy wrote the earlier work and Frank Williams or John Bennoch the latter ones.

The New York Public Library has an incomplete set of the *Jones & Baker Curb News* and several of the firm's pamphlets, including *Investors and Traders Guide* (1919) and *Profits and Dividends of America's Second Market* (1920). I found the New York *Herald, The New York Times,* New York *Tribune,* New York *Sun,* and New York *World* invaluable in tracing the important news stories of the early twentieth century. Such familiar sources as *The Wall Street Journal* and *Barron's* were far less informative.

Unfortunately, I have been unable to locate a single member of the Consolidated Stock Exchange. Searches of old rosters and newspapers, as well as leads provided by members of the New York and American Stock Exchanges, all proved fruitless. In all probability there are several former Consolidated members still alive—the organization lasted until 1927, and young brokers of that period would still be in their sixties and seventies today—but their names and whereabouts are unknown to all the people I met in the financial district who might have known of them. In addition, all the records of the Consolidated have been either lost, discarded, or destroyed. The New York Public Library has copies of the *Constitution and Bylaws of the Consolidated Stock and Petroleum Exchange,* dated 1902, and a *Directory* for 1900. S. A. Nelson's short book, *The Consolidated Stock Exchange* (New York, 1907) is useful but spotty, and reads more like a publicity release than a critical work. Thus, the history of that organization must be drawn from the public record, a short book, and a handful of court decisions.

After this manuscript was completed, copies were given to several experienced brokers as well as some of those at the American Stock Exchange who are most familiar with its history. These individuals then made comments and offered criticisms on what they considered inaccuracies in stress and, in a few cases, omissions. Then followed the task of investigating new leads, making changes, and submitting a final draft. In all this time no Exchange member, or anyone else who offered assistance, attempted to have a portion omitted that seemed unfavorable to their friends, or in any other way, directly or indirectly, tried to censor material. As I indicated earlier, the author-subject relationship in the preparation of the book left nothing to be desired.

APPENDIX I

Testimony of George W. Ely, Secretary of the New York Stock Exchange, before the Subcommittee of the Committee on Banking and Currency of the House of Representatives (Money Trust Investigation), June 11, 1912.

Mr. UNTERMYER. Is there another exchange in the city of New York known as the Consolidated Exchange?

Mr. ELY. Yes, sir; the Consolidated Stock Exchange.

Mr. UNTERMYER. Do you know what its membership is?

Mr. ELY. No, sir.

Mr. UNTERMYER. Do you know anything about it?

Mr. ELY. No, sir.

Mr. UNTERMYER. How long has that been in existence?

Mr. ELY. A good many years; I do not know how many.

Mr. UNTERMYER. But it is a small affair alongside of your institution, is it not?

Mr. ELY. That is a matter of conjecture.

Mr. UNTERMYER. What is it?

Mr. ELY. That is a matter of conjecture.

Mr. UNTERMYER. Conjecture?

Mr. ELY. Yes.

Mr. UNTERMYER. You know it is, do you not?

Mr. ELY. I do not know anything about it.

Mr. UNTERMYER. Then, so far as you know, it is a still larger affair than the New York Stock Exchange?

Mr. ELY. I do not know anything about it.

Mr. UNTERMYER. You have no impressions on the subject?

Mr. ELY. I have impressions.

Mr. UNTERMYER. We would like to have your impression.

Mr. ELY. I do not know what my impressions are.

Mr. UNTERMYER. You do not know what your impressions are?

Mr. Ely. I do not care to tell my impressions.

Mr. Untermyer. You do not?

Mr. Ely. No, sir. I am here to state facts. My impressions are worth nothing.

Mr. Untermyer. Yes, your impressions are the nearest you can come, sometimes, to stating the facts.

Mr. Ely. Yes.

Mr. Untermyer. I want to know what your impressions are as to the relative size of the business of two exchanges.

Mr. Ely. It is not as large as ours.

Mr. Untermyer. Of course not. It is a mere fraction of yours?

Mr. Ely. I do not know what fraction. I could not state that.

Mr. Untermyer. How small a fraction is it?

Mr. Ely. I do not know.

Mr. Untermyer. Tell us approximately?

Mr. Ely. I cannot tell you. I do not know.

Mr. Untermyer. Does it do one-tenth of the business that the New York Stock Exchange does?

Mr. Ely. I cannot tell you.

Mr. Untermyer. Does it do one-fiftieth of the business?

Mr. Ely. I do not know.

Mr. Untermyer. Does it do one-hundredth of the business?

Mr. Ely. I do not know.

Mr. Untermyer. Does it do as much as one-half of the business?

Mr. Ely. I do not know.

Mr. Untermyer. Does it do as much as you do?

Mr. Ely. No; it does not do that.

Mr. Untermyer. It does not? I thought you said a moment ago that it did less than the New York Stock Exchange.

Mr. Ely. What is that?

Mr. Untermyer. I thought you said it did less than the New York Stock Exchange, a moment ago.

Mr. Ely. It is a smaller exchange than ours.

Mr. Untermyer. The New York Stock Exchange has a listing department, does it not?

Mr. Ely. A committee on stock list.

Mr. Untermyer. It also has what is known as a listing department, has it not?

Mr. Ely. Well, the committee on stock-list department; that is the same as the committee on stock list.

Mr. Untermyer. And it has maintained such a committee on stock list to pass on applications for admission of stocks to the list for how many years?

Mr. ELY. As long as I can remember.

Mr. UNTERMYER. What is the procedure required by the exchange in order to admit a stock to what is called the regular or official list of the exchange?

Mr. ELY. Application is made to the committee.

Mr. UNTERMYER. Written application?

Mr. ELY. Written application is made to the committee, and it is submitted to the committee, and an officer of the company appears before the committee, and they go into the matter, and finally it is recommended to the governing committee.

Mr. UNTERMYER. This application involves a disclosure by the corporation, does it not, of its assets, its liabilities, and practically of all its affairs? Have you a form of the application here?

Mr. ELY. I have a form of requirements.

Mr. UNTERMYER. For listing?

Mr. ELY. Yes, sir.

Mr. UNTERMYER. I offer this in evidence.

Mr. UNTERMYER. Is there also a prescribed form of application?

Mr. ELY. Not prescribed, no.

Mr. UNTERMYER. Is there not a printed form of application?

Mr. ELY. No; each application is printed.

Mr. UNTERMYER. Each application is separately printed?

Mr. ELY. Is separately printed.

Mr. UNTERMYER. When a corporation desires to have its stock or its bonds or securities listed on the exchange and files its application that application then goes before the committee on stock list?

Mr. ELY. Yes.

Mr. UNTERMYER. And before going there do you examine to see whether the requirements of the exchange as to the information necessary to be given are contained in the application?

Mr. ELY. My clerk does.

Mr. UNTERMYER. Yes.

Mr. ELY. As far as possible.

Mr. UNTERMYER. What?

Mr. ELY. As far as possible, yes.

Mr. UNTERMYER. Then the committee makes a like examination, does it?

Mr. ELY. Yes, sir.

Mr. UNTERMYER. Are the members of the exchange permitted to deal on the exchange in any securities that are not listed on the regular list?

Mr. ELY. I do not know of any.

Mr. UNTERMYER. They are forbidden to deal on the exchange in any securities other than those that are on the list?

Mr. ELY. I do not know of any law that forbids it, but it is not customary to deal in them. I do not think it would be permitted. It has not been tried.

Mr. UNTERMYER. You know, do you not, that the admission of a security to the stock list is one of the requirements made by the great banks and trust companies, as a rule, before they lend on that security?

Mr. ELY. I do not know that.

Mr. UNTERMYER. You do not know that?

Mr. ELY. No.

Mr. UNTERMYER. Do you not know that in order to make a good collateral it is necessary that the stock shall be listed?

Mr. ELY. I do not know anything about the banks' rule; no, sir.

Mr. UNTERMYER. Are all the interstate corporations of the country, the stocks of which are listed on the New York Stock Exchange, required to make applications in conformity with this Exhibit No. 24 before their securities can be listed?

Mr. ELY. What do you mean by "interstate?"

Mr. UNTERMYER. Do you not know what an interstate corporation is?

Mr. ELY. Do you mean a railroad corporation?

Mr. UNTERMYER. I mean an interstate railroad corporation, or an industrial corporation engaged in interstate commerce.

Mr. ELY. Any security, to be listed, has to be applied for in that way.

Mr. UNTERMYER. Your regular stock list includes, does it not, practically all the great interstate corporations—railroad and industrial—so far as you know?

Mr. ELY. All over the United States?

Mr. UNTERMYER. Yes; so far as you know.

Mr. ELY. I do not know whether it does or not.

Mr. UNTERMYER. Will you please furnish us a list of the listed securities?

Mr. ELY. The securities listed?

Mr. UNTERMYER. Yes.

Mr. ELY. Yes.

Mr. UNTERMYER. Have you it with you?

Mr. ELY. No.

Mr. UNTERMYER. Please make a note and bring that tomorrow.

Mr. ELY. I will.

Mr. Untermyer. Is there a printed list of that kind?

Mr. Ely. There is a regular printed list; yes.

Mr. Untermyer. Separating the stocks from the bonds?

Mr. Ely. Yes, sir.

Mr. Untermyer. Please let us have such of those lists as are in your possession.

Mr. Ely. Yes. I can send for it now if you want it.

Mr. Untermyer. Very well, if you will; and if it will not inconvenience you.

The securities of national banks are also listed on the exchange, are they not?

Mr. Ely. We have some; yes.

Mr. Untermyer. In order to secure a listing of its securities on the exchange is every corporation bound to have a tranfer agent and a registrar located in the city of New York?

Mr. Ely. Yes, sir.

Mr. Untermyer. And that is without regard to where the corporation is located, is it not?

Mr. Ely. Yes, sir.

Mr. Untermyer. Is it also required that the transfer agent and registrar shall both be corporations.

Mr. Ely. No, sir.

Mr. Untermyer. Is it required that either shall be a corporation?

Mr. Ely. What does it say there? I have forgotten what it does say.

Mr. Untermyer. Do you know of any stocks of interstate corporations listed on the exchange that have a transfer agent or registrar rather than a corporation?

Mr. Ely. I do not happen to think of one now.

Mr. Untermyer. There are stock exchanges in other great cities in this country, are there not?

Mr. Ely. Yes, sir.

Mr. Untermyer. There is one in Chicago that does a large business, is there not?

Mr. Ely. There is one in Chicago.

Mr. Untermyer. There is one in Boston?

Mr. Ely. One in Boston, one in Philadelphia, and one in Pittsburgh.

Mr. Untermyer. And one in Baltimore?

Mr. Ely. I believe there is one in Baltimore.

Mr. Untermyer. And one in New Orleans?

Mr. Ely. Yes.

Mr. Untermyer. What would be the effect of all these exchanges requiring that the securities of corporations listed on its exchange should be signed by a transfer agent and registrar located in their particular city?

Mr. Ely. I do not know.

Mr. Untermyer. That regulation practically means, does it not, that an interstate-commerce corporation cannot have its securities listed upon any exchange other than the New York Stock Exchange, if the other exchanges make the same exaction?

Mr. Ely. I do not know, really.

Mr. Untermyer. There is no relaxation of that rule in favor of corporations that have their business in other localities, is there?

Mr. Ely. No; not that I know of.

Mr. Untermyer. I notice Exhibit 24 also contains requirements with respect to the engraving of certificates. Those certificates, under the rules of exchange, have got to be engraved by companies which are approved and admitted to the privilege of engraving by the New York Stock Exchange, are they not?

Mr. Ely. They have to be printed by such companies as the governing committee permits the committee on stock list to pass upon.

Mr. Untermyer. In other words, the committee on stock list cannot consider the application of any corporation to list their securities on the New York Stock Exchange unless the certificates have been engraved by an engraving company that has been approved by the governing committee of the stock exchange?

Mr. Ely. Yes.

Mr. Untermyer. That is right?

Mr. Ely. Yes.

Mr. Untermyer. The same is true as to bonds, is it not?

Mr. Ely. Yes, sir.

Mr. Untermyer. I offer in evidence the constitution and rules for the government of the stock exchange and ask that it be marked.

[The book in question, Constitution of the New York Stock Exchange, was marked "Exhibit No. 25, June 11, 1912."]

Mr. Untermyer. I call attention to the regulation dated May 19, 1909, on pages 87 and 88 of the book, and I ask you whether that rule is still in force in the New York Stock Exchange. It reads:

That any connection, direct or indirect, by means of public or private telephone, telegraph wire, or any electrical or other contrivance or device or pneumatic tube or other apparatus or device whatsoever, or any communication by means of messengers or clerks, or in any other manner, direct or indirect, between the New York Stock Exchange Building, or any part thereof, or any office of any member of said New York Stock Exchange, and any building of the Consolidated Stock Exchange, or any part thereof, or any room, place, hallway or space occupied or controlled by said Consolidated Stock Exchange, or any office of any member of said Consolidated Stock Exchange, who is engaged in business upon said Consolidated Stock Exchange, or any transmission, direct or indirect, of information from said New York Stock Exchange Building, or from the office of any member of said New York Stock Exchange, to the said Consolidated Stock Exchange, or to the office of any member of said Consolidated Stock Exchange, through any means, apparatus, device, or contrivance as above mentioned, is detrimental to the interest and welfare of this exchange and is hereby prohibited.

Resolved, That any member of this exchange who transacts any business, directly or indirectly, with or for any member of said Consolidated Stock Exchange who is engaged in business upon said Consolidated Stock Exchange, shall, on conviction thereof, be deemed to have committed an act or acts detrimental to the interest and welfare of this exchange.

Is it possible that regulation is in existence today?

Mr. ELY. You read it.

Mr. UNTERMYER. I say, Is it possible that that regulation is in existence today?

Mr. ELY. You have just read it; yes.

Mr. UNTERMYER. Just that way, is it?

Mr. ELY. Yes; just that way, exactly.

Mr. UNTERMYER. And any man who is a member of the stock exchange, who sends a message or a clerk from his own office to the office of a man who happens to be a member of the Consolidated Exchange, is guilty of violating this rule and is liable to expulsion from the stock exchange, is he not?

Mr. ELY. That is the book, what it says there. I do not want to add to or take from it.

Mr. UNTERMYER. You know that men have been punished for it, do you not?

Mr. ELY. For that?

Mr. UNTERMYER. Yes.

Mr. ELY. Yes.

Mr. UNTERMYER. Members of the New York Stock Exchange have been punished and disciplined for sending a messenger or clerk or telephoning from their own office to the office of a man who was a member of the Consolidated Stock Exchange; that is so, is it not?

Mr. ELY. Yes.

Mr. UNTERMYER. You talk of that as if it is a proper thing.

Mr. ELY. It is such a foolish question to ask me—if it has been done.

Mr. UNTERMYER. Will you tell me the reason for that benign resolution?

Mr. ELY. I have never heard of any.

Mr. UNTERMYER. You do not know that there is any?

Mr. ELY. No.

Mr. UNTERMYER. But still they punish members of the stock exchange for that?

Mr. ELY. Yes.

Mr. UNTERMYER. And deprive them of their seats?

Mr. ELY. No.

Mr. UNTERMYER. Suspend them?

Mr. ELY. Well——

Mr. UNTERMYER. Suspend them from doing business?

Mr. ELY. Yes.

Mr. UNTERMYER. And they suspend the partner of a man who communicates from his own office to the office of a Consolidated Exchange broker, do they not? The whole firm is suspended, is it not?

Mr. ELY. Yes.

Mr. UNTERMYER. And yet you say my question is a foolish question?

Mr. ELY. Yes; because it is in there.

Mr. UNTERMYER. Anything that is in there is gospel, is it not?

Mr. ELY. As far as I am concerned, yes.

Mr. UNTERMYER. Have you ever stopped to consider whether that is a reasonable regulation?

Mr. ELY. It is not within my province.

Mr. UNTERMYER. You have never stopped to think about it?

Mr. ELY. Stopped to consider this?

Mr. UNTERMYER. Have you ever stopped to consider what that means?

Mr. ELY. It does not concern me.

Mr. UNTERMYER. You have never considered it, have you?

Mr. ELY. No.

Mr. UNTERMYER. In all the 35 or 36 years you have been there?

Mr. ELY. No. It is good enough for me.

Mr. UNTERMYER. And that sort of action of the New York Stock Exchange is not now the subject of judicial review, is it?

Mr. ELY. It is subject to judicial review. Everything that we have got there is subject to judicial review.

Mr. UNTERMYER. Do you not know that they cannot interfere with those regulations?

Mr. ELY. I do not know anything of the kind. I think there was a case about it in regard to this——

Mr. UNTERMYER. In which they said they could not interfere, did they not?

Mr. ELY. I do not know what they said; but it is subject to the court's decision——

Mr. UNTERMYER. You mean any man can get into court, but he cannot get any relief from court?

Mr. ELY. I do not know that.

Mr. UNTERMYER. You know men have tried to do so.

Mr. ELY. Yes.

Mr. UNTERMYER. And have not succeeded?

Mr. ELY. A good many of them have not succeeded.

Mr. UNTERMYER. You say you do not know the reason?

Mr. ELY. No; I do not know the reason.

Mr. UNTERMYER. The Consolidated Exchange is an incorporated institution, is it not?

Mr. ELY. Is it?

Mr. UNTERMYER. Do you not know?

Mr. ELY. I do not.

Mr. UNTERMYER. You never heard of it?

Mr. ELY. No; I never heard of it; I do not know.

Mr. UNTERMYER. Do you know whether it is or not?

Mr. ELY. I do not.

Mr. UNTERMYER. Mr. Taylor tells me it is not, and upon his statement I will assume that it is not.

Mr. ELY. I do not know.

Mr. UNTERMYER. You know, do you not, that there are a great number of securities on the New York Stock Exchange that are not listed on the Consolidated Stock Exchange?

Mr. ELY. I do not know what is listed on the Consolidated Stock Exchange.

Mr. UNTERMYER. Now, Mr. Ely——

Mr. ELY. I do not know, and consequently I cannot answer the question.

Mr. UNTERMYER. Do you mean to have us understand that you have no information as to what securities are listed on the Consolidated Exchange?

Mr. ELY. I have no knowledge of it.

Mr. UNTERMYER. Do you not know that their quotations are a matter of daily record?

Mr. ELY. I see some quotations——

Mr. UNTERMYER. And you know, as a matter of fact, do you not, from general knowledge and information, that only a small proportion of the securities listed on the New York Stock Exchange are listed on the Consolidated Exchange?

Mr. ELY. I do not know it.

Mr. UNTERMYER. You know that they are not all listed there?

Mr. ELY. I do not know that.

Mr. UNTERMYER. You know they cannot be listed in both places?

Mr. ELY. I do not know that. I do not know anything at all about what is listed there.

Mr. UNTERMYER. And you do not want to know?

Mr. ELY. I do not want to know; that is right, too. I do not want to know anything about it.

Mr. UNTERMYER. What is the matter with them?

Mr. ELY. They do not interest me.

Mr. UNTERMYER. The Consolidated Exchange has interested the New York Stock Exchange very considerably for a great many years, has it not; to such an extent that they have been litigating right along?

Mr. ELY. I do not think they have been litigating right along.

Mr. UNTERMYER. Have they not been litigating over the ticker?

Mr. ELY. Oh, that was some years ago. You asked if they had not been litigating right straight along.

Mr. UNTERMYER. When did that litigation end?

Mr. ELY. Back in the eighties, I think. I have forgotten just when.

Mr. UNTERMYER. You think it ended in the eighties?

Mr. ELY. I think somewhere along there. I really do not know just when.

Mr. UNTERMYER. Will you tell me this: How would a man who happened to be a member of the Consolidated Stock Exchange and happened to have, we will say, a hundred shares of New York Central in his own name and right be able to sell that stock to any broker of the New York Stock Exchange as the law of your exchange stands today?

Mr. ELY. Let him sell them in his own exchange.

Mr. UNTERMYER. Suppose they were not listed on his own exchange, where would he sell them?

Mr. ELY. He could sell them anyplace.

Mr. UNTERMYER. But not on the stock exchange?

Mr. ELY. He could not sell them through a member of the exchange on the floor, no; but there are a thousand other places where he could sell them.

Mr. UNTERMYER. Where?

Mr. ELY. Plenty of places over the counter—

Mr. UNTERMYER. Over whose counter?

Mr. ELY. Anybody's counter who deals in stocks.

Mr. UNTERMYER. He could not sell them to a New York Stock Exchange member over that man's counter, could he?

Mr. ELY. No, sir.

Mr. UNTERMYER. Or in his private office?

Mr. ELY. Not one hundred shares of stock in his own name; no.

Mr. UNTERMYER. Or any other stock?

Mr. ELY. He could sell bonds.

Mr. UNTERMYER. A member of the Consolidated Exchange could sell bonds to a member of the New York Stock Exchange, could he?

Mr. ELY. He could; yes.

Mr. UNTERMYER. Without being disciplined?

Mr. ELY. Yes; he could.

Mr. UNTERMYER. Well, could he?

Mr. ELY. Yes.

Mr. UNTERMYER. But he could not sell stock?

Mr. ELY. Because there—

Mr. UNTERMYER. Suppose they were bonds that were listed on the New York Exchange; could he sell them to him?

Mr. ELY. Yes; he could.

Mr. UNTERMYER. Suppose a member of the Consolidated Stock Exchange owned a thousand-dollar bond that was listed on the New York Stock Exchange?

Mr. ELY. Yes.

Mr. UNTERMYER. Could he sell that bond to your stock exchange?

Mr. ELY. No; he could sell it to a member over the counter—

Mr. UNTERMYER. Could he sell it to a member of the New York Stock Exchange?

Mr. ELY. Not on the floor; no.

Mr. UNTERMYER. Suppose he had a hundred shares of stock; could he sell it anywhere to any New York Stock Exchange broker?

Mr. ELY. To a stock-exchange broker?

Mr. UNTERMYER. Yes.

Mr. ELY. Not if the stock-exchange broker knew he was a Consolidated Exchange man; but there are plenty of ways of selling——

Mr. UNTERMYER. You do not call that blacklisting a man, do you?

Mr. ELY. No.

Mr. UNTERMYER. Why should not a New York Stock Exchange broker be able in his own office to buy a hundred shares of stock from a man that happened to be a member of the Consolidated Stock Exchange?

Mr. ELY. Because it is against the law.

Mr. UNTERMYER. It is what?

Mr. ELY. It is against the law.

Mr. UNTERMYER. Because of that gospel?

Mr. ELY. Yes; that is it.

Mr. UNTERMYER. But you do not think the New York Stock Exchange ought to be incorporated, do you, and subjected to legislative and judicial control as to the kind of business it ought to do?

Mr. ELY. I have never thought about that.

Mr. UNTERMYER. You have no opinion in regard to that?

Mr. ELY. I have no opinion on that. I would like to call attention to the answer of the stock exchange to that question in the proceedings of the Hughes committee.

Mr. UNTERMYER. Where is that answer?

Mr. ELY. I gave you one.

Mr. UNTERMYER. You did not give me an answer.

Mr. ELY. Yes; I gave you an answer.

Mr. UNTERMYER. Well, will you furnish another?

Mr. ELY. I gave you an answer.

Mr. UNTERMYER. Will you furnish another?

Mr. ELY. Oh, yes.

Mr. UNTERMYER. In order that a man may become a member of the New York Stock Exchange, there has to be a vacancy or he has to buy somebody else's membership, does he not?

Mr. ELY. Yes.

Mr. UNTERMYER. Then he can only be admitted after he has been voted on. Is not that so?

Mr. ELY. He is admitted by a ballot of the committee.

Mr. UNTERMYER. The governing committee?

Mr. ELY. The committee on admission.

Mr. UNTERMYER. What is the membership of the committee?

Mr. ELY. Fifteen.

Mr. UNTERMYER. Does he have to pass the governing committee, too?

Mr. ELY. No.

Mr. UNTERMYER. In order to be admitted to membership, what vote does he have to have?

Mr. ELY. He must receive ten white ballots.

Mr. UNTERMYER. Before he can become a competitor of the members who are in the exchange?

Mr. ELY. Before he can be admitted to membership.

Mr. UNTERMYER. That is, before he is allowed to compete?

Mr. ELY. Before he can become a member.

Mr. UNTERMYER. I want you to answer the question I ask.

Mr. ELY. I have nothing to say about competing. Let me ask you—

Mr. UNTERMYER. I want you to answer my questions. Now, he cannot compete with the existing members until he becomes a member, can he?

Mr. ELY. He cannot become a member until he receives ten white ballots.

Mr. UNTERMYER. Until he becomes a member he cannot compete for business, can he?

Mr. ELY. He cannot do any business on the exchange.

Mr. UNTERMYER. You look on this exchange as a sort of a private club, do you not?

Mr. ELY. No.

Mr. UNTERMYER. Do you not realize that it has a vast and important public function to perform in interstate commerce?

Mr. ELY. I do not know.

APPENDIX II

Testimony of James B. Mabon, President of the New York Stock Exchange, before the Subcommittee of the Committee on Banking and Currency of the House of Representatives (Money Trust Investigation), June 13, 1912.

Mr. UNTERMYER. I think you were describing the process of listing securities and the requirements at adjournment.

Mr. MABON. Yes, sir.

Mr. UNTERMYER. Did you get some data that you want to submit on that subject?

Mr. MABON. No; this is the same paper that you have.

Mr. UNTERMYER. You remember the panic period in 1907, do you not, Mr. Mabon?

Mr. MABON. I do; yes, sir.

Mr. UNTERMYER. Do you remember whether or not the beginning of the panic had been preceded by a period of very wild speculation and inflation; very high prices of securities?

Mr. MABON. You mean the panic of October, 1907?

Mr. UNTERMYER. Yes; just before that.

Mr. MABON. That was not my impression. I thought there had been a preceding small panic in the spring of that year; that was my impression.

Mr. UNTERMYER. Do you not remember in August, 1907, securities were very high?

Mr. MABON. I do not remember.

Mr. UNTERMYER. You do not remember that?

Mr. MABON. No, sir.

Mr. UNTERMYER. I want to call your attention to your testimony of yesterday concerning the produce exchange, and in that connection to call your attention to Article XVII, and ask you whether you care to correct your testimony on that subject after having your attention called to Article XVII. Section 4 of Article XVII of the constitution of the New York Stock Exchange reads as follows:

Any member who shall be connected directly, or by a partner, or otherwise, with any organization in the city of New York which permits dealings in any securities or other property, admitted to dealing in any department of this exchange, shall be liable to suspension for a period not exceeding one year, or to expulsion, as the governing committee may determine.

Mr. MABON. What was my testimony, Mr. Untermyer? I have not read it over.

Mr. UNTERMYER. I may not have correctly understood it, but I understood you to say that the stock exchange had taken no action inimical to the attempt of the produce exchange to deal in securities that are dealt in on the stock exchange.

Mr. MABON. The effort of the produce exchange, as I remember it, was distinctly to trade in securities that are not admitted in the list on the New York Stock Exchange, and it was on that basis that I made my reply.

Mr. UNTERMYER. Do you not know that any member of your exchange who remained a member of the produce exchange, if he undertook to deal in any security that is dealt in on your exchange, would be liable to expulsion from your exchange?

Mr. MABON. Yes; but they did not attempt to deal in securities that are dealt in on our exchange.

Mr. UNTERMYER. Are you not mistaken about that?

Mr. MABON. That is my impression, Mr. Untermyer. If I am mistaken, I certainly will change it.

Mr. UNTERMYER. At any rate, it would not be possible for the produce exchange to deal in any security dealt in on your exchange without your requiring every member of your exchange to resign from the produce exchange?

Mr. MABON. Yes.

Mr. UNTERMYER. That is so, is it not ?

Mr. MABON. That is true, yes, sir.

Mr. UNTERMYER. And how many members of your exchange are members of the produce exchange?

Mr. MABON. I think a very small number, compared with the membership of the produce exchange.

Mr. UNTERMYER. What proportion would you say? Twenty-five per cent or more?

Mr. MABON. I should say, without knowing at all and without having any means of knowing, that there probably were not more than sixty or seventy members of the produce exchange, if as many as that, who are members of the New York Stock Exchange; and I understand the membership of the New York Produce Exchange is a very large one.

Mr. UNTERMYER. You never have made any investigation of the subject?

Mr. MABON. I have not.

Mr. UNTERMYER. All the bankers and brokers who deal in cotton are members of the produce exchange, are they not?

Mr. MABON. I should say all the bankers and brokers who deal in cotton are members of the cotton exchange.

Mr. UNTERMYER. And are they not nearly all members of the produce exchange also?

Mr. MABON. I should say not, although I do not know.

Mr. UNTERMYER. You know what the curb is, do you not?

Mr. MABON. In a general way.

Mr. UNTERMYER. Have you never dealt on the curb?

Mr. MABON. Personally, no.

Mr. UNTERMYER. You have given plenty of orders for securities dealt in on the curb, have you not?

Mr. MABON. I have given some orders; yes, sir.

Mr. UNTERMYER. And that is part of your regular business, is it not?

Mr. MABON. A very small part of it.

Mr. UNTERMYER. What?

Mr. MABON. A very small part. I presume you are asking about my personal business?

Mr. UNTERMYER. The business of your firm.

Mr. MABON. My firm almost wholly deals in bonds that are listed on the New York Stock Exchange.

Mr. UNTERMYER. But you deal in new bonds, too, do you not?

Mr. MABON. Very rarely.

Mr. UNTERMYER. You mean you do not deal in any new issues at all?

Mr. MABON. New issues occasionally, but not to any large extent.

Mr. UNTERMYER. New issues are dealt in on the curb before they can be listed on the stock exchange, are they not?

Mr. MABON. Yes.

Mr. UNTERMYER. So that you are familiar with the business of the curb?

Mr. MABON. Oh, yes; in that respect.

Mr. UNTERMYER. There is nothing to prevent a stock-exchange member from dealing on the curb, is there?

Mr. MABON. No.

Mr. UNTERMYER. And many of them do, do they not?

Mr. MABON. Yes; I imagine so.

Mr. UNTERMYER. But the curb is not allowed, is it, to deal in any security that is dealt in on the exchange?

Mr. MABON. No.

Mr. UNTERMYER. And the curb is not allowed to get under roof, is it?

Mr. MABON. I cannot answer that question.

Mr. UNDERMYER. You are a member of the governing committee, Mr. Mabon, and you can tell us whether or not the stock exchange does not prohibit the curb from taking shelter under roof ?

Mr. MABON. I cannot.

Mr. UNTERMYER. Do you not know that the subject has been up for discussion?

Mr. MABON. I know it has been up for discussion.

Mr. UNTERMYER. Do you not know the curb has organized into an association?

Mr. MABON. I understand so from the papers.

Mr. UNTERMYER. Do you not know the subject of discussion has been whether the stock exchange shall allow the curb brokers to go in out of the rain, and have a roof over their heads?

Mr. MABON. Not for some time.

Mr. UNTERMYER. When was that discussed?

Mr. MABON. I should say two years ago.

Mr. UNTERMYER. What did the stock exchange then decide?

Mr. MABON. I think they made no decision.

Mr. UNTERMYER. Do you not know they told them they could not do it?

Mr. MABON. I do not.

Mr. UNTERMYER. What other reason is there for their dealing in the rain?

Mr. MABON. I do not know.

Mr. UNTERMYER. What is the point of the objection to the curb getting into a building, provided it observed the rule not to deal in securities that are dealt in on the exchange?

Mr. MABON. I do not know, Mr. Untermyer.

Mr. UNTERMYER. You are a member of the governing committee, are you not?

Mr. MABON. I am.

Mr. UNTERMYER. And you know the subject has been under discussion?

Mr. MABON. Yes.

Mr. UNTERMYER. You know there has been an application by a committee of the curb, do you not?

Mr. MABON. No; I do not know that there has been.

Mr. UNTERMYER. You never heard of it, did you?

Mr. MABON. No.

Mr. UNTERMYER. Nothing of the kind?

Mr. MABON. No.

Mr. UNTERMYER. How did it come up for discussion?

Mr. MABON. I do not remember how it did come up for discussion.

Mr. UNTERMYER. Did it not come up through a committee of the curb calling on the committee of the stock exchange for the purpose of procuring such permission?

Mr. MABON. I do not know.

Mr. UNTERMYER. Do you know anything about it?

Mr. MABON. I do not.

Mr. UNTERMYER. Who would know?

Mr. MABON. I suppose the records of the exchange would tell.

Mr. UNTERMYER. Is there anybody here with them?

Mr. MABON. Mr. Martin, have you any records bearing on that subject?

Mr. MARTIN. I have the governing committee minutes.

Mr. UNTERMYER. Will you get them, please? What is the membership of the curb?

Mr. MABON. I do not know.

Mr. UNTERMYER. What would be the effect of an attempt on the part of the curb brokers to deal in a security that was dealt in on the exchange?

Mr. MABON. What would be the effect on the stock exchange of the action?

Mr. UNTERMYER. Yes.

Mr. MABON. I suppose the exchange would act under the provisions of the constitution, and I do not know how they would apply in that particular instance.

Mr. UNTERMYER. Do you not know they would apply so that the man who continued to have anything to do with a curb broker would be suspended or expelled from the exchange?

Mr. MABON. I assume so.

Mr. UNTERMYER. Are any of the members of the stock exchange members of the curb?

Mr. MABON. I do not know. Presumably, yes.

Mr. UNTERMYER. The curb is a regular organization, is it not?

Mr. MABON. I understand so, Mr. Untermyer, from the papers. That is all I know.

Mr. UNTERMYER. It has been incorporated, has it not?

Mr. MABON. I doubt it very much.

Mr. UNTERMYER. It has a membership, and has initiation fees and yearly dues, has it not?

Mr. MABON. I do not know.

Mr. UNTERMYER. You do not know anything about it?

Mr. MABON. I do not know anything about it. The only thing I have seen has been the newspaper statements some time ago.

Mr. UNTERMYER. And you see it before your eyes in operation every day, do you not?

Mr. MABON. I do not.

Mr. UNTERMYER. Where is your office?

Mr. MABON. No. 45 Wall Street.

Mr. UNTERMYER. And where is the curb?

Mr. MABON. It is in lower Broad Street.

Mr. UNTERMYER. Right around the corner from you, is it not?

Mr. MABON. It is in lower Broad Street.

Mr. UNTERMYER. You say you do not see it in operation?

Mr. MABON. I do not.

Mr. UNTERMYER. You never do?

Mr. MABON. I do not think I have ever seen it in operation.

Mr. UNTERMYER. How can you go from your office in Wall Street to Broadway without seeing it in operation?

Mr. MABON. Mr. Untermyer, I would like you to describe how you can see it in operation from Wall Street to lower Broad Street. If you can see it from that distance—

Mr. UNTERMYER. I say how can you go from your office in Wall Street to Broadway, through Wall Street, without seeing the curb in operation on Broad and Wall Street.

Mr. MABON. The curb is not on Broad and Wall Streets. It is on lower Broad Street.

Mr. UNTERMYER. It is on Broad Street between Wall Street and Exchange Place, is it not?

Mr. MABON. It is not.

Mr. UNTERMYER. Where is it?

Mr. MABON. Lower Broad Street.

Mr. UNTERMYER. Between what streets?

Mr. MABON. Between Beaver Street and Exchange Place.

Mr. UNTERMYER. I thought it was opposite the Mills Building. Is it not?

Mr. MABON. I have just said where it was, Mr. Untermyer.

Mr. UNTERMYER. It used to be opposite the Mills Building, did it not?

Mr. MABON. Yes, sir.

Mr. UNTERMYER. It is a railed-in space; that is, it is a space that is simply confined by ropes and posts, is it not?

Mr. MABON. I do not know whether there are any ropes or posts there.

Mr. UNTERMYER. You do not know anything about it?

Mr. MABON. No, sir.

Mr. UNTERMYER. How often do you have dealings on the curb?

Mr. MABON. I do not know how often my office has, but very rarely.

Mr. UNTERMYER. Have you those references there?

Mr. MARTIN. I have several of them; yes, sir.

Mr. UNTERMYER. I would like to have them. If you will just give us the numbers, we will read them as we go along.

Mr. MARTIN. Page 232 is the first.

Mr. UNTERMYER. We will read these references in evidence:

Mr. Sturgis offers the following: "*Resolved,* That the committee on unlisted securities consider the question of adding to the present list all the more important securities now dealt in upon the curb, with such regulations as they may deem for the best protection of the stock exchange, if any should be required, and that they report the result of their deliberation to the governing committee at the earliest possible date." Seconded.

Mr. Maury moved as an amendment that two members of the governing committee be added to the committee in the matter. Seconded.

Mr. Sturgis accepted the amendment, and it then became a part of the original resolution, which was put to vote and carried.

The president appointed Messrs. Sturgis and Thomas as the additional members.

That resolution is dated March 21, 1906.

That resolution, if carried, would have wiped out the curb and the curb brokers, would it not?

Mr. MABON. Not necessarily.

Mr. UNTERMYER. What if the stock exchange undertook to establish——

Mr. MABON. You read the resolution.

Mr. UNTERMYER (continuing). All the more important securities now dealt in on the curb in a department of its own, would it not have wiped out the curb?

Mr. MABON. I would say not.

Mr. UNTERMYER. What would have been left?

Mr. MABON. There would have been others left, as I take it from that resolution.

Mr. UNTERMYER. Other what?

Mr. MABON. Securities.

Mr. UNTERMYER. The curb could have dealt in any that the stock exchange did not want to put on its list, is that it?

Mr. MABON. Presumably.

Mr. UNTERMYER. And you think they could have lived on that?

Mr. MABON. There would be new things coming on.

Mr. UNTERMYER. And would not the stock exchange take the same jurisdiction over the new things that it considered important?

Mr. MABON. That is a matter that I——

Mr. UNTERMYER. You know perfectly well, do you not, the adoption of that resolution would have wiped out the curb?

Mr. MABON. I do not agree with you.

Mr. UNTERMYER. And you do not think so?

Mr. MABON. I do not think so.

Mr. UNTERMYER. If you took over onto the stock exchange the more important securities that are dealt in on the curb, it would not wipe out the curb?

Mr. MABON. I should say not.

Mr. UNTERMYER. You would not have allowed them to deal in those you took yourself, would you?

Mr. MABON. No.

Mr. UNTERMYER. I now read this in evidence:

Mr. Sturgis for the law committee also presented the following resolution, which was unanimously adopted: "That the matter of adopting a quotation in this exchange of securities traded in on the curb be referred to a special committee composed of the law committee and the committee on unlisted securities with instructions to consider the subject and to make prompt report thereon to the governing committee."

Mr. UNTERMYER. I read from the minutes of meeting of May 19, 1909:

Special committee composed of the law committee and the committee on unlisted securities make the following report:

"*Resolved,* That the governing committee refer back to special committee the following questions for examination and report on or before October 15, 1909:

"'Shall the members of the New York Stock Exchange be prohibited, after a certain date, say December 31, 1909, from dealing, directly or indirectly, in the market known as the curb? And further, shall said special committee consider and report upon any and all matters connected with this subject?'"

Mr. Sturgis moved that the report be received and the resolution adopted.

Seconded and carried unanimously.

Meeting of June 27, 1909:

The secretary submitted a communication from E. S. Mendel regarding meeting on curb, and, on motion of Mr. Groesbeck, said communication was referred to special committee consisting of the law committee and the committee on unlisted securities.

I offer in evidence from the book of minutes of the governing committee the meetings of January 19, 1910, resolutions and recommendations with respect to the curb.

I will read the last recommendation:

That the committee on stock list be requested and empowered to examine into and report upon the desirability of placing upon the floor of the stock exchange, for dealings under the restrictions provided in section 2 of this report, of any bonds or shares of stock, either of mining companies or otherwise, that they may deem advisable to recommend, even if such corporations have not made application for listing to the stock list committee of their own accord, the object of this recommendation being to bring before the governing committee from time to time the possible advantage of dealing in certain securities now dealt in upon the curb, but which, for some specific reason, have never applied for or been eligible to the regular list. It is thought if this course be pursued a gradual system of elimination, in so far as the curb market is concerned, will be put in process, and that it will result in transferring to the exchange from time to time all the real or desirable securities dealt in permanently on the Street. Your committee realize that an open curb market in some form will always exist, but they think the course which they have recommended will gradually minimize the evil and convince the community that the governing committee of the stock exchange are determined to give to all securities as open a market as may be permissible, or consistent with proper precaution and due security. The committee believe that there are many securities, both of mining and other nature, that, by a modification of the commission law in so far as they are concerned, will seek the exchange floor of their own accord for the transaction of business.

You will note that this last was the recommendation of the special committee, not acted upon; but it was acted upon to some extent, was it not, Mr. Mabon? Mining shares were put upon the stock exchange, and the commission rate was changed as to them, was it not?

Mr. MABON. I do not know whether the action of the governing committee was based upon that particular——

Mr. UNTERMYER. Mining shares that had been listed and dealt in exclusively on the curb were placed upon the exchange list, were they not?

Mr. MABON. I do not remember whether mining stocks which were traded in on the curb——

Mr. UNTERMYER. Let us see. You remember the Utah Copper Co.?

Mr. MABON. Yes.

Mr. UNTERMYER. Was not that traded in on the curb until it was put on the list; and was not the Reno, and the Miami Copper Co.? Were they not all traded in on the curb until they were put on the exchange list on the basis of one-sixteenth of 1 per cent commission where they sold under $10 a share?

Mr. MABON. Yes.

Mr. UNTERMYER. And they sold for a long time under $10 a share, did they not?

Mr. MABON. Some of them.

Mr. UNTERMYER. All of them, did they not?

Mr. MABON. I do not know whether the Utah sold under $5.

Mr. UNTERMYER. Was not that a $5 per share par value security?

Mr. MABON. Yes; but the basis of commission is not on the par value of mining stocks.

Mr. UNTERMYER. I know.

Mr. MABON. That is what I wanted to bring out.

Mr. UNTERMYER. That had been dealt in on the curb, as had these other mining stocks, until the governing committee changed its policy and took them on the basis of one-sixteenth when they were selling under $10 a share?

Mr. MABON. Yes.

Mr. UNTERMYER. And in that way they took all that business away from the curb, did they not?

Mr. MABON. Not all the business; no.

Mr. UNTERMYER. All that business, that particular business that they took unto themselves by listing them on the exchange?

Mr. MABON. Very likely a great deal of that business that was done on the curb was done by the stock-exchange houses, so that it is quite unfair to say that stock-exchange houses took business away from themselves.

Mr. UNTERMYER. The stock exchange as a stock exchange took that business away, did it not?

Mr. MABON. The stock exchange as a stock exchange listed these securities.

Mr. UNTERMYER. And took that business away from the curb, did it not?

Mr. MABON. I cannot say.

Mr. UNTERMYER. Was the curb ever thereafter allowed to deal in them?

Mr. MABON. No.

Mr. UNTERMYER. Do you not know whilst the curb was allowed

to deal in them anybody could deal in them on the curb; but he did not have to pay $70,000 to $90,000 for a seat in order to do it, did he?

Mr. MABON. No.

Mr. UNTERMYER. When that rule was changed, that business all disappeared from the men who had previously been permitted to do it, did it not?

Mr. MABON. To that extent.

Mr. UNTERMYER. From time to time you are taking mining stocks as they apply for admission and for listing and putting them on the list of the stock exchange, are you not?

Mr. MABON. Yes, sir.

Mr. UNTERMYER. And all the new issues of mining securities that apply for admission and are respectable you are putting on the stock exchange?

Mr. MABON. No, Mr. Untermyer; that is not quite true.

Mr. UNTERMYER. Are you not? What are you refusing? Will you give us the name of one you are refusing?

Mr. MABON. We have not had any applications, because the requirements—

Mr. UNTERMYER. I am asking you what you are refusing. I want my question answered.

Mr. MABON. I do not think we have refused any.

Mr. UNTERMYER. I guess not. Every one you take lessens the importance of the business of the curb, does it not?

Mr. MABON. In that respect.

Mr. UNTERMYER. It lessens it, does it not?

Mr. MABON. It lessens it to that extent; yes; but the curb may lose one today and the business increase by something new coming in tomorrow.

Mr. UNTERMYER. Until they put that on the exchange, and then it loses that, does it not?

Mr. MABON. Oh, yes.

Mr. UNTERMYER. I have not had those resolutions bearing on the application of the curb for permission to get a place. What was the date of that application to which you referred in your testimony a while ago?

Mr. MABON. I did not say there was any application.

Mr. UNTERMYER. Did you not?

Mr. MABON. I said I thought there was not an application.

Mr. UNTERMYER. I thought you said there had been, about two years ago.

Mr. MABON. There had been a discussion, I said. This was what I had in mind.

Mr. UNTERMYER. Discussion with whom?

Mr. MABON. With this very committee whose resolutions you have just read.

Mr. UNTERMYER. And a discussion of that committee and any committee of the curb?

Mr. MABON. I think not.

Mr. UNTERMYER. Or anybody representing the curb?

Mr. MABON. I think Mr. Mendel did voluntarily appear before the committee.

Mr. UNTERMYER. I did not mean to assume you dragged him there. Of course he voluntarily appeared; but he appeared on behalf of the curb, did he not?

Mr. MABON. I do not remember that he did.

Mr. UNTERMYER. For whom did he appear?

Mr. MABON. Personally, I believe.

Mr. UNTERMYER. He was a curb broker, was he not?

Mr. MABON. Yes.

Mr. UNTERMYER. And he appeared personally; for what purpose?

Mr. MABON. To discuss the matter of the curb; but I do not remember the details at all.

Mr. UNTERMYER. To discuss what matters of the curb; the idea of allowing it to get a place at which to do business?

Mr. MABON. I do not remember.

Mr. UNTERMYER. And he did not say he appeared for himself and his associates, did he?

Mr. MABON. That I do not remember.

Mr. UNTERMYER. What is the idea of fining a member $50 every time he deals in any securities on the exchange before 10 in the morning or after 3 in the afternoon?

Mr. MABON. The object is to have the dealings begin at a special time and end at a specific time.

Mr. UNTERMYER. What harm does he do if he wants to work overtime, beyond 3 o'clock?

Mr. MABON. There has to be a definite time for opening and closing the exchange.

Mr. UNTERMYER. Yes; but this is not a question of opening and closing the exchange; it is dealing on the exchange.

Mr. MABON. There are no dealings on the exchange until the hours fixed by the committee for dealing in securities.

Mr. UNTERMYER. That refers to making a transaction in the exchange outside these hours, does it?

Mr. MABON. I do not understand it so. What is your question?

Mr. UNTERMYER. It only refers to transactions that are made in the exchange in those hours?

Mr. MABON. Yes, sir.

Mr. UNTERMYER. It does not prevent transactions outside?

Mr. MABON. Oh, no.

Mr. UNTERMYER. All the obligations of one member of the exchange to other members of the exchange, in case of insolvency, take precedence over everybody else's claims against the insolvent member, do they not?

Mr. MABON. Yes.

Mr. UNTERMYER. If a member of the exchange converts stocks belonging to his customer or practices a fraud upon his customer the damage to that customer has to wait and be deferred until after that member has paid his debts to all the other members, does it not?

Mr. MABON. I never had any personal knowledge of that.

Mr. UNTERMYER. But that is the rule, and the seat of the member is sold, and all the proceeds are first applied to the debts to other members before any outside creditor can get a cent—is not that so?

Mr. MABON. That is the rule.

Mr. UNTERMYER. No matter whether it is a claim for fraud or anything else? Is that right.

Mr. MABON. That is the rule.

Mr. UNTERMYER. So that, in that respect, the law of your exchange is contrary to the law of the land, is it not?

Mr. MABON. I should say not.

Mr. UNTERMYER. You think not?

Mr. MABON. I do not think there is anything in that constitution that is against the law of the land.

Mr. UNTERMYER. I think there are a great many things. That is where we may differ. There is a clearing house for securities in the exchange, is there not?

Mr. MABON. There is a clearing house; yes.

Mr. UNTERMYER. Are you familiar with the mechanism of that department?

Mr. MABON. I am not.

Mr. UNTERMYER. Who would know of that?

Mr. MABON. Mr. Doremus, who is the chairman of the committee, and Mr. Geddes.

Mr. UNTERMYER. You know in a general way, though, what is required?

Mr. MABON. In a general way, yes.

Mr. UNTERMYER. What is the machinery, so far as you know?

Mr. MABON. So far as I know, the buyer exchanges his ticket with the seller. Those tickets are delivered to the clearing house——

Mr. UNTERMYER. You mean at the time of the transaction?

Mr. MABON. No; at the time of the transaction there is nothing.

Mr. UNTERMYER. At the time of a transaction between two members of the exchange, is anything exchanged between them?

Mr. MABON. No, sir.

APPENDIX III

Testimony of Marcus Heim, member of the Consolidated Stock Exchange, before the Subcommittee of the Committee on Banking and Currency of the House of Representatives (Money Trust Investigation), December 12, 1912.

Mr. UNTERMYER. Where do you live?

Mr. HEIM. In New York.

Mr. UNTERMYER. You have asked to be heard here today in connection with the relations between the New York Stock Exchange and the Consolidated Stock Exchange, have you not?

Mr. HEIM. Yes, sir.

Mr. UNTERMYER. Are you a member of the Consolidated Stock Exchange?

Mr. HEIM. I am.

Mr. UNTERMYER. And are you an investor?

Mr. HEIM. I am both an investor and a commission broker.

Mr. UNTERMYER. How long have you been engaged in business in New York?

Mr. HEIM. In New York? Forty years.

Mr. UNTERMYER. As an investment broker?

Mr. HEIM. No; only since 1879 in Wall Street.

Mr. UNTERMYER. Will you go on and state what you desire to say concerning the differences between you and the New York Stock Exchange?

Mr. HEIM. I supposed I was summoned here for that purpose. Do you wish me to state it in my own way or to answer questions?

Mr. UNTERMYER. Please go on and state the complaint you have to make.

Mr. HEIM. I have been a member of the Consolidated Exchange since the consolidation of 1885. I have been in Wall Street since 1879. I have always stood "A-1" financially; I have always been ready to meet every obligation on demand during all that time, in times of stress and otherwise—and we have had a great many during that time. I have had business relations with the New York Stock Exchange as an investor, as a speculator, and as a commission broker, during that time.

Mr. UNTERMYER. You mean with members of the stock exchange?

Mr. HEIM. With members of the New York Stock Exchange, placing orders there at times that I could not fill at any other exchange but the New York Stock Exchange. It was the only market in the world where those securities could be bought or sold. Therefore I was obliged to have an account or do business with stock-exchange members. I have had an open account practically since 1879 with possibly about half a dozen different houses.

Mr. UNTERMYER. You mean New York Stock Exchange houses?

Mr. HEIM. New York Stock Exchange houses. They were always ready to seek my business. Sometimes, as a matter of favor, I would open an account at certain houses for the asking. All my business arrangements have always been perfectly satisfactory to these brokers. I have paid the full commissions, as every other man did that traded in those offices. My accounts were conducted on the same lines. There was no difference, no variation whatever.

On May 19, 1909, the board of governors of the New York Stock Exchange, in meeting, passed a resolution that no member of the New York Stock Exchange should transact any business, directly or indirectly, with any member of the Consolidated Exchange.

Mr. UNTERMYER. Is this the resolution to which you refer? I think it is in the record, but I will read it here:

Resolved, That any connection, direct or indirect, by means of public or private telephone, telegraph wire, or any electrical or other contrivance or device or pneumatic tube or other apparatus or device whatsoever, or any communication by means of messengers or clerks, or in any other manner, direct or indirect, between the New York Stock Exchange Building or any part thereof, or any office of any member of said New York Stock Exchange, and any building of the Consolidated Stock Exchange, or any part thereof, or any room, place, hallway, or space occupied or controlled by said Consolidated Stock Exchange, or any office of any member of said Consolidated Stock Exchange who is engaged in business upon said Consolidated Stock Exchange, or any transmission, direct or indirect, of information from said New York Stock Exchange Building, or from the office of any member of said New York Stock Exchange, to the said Consolidated Stock Exchange, or to the office of any member of said Consolidated Stock Exchange who is engaged in business upon said Consolidated Stock Exchange, through any means, apparatus, device, or contrivance as above mentioned, is detrimental to the interest and welfare of this exchange and is hereby prohibited.

Resolved, That any member of this exchange who transacts any business, directly or indirectly, with or for any member of said Consolidated Stock Exchange who is engaged in business upon said Consolidated Stock Exchange shall, on conviction thereof, be deemed to have committed an act or acts detrimental to the interest and welfare of this exchange.

Is the Consolidated Stock Exchange incorporated?

Mr. HEIM. It is not.

Mr. UNTERMYER. That is the resolution to which you refer?

Mr. HEIM. That is the resolution to which I refer.

Mr. UNTERMYER. Go on and state what happened after that was passed.

Mr. HEIM. The day when that resolution was passed I saw it printed on the news ticker. I was astonished. The firm that I had an account with at the time called me up on the telephone and said they would like to see me. I said I would be over there after the close of business. They asked me, "Have you seen the resolution that the New York Stock Exchange has passed about doing business with an active member of the Consolidated Exchange?" I said, "Yes; I saw it on the ticker." They said, "What can we do about it?" I said, "I do not know what you can do about it, but it is up to you; you ought to fight your own battle on that."

Mr. UNTERMYER. I do not think it is necessary, Mr. Heim, to go into the conversation; just tell us what happened.

Mr. HEIM. They said we would have to close the account, and I told them that I did not propose to do it.

Mr. UNTERMYER. What happened?

Mr. HEIM. The partners had a little "confab" in the private office and then they came to me and called me in. They said, "Now, we cannot keep your account; it is forbidden by the New York Stock Exchange."

Mr. UNTERMYER. But will you not just tell us what happened? You see, relating the conversation will take a long time.

Mr. HEIM. They insisted upon closing the account, which I refused to do. In the course of a few days I went to my counsel; and, in fact, I told him that I would go to court on it, which I did.

Mr. UNTERMYER. Was that the only account that was closed?

Mr. HEIM. It was the only account I had open at the time. I went to my counsel and laid the matter before them and proceeded to get an injunction.

Mr. UNTERMYER. The injunction was dissolved, was it not?

Mr. HEIM. They got a temporary injunction, and then it was dissolved after that; and during the pendency of that temporary injunction they did no business for me—would not accept any business—and the account stood still as it was.

Mr. UNTERMYER. What has happened since?

Mr. HEIM. When the injunction was dissolved they insisted upon my taking up the account. Then, in order not to meet with terrible loss—I had a very large account there—I made myself an inactive member, which that resolution allowed. If I did no business on the consolidated exchange, I could do business with them, but as long as I did business on the consolidated exchange I was barred from them. So they asked me if I would put that in writing. They said: "We will take your word for it, but we want to have something to show in case any question arises." I said I would do so, and I gave them a letter.

Mr. UNTERMYER. You mean you gave it to the New York Stock Exchange?

Mr. HEIM. I gave the New York Stock Exchange member a copy of the letter stating that I was an inactive member. Here is the letter. Shall I read it?

Mr. UNTERMYER. Let me see it. [After examining letter.] Will you read it into the record, please?

Mr. HEIM. Yes, sir. After the injunction was dissolved, I made myself an inactive member in order to do business with them. [Reading:]

EXHIBIT No. 112, DECEMBER 12, 1912.

SEPTEMBER 7, 1909.

Messrs. ALBERT LOEB & Co.,
    32 Broadway, New York City.

GENTLEMEN: In view of the decision of the court in my case, and my personal interest being very much damaged in not being able to have members of the New York Stock Exchange to accept my orders to buy or sell securities, which are only traded in that exchange, I have decided to withdraw as an active member of the consolidated exchange, and therefore intend to continue my business relations with your firm and expect to continue to do my business with you as heretofore.

    Yours, very truly.

Mr. UNTERMYER. Please mark that as an exhibit.

The letter above referred to was marked "Exhibit No. 112, December 12, 1912."

Mr. HEIM. I continued then until October, and I think the firm was about to dissolve. They were split up there, and between the two partners they got into a controversy. They did not want that account any longer. Bear in mind that I was an inactive member, but still they insisted upon my taking up the account. I received a letter from them dated October 11, 1909, as follows:

EXHIBIT No. 113, DECEMBER 12, 1912.

[Albert Loeb & Co., 32 Broadway.]

NEW YORK, *October 11, 1909.*

Mr. MARCUS HEIM,
32 Broadway, New York City.

DEAR SIR: Will you please take up your account at your earliest convenience as we do not wish to carry it any longer, and oblige.

Yours, very truly,

ALBERT LOEB & Co.

The letter above referred to was marked "Exhibit No. 113, December 12, 1912."

Mr. HEIM. I was an inactive member at that time, and still I was obliged to take up the account. They did not care to carry it any longer for fear of getting into trouble. I obeyed that summons. I suppose it is necessary to tell you what kind of an account I had.

Mr. UNTERMYER. No; I do not think that is necessary.

Mr. HEIM. I brought it with me.

Mr. UNTERMYER. Had it been a satisfactory account to your brokers?

Mr. HEIM. I had an account there of something like over four thousand shares of stock.

Mr. UNTERMYER. There had been no default on your account, had there?

Mr. HEIM. Not at all. I took up the account. The day I got that letter I think was on a Friday, and on Monday I proceeded to take up the account. On Saturday we do not have any banking arrangements. There was a debit balance of two hundred and forty-three thousand and some odd dollars. On Monday I gave them a check for $80,000 and took up a portion——

Mr. UNTERMYER. I do not think that is necessary.

Mr. HEIM. All right. I simply want to show the size of the account.

Mr. UNTERMYER. We do not want to go into your private affairs any further than necessary.

Mr. HEIM. I merely want to show the size of the account; that is all. Then, being an inactive member, as I say—they refused it and did not care to carry the account any longer—I opened an account with Pearl & Co., who were anxious to do business for me as an inactive member. I continued that account there——

Mr. UNTERMYER. Is that a stock-exchange house?

Mr. HEIM. Yes, sir; that is a New York Stock Exchange house. I continued that account there for possibly about five or six months only. I then decided it was to my disadvantage to bar myself from my exchange, where I have been since 1885; and I then notified them that I was going to cease to be an inactive member and that if they wished to do business with me, all well and good; if not, I would have to take up the account. I notified them to that effect—that I was going to cease to be an inactive member—and I then closed the account. Since that time I have had no account with any stock-exchange house.

Mr. UNTERMYER. That is all, is it not?

Mr. HEIM. I received from time to time circulars from different stock-exchange houses making a bid for business, probably not knowing that I was a member of the Consolidated Exchange, or probably I would not have heard from them. But here a short time ago—this probably will be in point—the firm of Alexander & Co. advertised very extensively in the newspapers, and advertised a market circular on Chesapeake & Ohio Railroad. I happened to be interested very largely in the property, and they stated in their ad that it could be had on request. I wrote them and asked them if they would kindly send me this Chesapeake & Ohio circular letter, which, in the course of a day or two, I received, also with order blanks to take my orders and a letter expressing their desire to do business with me at any time or to give me any information I wanted.

Mr. UNTERMYER. When was this?

Mr. HEIM. That was here lately—in November. I think it was in November.

Mr. UNTERMYER. What was the date of that; November of this year?

Mr. HEIM. November of this year; yes; just here within a couple of months. After receiving this circular letter and this letter of theirs, I naturally, as a matter of common courtesy, acknowledged the receipt of it, thanking them for the same, and wrote, stating in the letter: "As per your request to do business, I will be pleased to open an account with you to do business for cash and for an open account if you are willing to accept my account. I am a member of the Consolidated Exchange"—not to deceive them at all. I received a letter in response to that as follows:

EXHIBIT NO. 114, DECEMBER 12, 1912.

JUNE 20, 1912.

Mr. MARCUS HEIM,
    32 Broadway, New York City.

DEAR SIR: We beg to acknowledge receipt of your favor of June 15, and regret that we are unable to do business for you as you are a member of the Consolidated Exchange.

    Yours, very truly,

ALEXANDER & CO.

The letter above referred to was marked "Exhibit No. 114, December 12, 1912."

Mr. UNTERMYER. By whom is that signed?

Mr. HEIM. That is signed by Alexander & Co., members of the New York Stock Exchange. This is the original letter.

Mr. UNTERMYER. Does that complete what you wanted to say?

Mr. HEIM. Unless you wish to notice the length of time—I have here the open account with this firm.

Mr. UNTERMYER. No; I do not think that is material.

Mr. HEIM. It is ten or twelve years.

Mr. UNTERMYER. Mr. Milburn, would you like to have us ask any questions of this witness for you?

Mr. MILBURN. No, sir.

Mr. UNTERMYER. Mr. Heim, are these the papers in the suit brought by you, and is this the opinion of the court in that action, that you furnished us [indicating papers]?

Mr. HEIM. I have a copy of the opinion. If you have not got it, you can have it.

Mr. UNTERMYER. No; you furnished it to us.

Mr. HEIM. I do not believe you have the opinion there.

Mr. UNTERMYER. Yes; the opinion is here.

Are there a number of interstate corporations the securities of which are listed on the New York Stock Exchange and not elsewhere listed?

Mr. HEIM. The Consolidated Exchange has a very small market. We practically try to trade in anything that brings an order in there. But the New York Stock Exchange is a broader market, and there are a great many stocks, hundreds of them, that are traded in there only and not elsewhere.

Mr. UNTERMYER. The question is whether or not there are a great many interstate corporations the securities, bonds, and stocks of which are listed only on the New York Stock Exchange.

Mr. HEIM. That is correct; yes, sir.

Mr. UNTERMYER. That find no other market?

Mr. HEIM. No other market.

Mr. UNTERMYER. There are how many members of the Consolidated Stock Exchange?

Mr. HEIM. At the present time—we have been reducing them by cancellation—there are about eight hundred.

Mr. UNTERMYER. Can a member of the Consolidated Stock Exchange who personally owns bonds or stocks that are listed only on the New York Stock Exchange sell them at any public market?

Mr. HEIM. Not in any public market that I know of except the New York Stock Exchange.

Mr. UNTERMYER. Can he sell them there?

Mr. HEIM. Probably, if you used someone else's name than your own, but not in your own name.

Mr. UNTERMYER. You could only sell them under cover; is that it?

Mr. HEIM. Under cover, possibly; yes.

Mr. UNTERMYER. I think that is all, Mr. Heim.

Witness excused.

APPENDIX IV

Testimony of Miguel E. De Aguero, President of the Consolidated Stock Exchange, before the Subcommittee of the Committee on Banking and Currency of the House of Representatives (Money Trust Investigation), December 12, 1912.

Mr. UNTERMYER. Mr. de Aguero, where do you live?

Mr. DE AGURRO. New York.

Mr. UNTERMYER. Are you the president of the Consolidated Stock Exchange?

Mr. DE AGUERO. I am.

Mr. UNTERMYER. What is your firm.

Mr. DE AGUERO. M. E. and J. W. de Aguero.

Mr. UNTERMYER. Are you stockbrokers?

Mr. DE AGUERO. Yes, sir.

Mr. UNTERMYER. How long have you been stockbrokers?

Mr. DE AGUERO. Since 1884. The firm was established in 1884.

Mr. UNTERMYER. And you have been continuously in existence all that time?

Mr DE AGUERO. We have; yes, sir.

Mr. UNTERMYER. Have the members of the Consolidated Stock Exchange experienced any difficulty or any discrimination on the part of great corporations in respect to transfers of securities bought on that exchange?

Mr. DE AGUERO. We claim that we have; yes, sir.

Mr. UNTERMYER. You claim that you are being discriminated against, as against the New York Stock Exchange, in such transactions?

Mr. DE AGUERO. We do; yes, sir.

Mr. UNTERMYER. Have you had the subject up with some of the corporations?

Mr. DE AGUERO. We have.

Mr. UNTERMYER. With what corporations?

Mr. DE AGUERO. I think you have a list there of the corporations. Perhaps I could give it to you here. This is a list of those who will not accept the guarantee of the exchange itself on certificates of stock for transfer.

Mr. UNTERMYER. And they do accept the guarantee of the New York Stock Exchange?

Mr. DE AGUERO. Yes, sir; so I am informed.

Mr. UNTERMYER. But you know they do not accept yours, do you not?

Mr. DE AGUERO. I do.

Mr. UNTERMYER. Just state the list of them; will you?

Mr. DE AGUERO. You have the list there. It is a pencil list.

Mr. UNTERMYER. I will read it into the record

Mr. DE AGUERO. If you please.

Mr. UNTERMYER. This is a list of transfer officers who will not accept the guaranty of the consolidated exchange: Pennsylvania Railroad, Lehigh Valley Railroad, Atchison, Topeka & Santa Fe, United States Steel Co., Harvey Fiske & Sons, the Bankers' Trust, the Manhattan Trust, and the Guaranty Trust.

Mr. DE AGUERO. Yes, sir.

Mr. UNTERMYER. Do the other corporations whose shares are dealt in on your exchange accept the guaranty of the exchange?

Mr. DE AGUERO. Yes, sir.

Mr. MILBURN. It is not the guaranty of the Consolidated Exchange.

Mr. UNTERMYER. No; of the members of the Consolidated Exchange.

Mr. DE AGUERO. No; I beg your pardon—of the exchange itself. That is a list of those who will not accept the guaranty of the Consolidated Stock Exchange itself, placed on the certificate by the chairman of the exchange under authority of the board of governors of the exchange.

Mr. UNTERMYER. In other words, you have offered the exchange's guaranty in addition to the guaranty of the members, have you not?

Mr. DE AGUERO. Yes, sir.

Mr. UNTERMYER. Have you had any correspondence on that subject?

Mr. DE AGUERO. We have.

Mr. UNTERMYER. With whom?

Mr. DE AGUERO. With the United States Steel Co., mostly.

Mr. UNTERMYER. Have you furnished the committee that correspondence?

Mr. DE AGUERO. I have, yes, sir; part of it.

Mr. UNTERMYER. Is this what you have furnished the committee [indicating papers]?

Mr. DE AGUERO. Yes, sir; it is.

Mr. UNTERMYER. That is it, is it?

Mr. DE AGUERO. Yes; that is it.

Mr. UNTERMYER. We will read that into the record.

Mr. DE AGUERO. Very well, sir.

Mr. UNTERMYER. Does that constitute all the correspondence on this subject?

Mr. DE AGUERO. No, sir, it does not.

Mr. UNTERMYER. Where is the rest of it?

Mr. DE AGUERO. The rest of the correspondence was had with the counsel of the exchange.

Mr. UNTERMYER. Would it not be fairer to have it all, Mr. de Aguero? These seem to be only letters from you to Mr. Gary, are they not?

Mr. DE AGUERO. Yes, sir.

Mr. UNTERMYER. Where are the replies?

Mr. DE AGUERO. We had no replies, as that shows, except this one, and one other; and the other I cannot find. This is the one reply; this is the only one I can find.

Mr. UNTERMYER. This is the only one you can find?

Mr. DE AGUERO. Yes, sir.

Mr. UNTERMYER. The United States Steel Corporation is its own transfer agent, is it?

Mr. DE AGUERO. Yes, sir.

Mr. UNTERMYER. Therefore you applied to it?

Mr. DE AGUERO. We did.

Mr. UNTERMYER. Do you remember what the other communication was, which you say you cannot find?

Mr. DE AGUERO. I think the answer there, as of February 15, 1910, will give you an idea.

Mr. UNTERMYER. We will read it over; and will you see if you can find the other letters, so as to have the correspondence complete?

Mr. DE AGUERO. I have looked for it, sir; and I cannot find it.

Mr. UNTERMYER. But you can tell us what its substance was when we get to it, can you not?

Mr. DE AGUERO. Very nearly.

[Mr. Untermyer thereupon read the following letter:]

EXHIBIT NO. 116, DECEMBER 12, 1912.

CONSOLIDATED STOCK EXCHANGE OF NEW YORK,
PRESIDENT'S OFFICE,
New York, January 3, 1910.

Mr. E. H. GARY,
Chairman United States Steel Corporation,
71 Broadway, New York City.

MY DEAR SIR: We have endeavored, over the telephone, for many weeks to get an appointment with you in order to reach some conclusion in regard to transferring stock for several of our leading commission houses who followed your suggestion by making a statement such as you outlined. These statements were sent to you a number of weeks ago.

Would it not be possible to arrange a meeting with us at your convenience when you could give the matter the consideration due and come to some conclusion, as our business in Steel is very large at the present time and our exchange is greatly in need of transfer facilities in the stock?

Small investors are now putting their money into Steel on the belief that it is one of the best investments of the day, and the Consolidated Exchange is probably handling more of the stock in small lots than all the other exchanges in the United States combined.

Awaiting your answer, I have the honor to remain,

Yours, very truly,

S. A. LUTHER,
First Vice and Acting President.

H. PLUMMER,
C. H. VAN BUREN,
Committee.

The letter above referred to was marked "Exhibit No. 116, December 12, 1912."

Mr. UNTERMYER. Were you away when this letter was written, or were you then the president?

Mr. DE AGUERO. I was not the president at that time. Mr. Badeau was president.

Mr. UNTERMYER. Was he away at the time?

Mr. DE AGUERO. He was away at the time.

Mr. UNTERMYER. What committee is that that signed this letter?

Mr. DE AGUERO. A special committee appointed to take up the subject with the United States Steel Corporation.

Mr. UNTERMYER [continuing reading]:

EXHIBIT NO. 117, DECEMBER 12, 1912.

CONSOLIDATED STOCK EXCHANGE OF NEW YORK,

PRESIDENT'S OFFICE,

New York, January 26, 1910.

Mr. E. H. GARY,
 Chairman United States Steel Corporation,
    71 Broadway, New York City.

DEAR SIR: We wrote you on the 3d instant concerning the matter of transfers for a few of our commission houses who at your suggestion prepared statements of their financial condition, which were delivered at your office several weeks ago. Many thousands of small investors in the United States Steel Corporation shares place their orders on the Consolidated Stock Exchange, which is an institution organized primarily to benefit business in fractional lots. In justice to these investors and the Consolidated Stock Exchange, we think the United States Steel Corporation, as represented by yourself, should make an early decision regarding this matter of transfers.

Trusting that you will fix a near-by date for an interview, we have the honor to remain,

  Yours, very truly,

     S. A. LUTHER,
    First Vice and Acting President.

     H. PLUMMER,
     C. H. VAN BUREN,
       Committee.

The above letter was marked "Exhibit No. 117, December 12, 1912."

EXHIBIT NO. 118, DECEMBER 12, 1912.

CONSOLIDATED STOCK EXCHANGE OF NEW YORK,

PRESIDENT'S OFFICE,

New York, February 9, 1910.

Mr. E. H. GARY,
 Chairman United States Steel Corporation,
    71 Broadway, New York City.

DEAR SIR: Your telephone message, refusing to grant transfer facilities to a number of our old-established commission houses, was received.

Your action reveals a most astonishing situation, that you, as head of one of the largest corporations in this country, should refuse to transfer stock for your own stockholders because they do business through the commission houses of the Consolidated Stock Exchange, an institution which is conducted on strictly business principles in every respect, and does the second largest business of any exchange in the United States, and probably the largest odd-lot business of any exchange in the world. Yesterday our official list of sales, which is inclosed, shows a total of between 82,000 and 83,000 shares of United States Steel common traded in on our floor, a showing which should command respect, as it is free from any matched orders, wash sales, or manipulative orders put in to influence prices.

When it becomes generally known that you have taken this stand against your own stockholders who trade through this exchange will you be backed up by your own board of directors, in view of the fact that you are the only corporation or railroad who refuses the privilege of transfer facilities to our members? Would the anti-Sherman Act and the general laws of the land allow you to "boycott" your own stockholders and our commission houses in this respect?

Some time ago we submitted, at your request, financial statements of some of our oldest commission houses. Will you kindly return these financial statements, as they are the property of the members who submitted the same, and should be justly restored to their possession if you do not propose to grant transfer facilities to them.

We feel the stand you have taken is unjust as discriminating against this exchange, which is organized especially for the benefit of the small investor.

It is unjust to you and your corporation to take a stand which places you in the position of not appreciating the fact that you are practically attempting to block the progress of increasing legitimate commission business in your own stock .

Don't you think this whole matter would be worth your reconsideration in view of all the agitation now before the public regarding stocks, stock transactions, and anticorporation legislation?

Awaiting your reply, we have the honor to remain,

Yours, truly,

C. H. BADEAU,
President.

C. H. VAN BUREN,
H. PLUMMER,
Committee.

The foregoing letter was marked "Exhibit No. 118, December 12, 1912."

Mr. UNTERMYER. I see you say, in this letter of February 9, 1910, that the United States Steel Corporation is the only corporation or railroad that refuses the privilege of transfer facilities to your members. Was that accurate at the time?

Mr. DE AGUERO. I suppose it was, sir. I really could not answer the question, because I did not write the letter.

Mr. UNTERMYER. The list you have given of those who refused is a list of those who now refuse, is it?

Mr. DE AGUERO. Yes, sir.

Mr. UNTERMYER [reading]:

EXHIBIT NO. 119, DECEMBER 12, 1912.

CONSOLIDATED STOCK EXCHANGE OF NEW YORK,

PRESIDENT'S OFFICE,

New York, February 15, 1910.

Mr. E. H. GARY,

Chairman United States Steel Corporation,

71 Broadway, New York City.

DEAR SIR: Your esteemed letter received. We are surprised that by your actions and words you seem to advocate the upholding of discriminations.

You state that one of your rules to be complied with is as follows: "In order to obtain a transfer, the assignment by the stockholder upon the back of the certificate must be acknowledged by him before a notary public or his signature must be guaranteed by a firm having membership in the New York Stock Exchange." The latter part of your rule is not in keeping with the progress of business in Wall Street. It has become too obsolete to meet the requirements of the business to-day. How can you reconcile your statement, "it seemed necessary for the protection of the corporation and its stockholders to limit as far as possible the responsibility of our transfer office," when you take the unquestioned guaranty of every member of the New York Stock Exchange? What protection has that been to your corporation and its stockholders under existing business conditions in the past few years? What protection did your corporation and its stockholders receive from the guaranties of such New York Stock Exchange firms as A. O. Brown & Co., T. A. McIntyre & Co., Coster, Knapp & Co., Marshall Spader & Co., Tracy & Co., Otto Heinze & Co., Meadows, Williams & Co., Freeman, Rollins & Co., Fisk & Robinson, J. M. Fiske & Co., Robert, Hall & Criss, and Lathrop Haskins & Co.? The combined indebtedness of the above concerns alone would amount to more than the total of all the failures which have ever occurred on the Consolidated Stock Exchange since its formation in proportion to the business executed on the respective floors of the two exchanges.

We fail to see any corroboration "that the wisest course for the Steel Corporation to pursue is to abide by the rule regarding transfer of stock which has heretofore been followed" when you carefully consider the disastrous consequences of the guaranties of these New York Stock Exchange firms as a necessity to protect the interest of your stockholders.

You need to bring your transfer methods up to date, to conform to the methods of other principal railroads and corporations, if you wish to be abreast of the present times.

We concur when you state that the request which was made to your corporation was on behalf of certain individual firms and not on behalf of the exchange itself or all of its members, but we can not agree when you state, "upon reflection you will see that to extend the limits of the rule to certain members of the Consolidated Stock Exchange and not to others would be much more of a discrimination than is the rule as it exists at present," for the reason that the request was made only for firms who have stood the test of their responsibility during all the vicissitudes of Wall

Street for upwards of 17 years and should therefore be entitled to transfer facilities on their past and present reputation alone. How can it be considered a discrimination against other members who have only been in business for periods of much less time and have not so thoroughly proven the same standard of responsibility and are not in the same relative position? But when they have withstood the same test they should certainly be entitled to the same consideration. The test of merit should be based upon proven responsibility.

We maintain that every firm, or individual, who can satisfactorily prove their, or his, responsibility, whether they are members of an exchange, or do not belong to any exchange, are entitled, by right and by law, to transfer facilities for themselves and their customers, on their guaranty, and it is direct discrimination against them by refusing such transfer, simply because they are not members of the New York Stock Exchange. We are at a loss to understand how a man of your vast business experience and extensive legal mind can look at the situation with any other view. It is less than 30 years when leading railroad companies refused to transfer except for a few New York Stock Exchange firms, on their guaranty, but times have progressed since then, and are equally progressing to-day.

The Consolidated Stock Exchange is a young and a rising institution, and when you decide to use your power, and that of your corporation, to attempt to obstruct or curtail the building up of the legitimate business of our long-established commission houses by refusing transfer facilities to responsible concerns, you place yourself in the position of advocating the restraint of trade, and put a direct "boycott" by your action on members of the Consolidated Stock Exchange.

The request to transfer for seven long-established firms on the Consolidated Stock Exchange, in addition to the one you already take the guaranty of, is based simply on right, fairness, and a square deal, which we trust that you will appreciate and concede when you give your ever-busy mind the opportunity to thoroughly weigh in all its particulars, as has been done by some of the greatest interests in Wall Street.

We have the honor to remain,
Yours, very truly,

C. H. BADEAU,
President.
C. H. VAN BUREN,
H. PLUMMER,
Committee.

The above letter was marked "Exhibit No. 119, December 12, 1912."

EXHIBIT No. 120, DECEMBER 12, 1912.

CONSOLIDATED STOCK EXCHANGE OF NEW YORK
New York, March 2, 1910.

Mr. E. H. GARY,
Chairman, United States Steel Corporation,
71 Broadway, New York City, N. Y.

DEAR SIR: On February 15 we sent to your office, per messenger, an answer to your letter of February 12. Not having received a reply from you, or the return, requested by us on February 9, of the seven statements made to you in confidence, and at your special request, we can only infer that you have decided to give the matter of discrimination, by the United States Steel Corporation, against these seven concerns a thorough reconsideration.

Trusting to hear from you that such is the case, and that you have finally decided to grant so just a request, as we have made of you, we have the honor to remain,

Yours, very truly,

C. H. BADEAU,
President.
C. H. VAN BUREN,
H. PLUMMER,
Committee.

The above letter was marked "Exhibit No. 120, December 12, 1912."

EXHIBIT NO. 121, DECEMBER 12, 1912.

UNITED STATES STEEL CORPORATION,
New York, March 4, 1910.

Mr. C. H. BADEAU, President,
Messrs. C. H. VAN BUREN and H. PLUMMER, Committee,
Consolidated Stock Exchange of New York, New York.

DEAR SIRS: Referring to your letter of March 2, addressed to Mr. E .H. Gary, chairman, I am directed to return under seal the seven statements referred to and inclosed herewith, and to state that we can not see our way clear to change our position in the matter.

Yours, truly,   RICHARD TRIMBLE,
Secretary.

The above letter was marked "Exhibit No. 121, December 12, 1912."

This correspondence which I have just read refers to a letter of February 12 from Mr. Gary?

Mr. DE AGUERO. It is quoted from so largely that you may have a very good idea of what it said; of the contents of the letter.

Mr. UNTERMYER. Do you not think it is more just to have the letter?

Mr. DE AGUERO. If I had it, I should be very happy to give it to you. I have looked for it, but have not been able to find it.

Mr. UNTERMYER. May it then be understood, Mr. Chairman, that Mr. Gary will be invited to put that letter in the record, or that counsel for the stock exchange may do so?

The CHAIRMAN. Certainly; or a copy of it.

Mr. UNTERMYER. And that Mr. Gary's letter will go into the record.

Mr. DE AGUERO. I should be very happy to have it.

The CHAIRMAN. If they desire to avail themselves of the privilege.

Mr. DE AGUERO. May I state that we continued our efforts to get transfers from the United States Steel, and so from time to time it went along for a year and a half or more; and eventually we decided that we would address the chairman of the exchange to guarantee the signatures on certificates for all companies, and passed the resolution and sent a copy to the transfer officers. The United States Steel Corporation still refused, or would not transfer when certificates were sent over to them. They questioned, as this correspondence will show, the power of the board to pass the resolution authorizing the chairman to act for the exchange. We offered to have their counsel draw the resolution, and pass whatever they would draw. Notwithstanding that, they finally declined. They turned it over to the Guaranty Trust Co. as the registrar, and they finally declined to change their rule.

On the ninth of this month we had some steel to transfer, and I directed the chairman to send a certificate over to the United States Steel Corporation with the guaranty of the exchange on it. He did so. They returned it—would not transfer it. Then he put a notarial certificate on it, and it was, of course, transferred, which they must do according to law.

Mr. UNTERMYER. Yes. But they do not require these notarial certificates from the members of the New York Stock Exchange?

Mr. DE AGUERO. No, sir.

Mr. UNTERMYER. How does that requirement for a notarial certificate, if at all, embarrass business dealings in the stock?

Mr. DE AGUERO. In this way: A man must appear before the notary—in this case the chairman of the exchange himself—and give evidence to the fact that he is the signer, and he must be known to the notary.

Mr. UNTERMYER. He must do that as to every certificate?

Mr. DE AGUERO. He must do that as to every certificate. A man out of town sends his certificate in to New York to be sold by one of our houses, and that stock is sold, perhaps on order—telegraphic order over the wire—and when they receive the certificate it has no notarial certificate upon it, and that certificate must be returned to the owner, perhaps five hundred to one thousand miles away, to have that notarial certificate put upon it, and must be sent back to New York and then transferred to the man who buys the stock.

Mr. UNTERMYER. To what extent would any such requirement embarrass business on your exchange, as against the other exchange?

Mr. DE AGUERO. I do not know to what extent; but of course anybody can see that it does make a difference.

Mr. UNTERMYER. Would it make business practically impossible?

Mr. DE AGUERO. Not impossible, but it makes it very hard for our brokers out of town to receive orders to buy or sell stock when they must go to the owner of that stock and tell him that he must have a notarial certificate put upon it; or they must have the certificate returned and then go to him. He naturally comes to the conclusion that we have no standing in New York, and we have no right, therefore, to have stocks transferred.

We claim two things, Mr. Chairman. One is that these people are acting against the interests of their own stockholders, in that they force them to sell their securities through one exchange and one exchange only, because they give them no transfer rights if they sell through any other exchange; whereas they have the signature on their books of every one of their stockholders, and are best able to judge whether that signature is correct or not. Also gentlemen in our exchange, of good standing, sell their seats and join the New York Stock Exchange, and the next day they can transfer in the offices of all these railroads and the Steel Corporation. The day before they could not; although they had more money than they had the next day, because they had to pay for the seat in the exchange.

Mr. UNTERMYER. In making transfers on the books of the corporation of stocks sold through members of the New York Stock Exchange, does the New York Stock Exchange itself guarantee the genuineness of the signature?

Mr. DE AGUERO. I think not. I have never heard of it.

Mr. UNTERMYER. That rests upon the brokerage firm?

Mr. DE AGUERO. Yes.

Mr. UNTERMYER. Do I understand that, in the case of your exchange, in addition to the guaranty of the brokerage firm you offer the guaranty of the exchange itself?

Mr. DE AGUERO. Yes; with free assets of probably $600,000.

Mr. UNTERMYER. The Consolidated Exchange has free assets of $600,000?

Mr. DE AGUERO. Yes.

Mr. UNTERMYER. You own your own building, too, do you not?

Mr. DE AGUERO. Yes; and the land; mortgaged, of course. But I am speaking of free assets. I am talking about the equity in the building and the free assets.

Mr. UNTERMYER. Is this a certified copy of the resolution of the Consolidated Stock Exchange that you tendered to the United States Steel Corporation?

Mr. DE AGUERO. To the transfer officers; yes.

The paper referred to was marked "Exhibit No. 122, December 12, 1912," and is here printed in the record, as follows:

EXHIBIT NO. 122, DECEMBER 12, 1912.

Resolved, That Valentine Mott, as chairman of the Consolidated Stock Exchange of New York, be, and he is hereby, authorized and empowered, until the rescission or amendment of this resolution by the further resolution or resolutions of this board of governors, in the name and as the act and deed of the Consolidated Stock Exchange of New York, to guarantee the genuineness of any and all indorsements of certificates of stock; and be it further

Resolved, That each and every guaranty of the genuineness of the indorsement of a certificate of stock hereafter made or given by said Valentine Mott as such chairman, in the name of said exchange, be, and is hereby, ratified, approved, and confirmed as the act and deed of the Consolidated Stock Exchange of New York; and be it further

Resolved, That the secretary be, and is hereby, authorized to transmit to any corporation or to the transfer agent or agents thereof a duly certified copy of this resolution.

I, James E. Lynch, secretary of the Consolidated Stock Exchange of New York, do hereby certify this 29th day of November, 1912, that the foregoing is a full and correct copy of a resolution duly adopted at a meeting of the board of governors of the Consolidated Stock Exchange of New York, duly called and held on the 9th day of November, 1911, and that the same has not been rescinded or amended except the resolution attached.

JAMES E. LYNCH, *Secretary.*

I, Miguel E. de Aguero, president of the Consolidated Stock Exchange of New York, hereby certify, this 29th day of November, 1912, that the signature to the foregoing certificate is the signature of James E. Lynch and that said Lynch is the secretary of the Consolidated Stock Exchange of New York.

M. E. DE AGUERO, *President.*

Mr. UNTERMYER. Is this a copy of the resolution under which that was done?

Mr. DE AGUERO. The other is the resolution. This is a part of the resolution passed, for the information of the chairman himself. It does not apply to the resolution.

Mr. UNTERMYER. Will you tell me whether or not that is a list of corporations that accept the guaranty of the Consolidated [showing witness paper]?

Mr. DE AGUERO. It is; yes.

Mr. UNTERMYER. Is that a further list [referring to another paper]?

Mr. DE AGUERO. This is a list of those that accept the guaranty of the chairman without the guaranty of the exchange.

Mr. UNTERMYER. And the second is a list of those that accept the guaranty of the chairman accompanied by the guaranty of the exchange?

Mr. DE AGUERO. That is the first one.

Mr. UNTERMYER. I will read that [reading]:

EXHIBIT NO. 123, DECEMBER 12, 1912.

New York Central, Southern Pacific, Pacific Mail, Union Pacific, City National Bank, American Sugar, American Smelting & Refining Co., Consolidated Gas Co., Colorado Fuel & Iron, Central Leather, Canadian Pacific, Great Northern, Louisville & Nashville, Texas Pacific, Wabash, Denver & Rio Grande, and United States Rubber Cos.

That is the list of those that accept the guaranty of the house and that of the exchange together?

Mr. DE AGUERO. Yes.

The list referred to was marked "Exhibit No. 123, December 12, 1912."

Mr. UNTERMYER. Is this a list of concerns that accept the guaranty of the stock exchange house, without that of the exchange?

Mr. DE AGUERO. And the chairman. Mr. Mott signs it. They accept his signature.

Mr. UNTERMYER. Without the guaranty of the exchange?

Mr. DE AGUERO. Without the guaranty of the exchange; yes, sir.

Mr. UNTERMYER. I will read it [reading]:

EXHIBIT NO. 124, DECEMBER 12, 1912.

Rock Island; National Lead; Brooklyn Rapid Transit; Chesapeake & Ohio; Ontario & Western; Winslow, Lainer Co.; Central Trust Co.; Peoples Gas; J. P. Morgan & Co.; New York Air Brake Distillers' Securities; New York Trust Co.; Equitable Trust Co.

The paper referred to was marked "Exhibit No. 124, December 12, 1912."

Mr. UNTERMYER. I think that covers all that you wanted to say, does it not?

Mr. DE AGUERO. Yes, sir. There was one point that I would like to make, if I may.

Mr. UNTERMYER. Very well.

Mr. DE AGUERO. That is this: Can a man who belongs to our exchange sell securities in the New York Stock Exchange if he is appointed executor of a will?

Mr. UNTERMYER. We are not here to take up problems, Mr. de Aguero; but I suppose what you want me to ask is as to whether or not an executor of an estate would be able to sell his estate's securities on the Consolidated Stock Exchange?

Mr. DE AGUERO. Under the ruling, he would not.

Mr. UNTERMYER. That is a matter in which we are not concerned.

Mr. DE AGUERO. All right.

Witness excused.

APPENDIX V

Testimony of Frank Knight Sturgis, President of the New York Stock Exchange from 1892 to 1894, before the Subcommittee of the Committee on Banking and Currency of the House of Representatives (Money Trust Investigation), December 12, 1912.

Mr. UNTERMYER. Has the stock exchange enacted a regulation that prohibits brokers on the curb from dealing with the members of the Consolidated Stock Exchange?

Mr. STURGIS. Not to my knowledge.

Mr. UNTERMYER. They have a regulation, have they not, which——

Mr. STURGIS. The curb people?

Mr. UNTERMYER. Yes; the curb. Have you had any connection with the negotiations that have been carried on by the curb?

Mr. STURGIS. I think I have seen Mr. Mendel, the secretary of the curb, perhaps three times or four.

Mr. UNTERMYER. The New York Stock Exchange brokers are permitted to deal on the curb, are they not?

Mr. STURGIS. We take no cognizance of the curb. We do not forbid or sanction. They do as they like about that.

Mr. UNTERMYER. Do you not know that they are not permitted——

Mr. STURGIS. I do not know of any member of the exchange who is a member of the curb.

Mr. UNTERMYER. We are not speaking of members of the curb. I am referring to dealings by stock exchange brokers on the curb. What I want to know is whether or not there are any securities listed on the curb that are dealt in on the New York Stock Exchange.

Mr. STURGIS. Not to my knowledge.

Mr. UNTERMYER. Is it not a fact that the Curb Association is not allowed to list any securities there that are dealt in and listed on the New York Stock Exchange?

Mr. STURGIS. I do not know what their powers are, but I know they never do it.

Mr. UNTERMYER. Do you know why they never do it?

Mr. STURGIS. No; I could not answer that question.

Mr. UNTERMYER. Do you not know?

Mr. STURGIS. No.

Mr. UNTERMYER. Do you not know that it is because of your regulation that forbids any of your members dealing on any exchange where the securities are dealt in that are listed on your exchange?

Mr. STURGIS. Ah! But the curb has never been, so to speak, recognized by the stock exchange.

Mr. UNTERMYER. Has it not?

Mr. STURGIS. As an exchange, no; it has no housings.

Mr. UNTERMYER. Was not the following section of the constitution and by-laws of the curb market inserted as a result of negotiations with your committee?

Mr. STURGIS. Will you please read it?

Mr. UNTERMYER. Yes; section 2 of article 12:

Any person who shall be connected directly, or indirectly, or by a partner, with any association, corporation, or exchange other than the New York Stock Exchange of the city of New York, which permits dealings in any securities or property admitted to dealing in any department of the New York Stock Exchange shall be ineligible for membership.

Mr. STURGIS. On the curb?

Mr. UNTERMYER. Yes.

Mr. STURGIS. Mr. Untermyer, to the best of my recollection, the stock exchange had nothing to do with the framing of that.

Mr. UNTERMYER. Why should the curb have prevented any of its members from dealing with any member of the Consolidated Stock Exchange in any security that was listed on the New York Stock Exchange?

Mr. STURGIS. I was not even aware that they had, until you just read it to me.

Mr. UNTERMYER. You know, do you not, why the curb cannot get in out of the rain into a building.

Mr. STURGIS. No; I do not.

Mr. UNTERMYER. Do you not know that it is because of your regulation of 1909, which forbids any of your members dealing with any association—or having any connection, direct or indirect, with any association—that deals in securities?

Mr. STURGIS. That deals in our securities—the securities of the New York Stock Exchange?

Mr. UNTERMYER. No; that deals in any securities?

Mr. STURGIS. The members of the New York Stock Exchange do deal on the curb, through brokers.

Mr. UNTERMYER. Yes; but the question is why the curb does not get in out of the rain into a building.

Mr. STURGIS. I misinterpreted your question.

Mr. UNTERMYER. Is it not because of that regulation?

Mr. STURGIS. I could not say positively whether it is or not— whether that bears upon it or not. I really have not given the matter attention.

Mr. UNTERMYER. Give it a little attention just now, will you?

Mr. STURGIS. I will; I will go home and give it attention.

Mr. UNTERMYER. No, no; do not go home. We want you here.

Mr. STURGIS. Thank you.

Mr. UNTERMYER. Just read over that [handing paper to witness] and then tell me whether that is not the reason why the curb association cannot go into a building instead of staying out on Broad Street.

Mr. STURGIS. This resolution is headed "Consolidated Stock Exchange." It reads:

Resolved. That any connection, direct or indirect, by means of public or private telephone, telegraph wire, or any electrical or other contrivance or device, or any pneumatic tube——

Mr. UNTERMYER. Do not read it all over.

Mr. STURGIS I thought you asked me to read it.

Mr. UNTERMYER. Not aloud; read it to yourself.

The CHAIRMAN. It is in the record.

Mr. UNTERMYER. In connection with that, after having read it, will you please look at section 4 of article 17 of your constitution, which reads as follows:

Any member who shall be connected, directly or by a partner or otherwise, with any organization in the city of New York which permits dealings in any securities or other property admitted to dealing in any department of this exchange shall be liable to suspension——

And so forth?

Mr. STURGIS. Yes.

Mr. UNTERMYER. Do you see that?

Mr. STURGIS. That says he is liable to suspension.

Mr. UNTERMYER. That prohibits the curb, does it not, from dealing in any securities that are dealt in on the New York Stock Exchange?

Mr. STURGIS. No. The language is:

Any member who shall be connected, directly or by a partner or otherwise, with any organization in the city of New York which permits dealings in any securities or other property admitted to dealing in any department of this exchange.

Mr. UNTERMYER. Yes.

Mr. STURGIS. It prevents our own members from becoming members of an institution where these same stocks are dealt in. But the curb does not deal in our stocks.

Mr. UNTERMYER. But why?

Mr. STURGIS. That is their reason. I do not know why.

Mr. UNTERMYER. Do you not know that that is because your members could not deal on the curb or give them any business if they did deal in your stocks?

Mr. STURGIS. Certainly they would be very foolish to deal in our stocks.

Mr. UNTERMYER. Why would they be foolish?

Mr. STURGIS. Because the stock exchange does now furnish them with a very large amount of their business in the stocks that are not listed on the exchange.

Mr. UNTERMYER. I understand; and therefore they are not allowed to deal in your stocks?

Mr. STURGIS. That is their rule, not ours.

Mr. UNTERMYER. Now, about their getting in under a roof; have there been conferences—numerous conferences—between representatives of the curb association and the stock exchange?

Mr. STURGIS. On that subject?

Mr. UNTERMYER. On the subject of the relations between the two exchanges.

Mr. STURGIS. I told you that I thought I had had three that I recollect only.

Mr. UNTERMYER. Three conferences?

Mr. STURGIS. Three in which I personally participated.

Mr. UNTERMYER. Has the subject of the curb association getting quarters been discussed?

Mr. STURGIS. I think it was, once.

Mr. UNTERMYER. With you?

Mr. STURGIS. I think it was with the law committee; yes; on one occasion.

Mr. UNTERMYER. Who discussed it on behalf of the curb?

Mr. STURGIS. Mr. Mendel, I believe.

Mr. UNTERMYER. Did they not want to hire a place?

Mr. STURGIS. No; they did not particularly insist upon it.

Mr. UNTERMYER. But did they not say they would like to get in under a cover during the bad season?

Mr. STURGIS. On one occasion; and then they changed their minds and said they preferred not to.

Mr. UNTERMYER. Before they changed their minds, what did you say to them about it?

Mr. STURGIS. My recollection is not very clear.

Mr. UNTERMYER. But, generally, what was the decision of the law committee?

Mr. STURGIS. I think the decision was that they could do as they liked.

Mr. UNTERMYER. With what consequences?

Mr. STURGIS. Ah! That is their business, not ours.

Mr. UNTERMYER. I see. But what was said as to what would happen if they should take quarters?

Mr. STURGIS. They had the constitution of the exchange before them.

Mr. UNTERMYER. But what was said as to that?

Mr. STURGIS. I do not remember what was said.

Mr. UNTERMYER. What would happen if they took quarters?

Mr. STURGIS. If they dealt in our securities?

Mr. UNTERMYER. No. What would happen if they did not deal in your securities, but took quarters?

Mr. STURGIS. I think we should keep on sending our orders in there.

Mr. UNTERMYER. Did you say so to them?

Mr. STURGIS. Yes; as far as——

Mr. UNTERMYER. Then why do you not do that with the Consolidated Exchange?

Mr. STURGIS. May I give you, briefly, the history of the difficulty with the Consolidated Exchange?

Mr. UNTERMYER. Yes; I think it is only just that you should be allowed to do so.

Mr. STURGIS. The Consolidated Stock Exchange has always been a competitor for business, sometimes under very trying conditions and sometimes under circumstances that were very painful to both sides. There was a great deal of ill feeling and a great deal of quarreling, and I must say I think there was some disloyalty, perhaps, on the part of members of the Consolidated and, perhaps, on the part of some members of the regular exchange. That feeling became aggravated. The Consolidated Stock Exchange has two tickers of the Western Union on its floor, upon which, very largely, its daily fluctuations are based. When we made our contract with the Western Union an injunction prevented the taking out of those tickers, and they there remain, in a rival organization. It did not tend to promote a very kindly feeling to think they were using what we regarded as our property, against our wishes; and that aggravated the ill feeling, which continued to grow. I am not familiar with what occurred in 1909 when that resolution was passed, but it reached a point where the authorities of the stock exchange said that it was better to have no relations with the active—or, rather, with the members of the Consolidated Exchange that were engaged in the same business. They did not discriminate against those members of the Consolidated Exchange that were not engaged in active business, for instance like the late Mr. H. H. Rogers, who was a member of the Consolidated Exchange and operated very extensively on the floor of the New York Stock Exchange; and of course his orders were gladly received. There were others also.

Mr. Untermyer. He was a big trader, was he not?

Mr. Sturgis. Yes; and there were small traders, too, who did their business in that way. But when they went into the brokerage business and entered into direct competition with the members of the stock exchange the governing committee thought it was time to pass this resolution.

That is the history of it, as far as I recollect it.

Mr. Untermyer. They offered to pay, did they not, for the use of the ticker?

Mr. Sturgis. The ticker was not our ticker. It was the Western Union's ticker.

Mr. Untermyer. Yes; and they offered to pay the Western Union for it, did they not?

Mr. Sturgis. I presume they were willing to pay the Western Union for it.

Mr. Untermyer. Why should you object to their renting a ticker from the Western Union?

Mr. Sturgis. Would you want your materials, so to speak, in trade handed over to somebody else to make capital of?

Mr. UNTERMYER. But do you not think information of that kind, affecting the whole country as to the price of securities, is rather public property than mere private property?

Mr. STURGIS. Our courts so held, and decided in their favor.

Mr. UNTERMYER. Another thing. They decided in favor of the Consolidated?

Mr. STURGIS. They decided in favor of that injunction.

Mr. UNTERMYER. And you passed this resolution by way of reprisal, did you not?

Mr. STURGIS. The resolution was not passed until just after that.

Mr. UNTERMYER. You did pass it by way of reprisal, did you not?

Mr. STURGIS. I do not think so; but, as I told you, I was not familiar with the cause of the passage of that resolution.

Mr. UNTERMYER. Was not the friction and the hostility further increased by the fact that the Consolidated Exchange only charges one-half as much to buy or sell a share of stock as your exchange?

Mr. STURGIS. Very probably. There were a great many things. As I told you, the friction between the two institutions was constantly increasing.

Mr. UNTERMYER. But that was the main reason; because they did the service for the public for one-half of what you did?

Mr. STURGIS. No; there are a great many more reasons than that.

Mr. UNTERMYER. But they do the service for one-half what you do it for, do they not?

Mr. STURGIS. They do.

Mr. UNTERMYER. And you are trying to destroy them, are you not?

Mr. STURGIS. No. They have a right to go on with their business.

Mr. UNTERMYER. Is not every regulation that you have passed here directed toward destroying them?

Mr. STURGIS. Why should we assist to build up a rival organization?

Mr. UNTERMYER. I did not ask you that. I asked whether you were not trying to destroy them?

Mr. STURGIS. I said to you no, we are not. We are doing nothing with them. We are leaving them alone.

Mr. UNTERMYER. You are leaving them alone?

Mr. STURGIS. Yes, sir.

Mr. UNTERMYER. And forbidding your members from having anything to do with them?

Mr. STURGIS. Certainly; we are leaving them alone.

Mr. UNTERMYER. And you are compelling them to leave you alone, are you not?

Mr. STURGIS. It looks that way.

Mr. UNTERMYER. If they were willing to double their charge to the public so that it would be the same as the charge you were making for buying and selling stocks, your troubles would be over, would they not?

Mr. STURGIS. That is a suppositious question. I think if they were to take out their tickers that might have some influence upon the situation, but I cannot say. It is a question of opinion of the members of the governing committee.

Mr. UNTERMYER. If they increased their charges to the public that would have an effect, would it not, with you?

Mr. STURGIS. It would not personally with me, because I do not care much about it, either way.

Mr. UNTERMYER. I mean, with you as a governor of the exchange. I do not mean individually. That would solve it, would it not?

Mr. STURGIS. No; I do not think it would solve it. It would be a healing balm to some extent.

Mr. UNTERMYER. In other words, if they doubled the charge to the public you would regard it as a healing balm?

Mr. STURGIS. I think it would be helpful.

Mr. UNTERMYER. Are you familiar with the process of lending money on the stock exchange?

Mr. STURGIS. I am not; no.

Mr. UNTERMYER. Or with the movement of funds not dependent on the money market on the stock exchange?

Mr. STURGIS. No; I am not. I do not keep posted upon that situation.

Mr. UNTERMYER. What determines the availability of a security as collateral on the stock exchange—its activity?

Mr. STURGIS. No, Mr. Untermyer. Generally speaking, the credit of the corporation itself.

Mr. UNTERMYER. Is it not a fact that the most active securities have been those that never paid a dividend at times?

Mr. STURGIS. That is true.

Mr. UNTERMYER. Mr. McMorran, one of the members of the committee, would like to know whether the building is owned by the stock exchange, or whether you have organized a corporation that owns it?

Mr. STURGIS. Mr. Untermyer, the New York corporation, the Building Company, as it is called, that owns the Stock Exchange

Building, has been in existence since the construction of two exchanges before this.

Mr. UNTERMYER. And what you own is the stock of that corporation?

Mr. STURGIS. We own the stock of the building.

Mr. UNTERMYER. The stock of the building is owned by this voluntary association known as the stock exchange?

Mr. STURGIS. I think you have put it correctly. It is in the treasury of the exchange as an asset.

The CHAIRMAN. As an asset?

Mr. STURGIS. As an asset.

At 4 o'clock P.M. the committee adjourned until tomorrow, Friday, December 13, 1912, at 11 o'clock A.M.

APPENDIX VI

The Curb News, 1909-1911

IN 1909, several Curb brokers wrote and edited a small, four-page newsletter called *The Curb News*. It was released weekly, although several issues were skipped in the summer months, and a year's subscription cost $2. Those curbstone brokers who remember *The Curb News* are rather vague as to when and why it ceased publication, but all agree it was not being distributed by the eve of World War I.

Fragments of the journal remain on deposit at the American Stock Exchange Library, and these provide an interesting glimpse into the social life of the Curb in this period. Among other things, it indicates that some brokers were quite well-to-do, that although uneducated for the most part they were beginning to dabble in cultural affairs, but they remained substantially middle class in orientation and attitudes. Finally, the short paragraphs in *The Curb News* clearly indicate the existence of a social community at that market, one more closely bound together by ties of affection than the one that existed at the Stock Exchange in the same period. It was these ties, as much as if not more than the few rules and regulations of the Curb Market, that enabled the out-of-doors exchange to function smoothly.

The following are a series of excerpts from *The Curb News* of 1909–11. Particular care has been made to select those dealing with brokers mentioned in the body of this book. Exaggerations and humor notwithstanding, this small paper provides one of the best insights of Curb life extant.

273

William Marko has been very successful breeding mules for the army on his Long Island farm.

It is not generally known that Billy McGee is very artistically inclined; his six months sojourn in southern Italy watching the beautiful sunsets and imbibing the glorious air has filled him with so much poetical inspiration that the outcome is the cause of much concern to his Coney Island friends.

Since Andre Jacobi discovered that little French eating place in Englewood, we notice his early departure on Saturdays, sometimes with company.

We wish to deny the report that Tom Hall is engaged to be married. Did you ever see a fat man get fatter with a problem like that on his mind? A few more weeks of quick stomach growth and Tom will be unable to see his knee-caps.

Oscar Bamberger, director of mining reports, railroad analyst and statistician, bull lasooer and bull thrower, is possessed of a vocabulary as voluminous as that of a campaign orator. He has travelled a considerable distance with it, and was never sidetracked for lack of conversational salve.

Though the temperature registered 116 in the sun on the curb last Tuesday, the day was very eventful. The Board of Trade of Porcupine City, Canada, presented Norman DeMauriac with a beautiful porcupine cat. He was quite overcome with the weight of the honor and toasts to the cat were drunk with gusto. Arthur Weiner received from his affectionate Curb associates a regal floral horseshoe. There were no toasts drunk on this occasion.

Deacon Dick Carney, chair warmer, dealer in cigar coupons and guardian of the Curb mascot Agnes, is trying to dispose of a mummy picked up during his Egyptian travels a year ago. If he can't sell it, he may swap for a meal ticket in a first class boarding house in University Heights.

Reported to be the largest individual stockholder of the Tri-Bullion Mining Co., Ed McCormick has, in addition to this valuable asset, a propensity for wearing elaborate and ornate waistcoats and meandering up and down Fifth Avenue afternoons, mingling with the wealthy.

It is possible that we are a trifle premature in congratulating Sam "Kitty" Frank on his approaching marriage to a charming Miss living on upper Madison Avenue. There is something on his mind these days, chewing cigars and forgetting feeding time are almost conclusive symptoms. George Leslie, Jr., doesn't deny that he will "sign up" soon. He will get the usual rice pudding reception when the fatal day approaches.

For the past months there has been a big demand for archaic plug hats among the manufacturers of the country, and we find Louis Cartier wearing one of the by products; the soft black beaver hat he is now showing, is a thing of marked distinction.

Wash Content's valet Meyer, is the quickest man on his feet when lunch hour approaches, that we have in our midst; that pained look on his face is now chronic, and is done to match the times. The slightest suspicion of an order will make him dance about to such an extent, as to give the Major the impression that at last money is in sight, but also, there is nothing done.

Fritz Ackerman had the honor of taking George Leslie, Jr., to a nearby sarsaparilla emporium for his final bachelor drink. It is needless to say that the occasion will be a pleasant recollection to the embryo benedict.

The one only bull on the Curb, Cameron Blakie, has been exhaling optimistic oxygen for several weeks. He had planned extensive improvements in his home in Englewood, N.J., if the market does what he predicts, but of course "Cam" knows that bricklayers and carpenters fight shy of ninety day contracts.

Dudley Gray spent a very enjoyable vacation at Southhampton, L.I., with his family. His plump cheeks and springy step mixed with refreshing optimism speaks well for the rest he took.

Herbert Oppenheim, when not boxing all comers on the Curb devotes his spare time to fattening up the exchequer of Carl Pforzheimer. Who can tell, some day he might own an automobile, too.

A deadly feud is imminent between Bert Hedge and Lew Teichman, and it is with great tact that these two gentlemen have been kept apart. It is surmised that the light and gay hearted Bert has been encroaching on the territory of the undesirable and ingratiating Lew. These two old birds ought to know by this time of the proverbial fickleness of Broad Street typists.

Jack McCormack returned from his camp at Rangley Lake, Maine, brown as a berry, hard as nails, and just as amiable as ever. The Curb Association will now take up much needed reforms under the guidance of their estimable executive.

The baptism of Jonesy, chauffeur and one-time Curb messenger, was a lively incident in the history of Broad Street. Officer Bill Rohrs, wrapped up in dreams of the Elysian fields and the Battery Bath, was rudely disturbed by the high pitched snorts of an ocean going taxi-cab driven by Jonesy, who had acquired the machine through his eloquent and persuasive power taught by his Curb messenger experience and a couple of hundred dollars. The cab stopped still as a rock in front of the brokers who immediately pounced on the car. There was a scuffling in and out of the doors, hand springs were turned on its roof; poor Jonesy with the assistance of Billy Miller, a former director of the Packard Motor Car Co., started the ill-fated taxi again on its journey. The exhaust sputtered, and amid the grinding and chewing of the gears, the crippled oil carrier, with convulsive and snake-like movements, picked its way sorrowfully homeward, amid the gaping of the curious and idle rich who crowded the nearby windows and doors. Suddenly the poor old taxi again refused to come to life, a pained expression came over the ethereal and spiritual face of Jonesy. Mr. J. P. Morgan, from his window, directed the efforts of the motor experts gathered about, and after a lot of perspiration had been shed she moved laboriously, and Jonesy heaved countless sighs of relief. Thus ended the baptism of the one-time messenger who would be a chauffeur. The only damage reported was by Bert Hedge, who had his thumb squeezed in the gear-box, and Percy Guard confided to the police sergeant that in the excitement he lost his upper set of dining room furniture.

The fact that Stock Exchange seats are getting cheaper every day doesn't interest the average curb broker. He is a little curious as to the continuation of his purchasing power of meal tickets and sundry other things that tend to keep him alive.

Spencer Koch arrived from Europe, the early part of the week. Most of his time was spent with Admiral Togo, who promised to visit the Curb when he returned from Washington. The Admiral presented "Spinney" with a box of Japanese cigars which he distributed among his customers.

The first real fat order made its bow on the Curb last week, and it is worth while chronicling the fact. Aleck Gale was the broker and Inspiration Copper the stock, and the quantity, enough to choke a horse. It was a selling order, and the security is still limping as a result.

Seward Forster won two motor boat races at Bay Head, Barnegat Bay, a few weeks ago. His forty-foot power boat exceeded all speed expectations and may be heard of favorably in the big races coming off this month.

We hear that E. S. Mendels, the dean of the Curb, is in very serious condition; we hope though, that he will pull through, as he has done on numerous other occasions, and that we will soon again see his genial face and hear his friendly laugh.

It was shown conclusively a few evenings ago that twenty or thirty Curb brokers could get together and give a thoroughly enjoyable and up-to-date beefsteak dinner and entertainment; a repetition in the near future, but on a larger scale, is anticipated.

Gene Crassous, who bears a striking resemblance to a popular matinee hero, is contemplating buying a Curtiss aeroplane.

Al Sturges returned to the Curb last week after being absent for some time, combating a case of poison ivy. He looks none the worse for his experience.

What promises to be an event of great interest to baseball fans will be the attempt of Ben Manowitch to catch a baseball dropped from the roof of the Broad Exchange Building, some day next week, not selected as yet.

We noticed on the Curb one day last week three successful members of the Stock Exchange sunning themselves. They were old-time Curbites, Louis Heineman, George Leslie and Briggs Buchanan, and apparently were sniffing about too, seeing if they couldn't pick up a floating eighth.

Carl Pforzheimer and his army of assistants are still writing in their little books and smiling, so all is well, and the automobile will be kept in commission.

Hats off to Jack McCormack—this time a boy, and the lucky seventh, too.

Emanuel S. Mendels, Jr., more familiarly and lovingly known as "Pop" Mendels, departed from this life on October 16, 1911, after a seige of illness lasting many months, fighting the inevitable with the same bravery, pluck, good humor and perseverance that he showed in all matters during his earthly existence; now that he is gone, little intimate insights akin to his character come to light; his fighting spirit when antagonism developed, concerning the peace of his beloved foundation, the curb; his haste, good-will, and energy to fulfill a favor for anyone, his wide fund of experience in all financial matters to be had only for the asking, his keen sense of humor, with his storehouse of anecdotes of the street, when the curb veterans gathered about talking over bygone days, it was only to know him slightly to know him well, such was the man; there were a few who differed with him, but they see his goodness and well meaning now; the curb is sincerely bereaved to lose its staunch, militant, courteous and beloved pillar of strength and many a moist eye will glisten when fugitive thoughts of the many kindnesses of Ed Mendels creep upon them during his absence; he will always be missed, never forgotten, and his memory kept verdure clad by the universal opinion of the members of his beloved work and hope, the curb, in the sentiment, "Well done, good and faithful servant, enter though into the joys of the Lord."

Index

Index